MIKE PANNETT

t the Job, Lad

More tales of a Yorkshire bobby

JUST THE JOB, LAD

MIKE PANNETT

HODDER

First published in Great Britain in 2011 by Hodder & Stoughton
An Hachette UK company

First published in paperback in 2012

1

ISBN 978 1 444 70893 6

Typeset in Sabon MT by Palimpsest Book Production Limited,
Falkirk, Stirlingshire

Printed and bound by CPI Group (UK) Ltd, Croydon CR0 4YY

Hodder & Stoughton policy is to use papers that are natural, renewable
and recyclable products and made from wood grown in sustainable
forests. The logging and manufacturing processes are expected to conform
to the environmental regulations of the country of origin.

Hodder & Stoughton Ltd
338 Euston Road
London NW1 3BH

www.hodder.co.uk

In memory of John Corner.
A true Yorkshireman and dear friend.

With special thanks to Alan Wilkinson
and my wife, Ann.

Contents

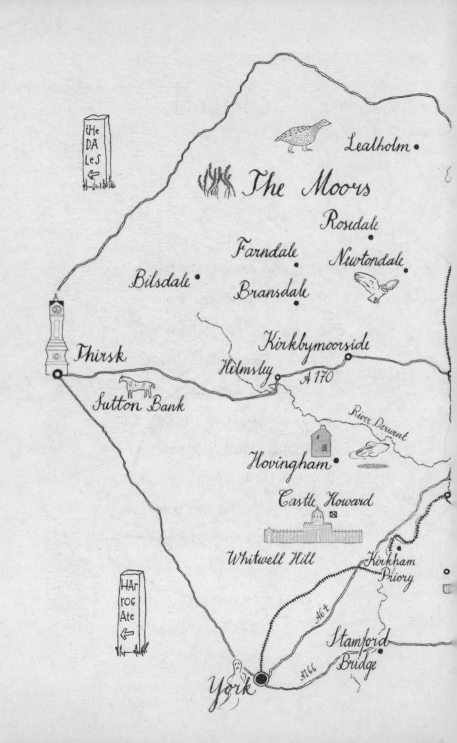

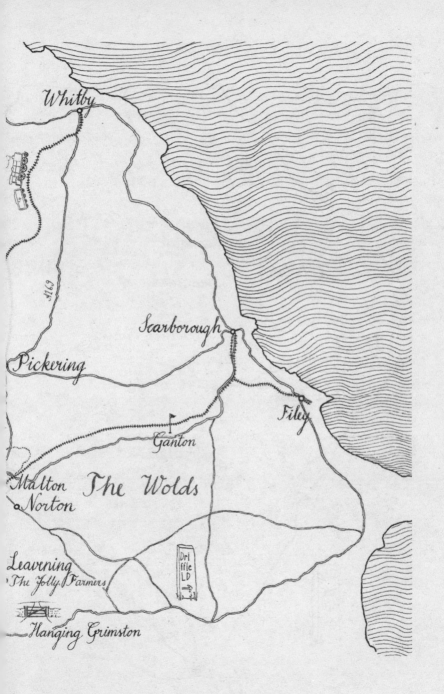

Whitby

A169

Scarborough

Pickering

Filey

Ganton

Malton The Wolds
Norton

Leavening
The Jolly Farmers

Dri
ffie
LD

Hanging Grimston

As in my previous books about policing in North Yorkshire, all the cases I deal with actually happened. I have changed the names of the characters – police as well as villains – and altered the locations and certain details but only when absolutely necessary to protect people's identities.

Policing procedures are always being updated; what you read here accurately reflects the way we operated at the time each event took place – which in every case is within the last ten years.

Mike Pannett
North Yorkshire

Chapter 1

Duty Calls

'Walt! Where are you, mate?'

All I could hear was the cawing of the rooks as they busied themselves high up in the sycamores. Spring was here, their young were hatching, and they were busy repairing their nests, rickety, fragile things perched among the topmost branches.

'Walt!' I pushed the wrought-iron gate open and squeezed into the yard. 'Come on now, let's be having you.' I knew he was there – somewhere. The car was parked in its usual place with the lid of the boot wide open, and the door of his shed was creaking as it swung this way and that.

'Come on out. It's no good hiding, mate.'

From inside the shed I heard a dull rumble, followed by clattering, as if a pile of loose slates was falling off a roof. A moment later a cloud of dust rolled out, followed by Walter, clutching a grubby red handkerchief to his mouth with one hand and holding a coil of frayed hempen rope in the other. It was a mild afternoon, despite the

wind, and the layer of grime that covered his bare forehead was streaked with sweat.

'Good job you're here, lad, 'cos I'm at the end of me
tether.' He paused to flick a cobweb off his waistcoat and
mop his face. 'I've had it up to here, lad.'

'Oh,' I said, eyeing the rope. 'Decided to end it all,
have you? Just because me and Ann took off for a few
days in the sun?'

''Tisn't a laughing matter, lad. Nearly broke me neck
looking for this here rope.' I'd never seen Walt scowl
before. He nodded towards the kitchen window, where I
could see Henry's head bobbing into view as he hurled
himself at the steamed-up glass. 'That blooming dog of
yours, why, he's led me such a dance.'

'Aye, he's a challenge. Bit of a slippery customer is our
Henry.'

'Slippery? He's like a blooming little eel – and crafty
with it.' Walt was shaking a tangle out of the rope. 'Why,
there's no controlling him. Pulled t'lead right out of me
hand this morning. Shot off across t'field and come back
two hours later without it.'

'So is that for me?' I said, holding my hand out.

'I'm goin' to lend you this rope, that's what I'm going to
do. While you buy a new lead – a strong 'un. If you want
my advice you'll get yourself down to Yates's and treat
yourself to one o' them chainlink jobs.' He led the way to
the back door, and kicked off his turned-down wellies.
'And I'll give you another tip while you're here. You want
to get that dog properly trained before you go traipsing off
abroad and dropping your friends in the mire. Why, he's
three sheets to t'wind.'

'He's a character all right.'

'A character? He's bloody cracked, that's what he is. You wanna get him to one of them – them pet psychics.'

'You mean psychiatrists, Walt.'

'You know what I mean. One of them as sorts his mind out.' Walt handed me the rope and opened the back door. Henry leapt out, almost taking me off my feet as he jumped up at me, licking my face.

'Right then,' I said, threading the rope through his collar and trudging towards the gate, 'I suppose I'll see you later.'

I had my hand on the latch when he called me back. 'Now then, don't be tekking it personal, lad. Let's not be falling out.' I turned around to see him forcing a resigned sort of grin. 'Tie him up to t'post yonder and come in the house. We'll have a cup of tea and a bit of a catch-up, shall we?'

'Good man.' I followed him inside, hung my jacket on the back of the door and sat myself down at the scrubbed wooden table. Walt filled the teapot from a simmering kettle and put two mugs and a plate of rock buns on the table. 'Them's me sister's,' he added. 'Fresh out of her oven this morning. Dig in, lad. They want eating.'

'I tell you what,' I mumbled through a mouth full of crumbs, 'that sister of yours can't half bake.'

'Aye well, she used to do it professionally. Still does a turn for family and friends. Weddings, christenings and suchlike.' He sat down and started drumming his fingers on the table. And whistling. Then he winked at me. 'How was your trip?'

'Oh. Grand, mate, grand.' I was looking at the teapot,

still on the stove. I fancied another cake but my mouth was dry as a bone.

'Got a cheap deal, did you?'

'An absolute bargain, Walt.'

'Aye, and no kennel fees or owt.' He was drumming his fingers and whistling again.

'Oh hell, Walt!' I went over to the door and reached inside my jacket pocket. 'Here,' I said. 'Almost forgot.' I handed him the duty-free Ann and I had brought back for him.

He tore the wrapping paper off and stared at the Greek writing on the bottle. 'Why, what sort of concoction is this?' He unscrewed the top and was sniffing at the contents.

'It's all the rage over there, mate. Ouzo.'

'Ouzo you say? Smells like blooming aniseed balls to me.'

'Aye, it does. And you wanna go steady with it. Just a little splash in the bottom of your glass and top it up with water. Treat it like medicine. Like the doctor says. One spoonful at bedtime – or as required. It'll calm your nerves after all the excitement.'

Walt just grinned and put the bottle in his cupboard. 'Aye well,' he said, 'I suppose I shall have to forgive you now. But don't forget what I said about a lead. Chainlink, that's what you want.'

As I walked back down the hill half an hour later, with Henry tugging away at his rope, I still felt a twinge of guilt, but I knew Walter wasn't one to bear a grudge. We'd had a really good holiday, me and Ann. And we'd needed it. We'd timed it to perfection. The end of April had seen a cold wind sweeping down from the north, and we'd grinned smugly all the way to Cyprus, supping our duty-free; and as we lazed away the afternoons on the beach we scanned the English papers, day after day, relishing the reports of record low temperatures, and the familiar photographs of snow-covered daffodils. How lucky can you get? By the time we arrived home the sun was shining, the fields were greening up, and the birds were singing. Spring was in the air, and the best of it was, I could look forward to another day off before I was due back at work. No such luck for Ann though; she was starting that same night, ten o'clock, and wasn't feeling like it. At all.

'Tell you what,' I said, as we strolled along the brow above Wharram Percy with Henry tugging at Walter's rope. It was getting on for teatime, and I was thinking about food. 'I'll make you a nice pack-up to take into work tonight, something to look forward to. Then maybe this evening I'll pop over to my mum's. Catch up with her, show her a few holiday pictures. I'll download 'em onto a CD for her.'

'Just mind your mum doesn't keep you nattering till the small hours,' Ann said. 'I know what you two are like, once you start reminiscing.'

'I'll be all right,' I said. 'I don't have to be up early.'

As ever, Ann was right. Mum and I chatted long into the night. We talked about everything under the sun, as we always do, and I never did get to show her the photographs. It was past midnight when I set off for home. Tired as I was, I was already starting to think about work, and what might be in store for me after a ten-day break.

You try and switch off when you're away from the job, but of course you never manage to tidy all the loose ends before you sign off. I'd left a few unresolved problems, one of which was a series of thefts that had plagued our area over the winter. This wasn't small-scale stuff. It was trailers, horseboxes and the like, with the odd four-wheel-drive vehicle thrown in. We'd had bits and pieces of intelligence but no substantial leads, and our inspector had got on the case, demanding that we come up with something – soon.

Some people say you shouldn't take your work home with you, but I've never really seen the sense in that, certainly not for a rural officer. The people I socialise with are the same people I 'protect and serve', as we like to say – unlike in London, where you tend to live outside of the area you work in. So anything my friends complain about when we're out at the pub of an evening, or when I pop into the village shop – even when we're out fishing – it all goes into my own personal database. Much as I like my time off, a part of my brain is always on duty. Always has been. As far as I'm concerned, if you're a police officer that's what you are. An upholder of the law, twenty-four seven. There's no getting away from the job. You expect people to confide in you – the same as they would if you were a doctor, I dare say. You may not always be conscious of it, but as a copper you're always absorbing bits and pieces of information. And I'm always observing, taking mental notes. I don't mean to. It's just the way I am. In fact, thinking back, I sometimes wonder which came first – an observant, inquisitive nature or the ambition to be a copper. Because I was always interested in what was going on around me. Always will be. Besides, I joined up to catch criminals. Don't get me wrong, I don't go around looking for it off duty, but if something happens I'm not one to turn a blind eye.

I'd made my way onto the A64 and was just approaching the Little Chef, near the lane that takes you down to Claxton, and there, parked up next to the filling station, I spotted a little yellow Datsun. I wouldn't normally have taken much notice, tired as I was, but as I passed it a match flared up in the cab and illuminated three faces, all male. Now, if it had been a car, and if they'd been youngsters, I might have assumed they were on their way home from a night out, or maybe on their mobiles trying to find out where the party was. But this was a rusty old pick-up, and they were all grown men, in their thirties or maybe older. They didn't look like lads on a night out. And the petrol station was closed. Closed at half ten as far as I could recall. So the thought sort of skittered across my mind: what were they up to? No question about it: they looked dodgy.

Even as I hesitated, and then drove on towards the dual carriageway, I remembered something Ed had mentioned just before I went on leave. Something about a pick-up truck that had been seen in the vicinity of a recent trailer theft. As I thought about what he'd told me my foot hovered over the brake. He'd said it was a yellow one. And a Datsun.

To tell the truth, at that moment I clean forgot I was off-duty. I went onto automatic pilot. I checked the rear-view mirror. There was nothing behind me. I drove on a few hundred yards until the road curved and I was sure

I would be out of sight, then turned around and headed back towards York. I slowed as I approached the filling station, hoping to get a better look at the truck and the occupants, and maybe get their registration number. But they'd gone – and in the distance I caught just a brief glimpse of their rear lights before they disappeared from sight.

It was at this point that I realised the position I was getting myself into. One, I was off duty. Two, I was in my own car, which wasn't the nippiest. And three, I had none of my equipment with me. No handcuffs, no CS gas – and, of course, no uniform to identify myself as a copper, although as always I had my warrant card in my wallet. All I had was an unreliable mobile phone – and here I was out in the country where the signal came and went on a whim. This was not the type of situation you would want to be in when you were on your own, not even if you were on duty.

I drove on, at speed. A mile further, at the junction where I'd joined the main road, I saw the pick-up signalling right for Flaxton and Sheriff Hutton. I slowed instantly. I had been surveillance trained in the Met, and had a fair bit of experience involving follows of suspect vehicles. I'd learned to be cautious. The last thing you want is to alert a driver to the fact that they're being followed, because as often as not it'll panic them and blow your cover. They end up spooked, and that's the end of the job.

So there was no way I was going to telegraph my intentions by switching on my indicators and following them down the lane. Instead I would drive on past the junction totally naturally, give them time to get ahead and out of sight, then turn round and pick them up some-where down the minor road. But as I watched them swing off to the right I saw two cars approaching me from the direction of York – and both of them slowed, signalled, and turned towards Flaxton.

Perfect, I thought. Cover for me. I signalled, pulled to the right, and braked as they made their manoeuvre. I noted that the first was an old Mondeo with a single male occupant. The second was a battered Cavalier. I followed it into the lane. I could clearly hear that its exhaust was blown. That's when I started to get the feeling that there was something wrong. Something in my gut – something about the type of cars and the look of the occupants – was telling me that the three vehicles were actually together. I picked up my mobile from the seat beside me and punched the autodialler, hoping that the night-duty staff in the control room weren't too busy.

I was in luck. The control-room staff responded quickly.

'*Mike?*'

'Yeah Brian, it's me.'

'*Thought you were on leave.*'

'I was. Still am, in fact. But listen, I'm out and about and I've just spotted sommat.'

'*Fire away.*'

'I've got three vehicles in front of me heading from the A64 towards Flaxton. There's something not right about them. Can you get somebody out here?'

I gave Brian the number of the Cavalier, which was barely fifty yards ahead of me and travelling at a steady 30 or 40 mph, which, given the time of night, seemed slow.

It didn't take Brian long to come back. '*Yeah, we've*

had intelligence reports on this one, Mike. Owned by a known associate of . . .' The name he gave me sent a shock wave through me. It was a member of a notorious gang, an extended family from one of the York estates. They were into a wide range of criminal activities and had a record of vicious and violent assaults.

My hands tightened on the wheel. 'Right,' I said, 'he's in a convoy of three vehicles, and I'm pretty sure the first vehicle is also suspect. It's a yellow . . .'

I got no further. The familiar whine from my phone told me I'd lost my signal. I dropped it onto the seat beside me and concentrated on keeping a safe distance – a discreet distance – from the cars ahead of me. Maybe I should have turned round and gone back to where I was getting reception, but I was determined not to lose this lot. If they were up to something perhaps this was a chance to collar them in the act and put them out of circulation for a while. The area would certainly be a safer place. Besides, by this time the adrenaline was flowing through my veins and I was smelling a result.

We were approaching Flaxton now, and I'd relaxed a little. I expected them to carry on to Sheriff Hutton or beyond, but suddenly they pulled in at a gated entrance to a field, one after the other. I wondered whether they suspected me and wanted to get me out of the way. If I'd had any doubts up to now, this at least confirmed that the three were operating together. I drove on past at a steady speed, looking straight ahead all the way. That's another surveillance tip: never show any obvious interest in the suspect. What you need to do is act as normal as possible.

The question now was what should I do? I got into the village, passed the first few houses and then, as the road curved, I stopped, backed into an empty driveway and switched off the engine. Then I lowered the window and listened. The wind had dropped by now and it was a still, cool night. High in the sky a full moon was peering through broken cloud. Somewhere, perhaps a mile or so away across the fields, a fox was yipping; otherwise it was perfectly quiet. I put my seat right down and lay back. If they happened to come by on foot they shouldn't see me. I certainly hoped not. I felt in my inside pocket to make quite sure I did have my police warrant card on me, just in case the occupants of the house came out to see who I was. I picked up the mobile again, and swore under my breath. Still no signal.

I sat there, listening to the gurgle of fluids and the tick-tick-ticking as the engine started to cool. I couldn't have been there more than three or four minutes, but that's a long time when you're on your own waiting and wondering what's going to happen. As well as worrying about what the suspects were up to, I was frustrated that I couldn't relay the information back to Brian and update the troops. Then I heard a vehicle approaching. At the same time a tall cypress hedge opposite was illuminated by headlights. It was the yellow pick-up coming round the corner, followed by the other two cars.

Raising my head an inch or two so that I could see over the dashboard, I watched them all cruise slowly past, then eased myself upright, ready to start the engine and follow them. But they stopped in a line, right opposite the Blacksmiths Arms, not fifty yards from where I was parked. I suddenly felt very vulnerable. Had they spotted me? Had I inadvertently parked right next to the target premises? This was not a good situation. I was out of range and couldn't contact the control room, and if these people had seen me and decided to challenge me I had no means with which to protect myself. I could be in grave danger. I needed an exit strategy, and the only one that made any sense was the obvious one. Flight. I pressed my foot down on the clutch, eased the gear lever into first and closed my fingers on the ignition key. If they got out of their cars and approached me there was no doubt in my mind what I would do. Fire up and drive off, fast – and let them do the worrying. I wasn't going to attempt any heroics. Not with that lot.

Keeping my head as low as I could, I watched as the pick-up doors opened and the three occupants got out. Would they be heading my way? My fingers tightened on the key, then relaxed a shade as I saw them approach the rearmost of the three vehicles, the Mondeo. What was puzzling me was, why the three-vehicle convoy? Was one going to be deployed as a look-out? A decoy? Or what?

The guy in the Mondeo just sat there, his window half open. He seemed nervous, pulling on a cigarette and flicking the ash onto the road with his forefinger more often than seemed necessary. I now saw that his car was fitted with a stout towbar.

The other four were clearly conferring, plotting their next move – but what had they got in mind? The pub? Maybe the antique shop further along the road. There had been a smash-and-grab there a few years earlier. I tried to make a mental note of each man's height, weight, clothing and so on, but they were all dressed in similar fashion: jeans, sweatshirts or loose jumpers, and trainers. They all had woollen hats pulled down low, so that it was hard to see their faces.

Whatever they had been discussing they'd clearly made up their minds as to their next move. The three men were heading briskly back to the pick-up. They got in and set off out of the village with the other two vehicles following.

I gave them a minute or so, then set off, my heart thumping. Once again, I broke the rules. It's just something you have to do from time to time. I'd already used my phone while at the wheel, and now I switched off my lights and drove by the light of the moon, which had broken through the clouds. The landscape was brightly illuminated, and I could clearly see the convoy up ahead, their brake lights glowing red as they hit the bends. I was feeling a little less vulnerable now, and a broad grin broke across my face as I remembered similar surveillance jobs in my Met days. The thrill of the chase – although in those days I was always part of a team, with all-important backup. This was different.

I still hadn't a clue where the convoy was going. Up ahead was West Lilling, and beyond that Sheriff Hutton. I knew I'd get a signal there, if not earlier, and that was my second priority – to contact control as soon as possible and alert them to what was going on. The first, though, was not to lose contact with the three vehicles. They were now round the bends and out of sight. It was make-your-mind-up time. I switched the headlights on. My best strategy now was to act as an ordinary member of the public on his way home. I got my foot down and started to gain on them, picking up the phone as I did so. Thank God for that. The full five bars.

'Hello Mike, you all right? We were getting worried.'

'Bloody signal's hopeless round here, Brian. Listen, I've just left Flaxton, en route to Sheriff Hutton and – whoa, hang on!'

I was just passing a gateway that led into a field of oilseed rape – and there was the pick-up, with nobody in it. I drove on by, maintaining a steady forty to fifty. Barely two hundred yards later I slowed on the approach to the crossing that takes you over the York to Scarborough line. On either side are a number of business premises – and on my right was the entrance to a small engineering works. And there, at the metal gates, and armed with a hefty set of boltcutters, were the three men from the pick-up. The Mondeo was tucked away just beside the gates, almost out of sight from the road. I might not have noticed it if the driver hadn't just blown a cloud of smoke out through his side window.

Bumping over the crossing I saw the other back-up vehicle. I drove on, looking straight ahead, keeping an eye out for somewhere I could pull over and renew contact with control. But that's when Sod's Law kicked in. The road ran straight as a die for a mile or so and I had no choice but to keep going. When I did finally get round a bend and out of sight, I picked up the phone to find I was out of credit.

It's at times like this that you thank your lucky stars for your backroom staff. I'd been sitting there less than a minute, cursing my luck and wondering what to do next, when the phone rang.

'*Mike, it's Brian.*'

'You played a blinder there, mate. Bloody phone's out of credit.'

'*Right, well, stay tuned. We don't wanna lose contact. Any developments?*'

I filled him in on what I'd seen at the crossing, which was effectively a break-in in progress – and I reminded him I was still off duty, in civvies and unprotected. '*Well,*' he said, '*I've got backup organised but you're looking at – at least ten, maybe fifteen minutes. There's an armed response vehicle en route from the York area, and a Malton car – but that's coming from Heslerton. Not even on the bypass yet.*'

I needed to gather my thoughts. Because my problem is I'm inclined to get carried away. Overenthusiastic, you might say. Right now, above all, I needed to stay calm, which wasn't easy. I was sweating, and my heart was thumping. You very rarely come across villains in the act of committing a crime, and if these were the people who'd been plaguing us over the past few months, ripping off trailers and horseboxes, well, it could be a major clear-up. But what was I to do? Should I stay put and risk losing them completely, or go and see what they were up to? I had no way of knowing whether they were armed or not, but just the thought of those boltcutters was enough to make anyone think twice about approaching them.

I put the car into gear and let out the clutch. Bugger it, I thought. What's the worst that can happen? So long as I don't get out of the car.

'Brian, I'm heading back to see where they are. If I lose my signal again, just keep ringing, will you?'

'*Mike, whatever you do, do not go jumping in. Keep your . . .*' – he was fading again – '*distance and be care . . .*' The signal was lost. Back over the railway crossing I found that the gates to the works were closed, and the two vehicles that had been there earlier were nowhere to be seen. The third one, the Cavalier, was still on the road-side, with just the driver in it. Were the others inside the premises, or had they got what they were after and gone?

I barely had a few seconds to take all this in, maintaining my speed as I was. I drove on by, back towards Flaxton. There I looked ahead, checked my mirror, and pulled into the same driveway I'd used earlier, glancing up at the bedroom windows, hoping the occupants hadn't heard me. I crouched behind the dashboard and wound my window down a few inches, listening intently.

I'd only been there a couple of minutes when I heard the roar of the dodgy silencer. Moments later the Mondeo came hurtling through the village, swaying to left and right, its headlights dazzling me briefly. It was pulling a brand-new Ifor Williams trailer – and looking as though it would part company with it at any moment. Hard on its heels was the pick-up, followed in turn by the Cavalier. These lads weren't hanging about now.

I started the engine, nosed forwards towards the road, and watched as the convoy disappeared from sight before following on behind. Thirty seconds or so later my phone rang.

'Brian.'

'*What's happening, Mike?*'

'All three suspect vehicles leaving Flaxton and heading towards the A64. The Mondeo is pulling a bloody Ifor

Williams trailer. Nicked. They'll hit the A64 any minute now.'

'*Right, Mike. The good news is the backup's not too far away. York car's just leaving the city centre. The Malton car's coming down Whitwell Hill.*'

I'd got the tail-lights of all three vehicles in view now. At the junction with the A64 the lead car was straight out, barely seeming to slow down. It swerved, wobbled, and raised a puff of smoke as the driver hit the brakes at the last moment to avoid toppling it over. The pick-up followed, then the Cavalier, but as I followed him out into the main road the driver of this one swung to the left, braked hard and pulled over onto the verge to let me pass. I had a fair idea what he was up to. He reappeared in my rear-view mirror a moment later. Where the hell was my backup?

My hands were now slipping on the steering wheel, my palms sweating and my heart racing. We were fast approaching the Hopgrove roundabout, just on the outskirts of York. The car behind had now closed right up behind me. In my rear-view mirror I could see the driver's face lit up by his dashboard lights, flushed red as I put my foot on the brake. At first I thought he was just trying to get a closer look at me, but his lights, reflected in my mirrors, were dazzling me. Was he planning to take me out?

'Brian, I've one on my tail – close up. Whoa, scrub that. He's turned off towards Stockton-on-the-Forest.' The question was, had he alerted the drivers in front on a mobile? They must know that something was up. I was directly behind the pick-up now, close enough to give

Brian the registration number, just as the driver pulled out, accelerated and passed the Mondeo.

'Yeah Mike, the pick-up has no registered keeper.'

'What's the backup situation, over?'

'Malton car'll be there in a minute or two. Just passing the Tanglewood. And you should see the York car any moment.'

'Hope you're right, mate. Hope you're right.'

I followed the pick-up onto the roundabout at speed. He didn't signal, just swung sharply off, taking the first exit.

'Brian, the pick-up's gone Leeds way. I'm following the Mondeo plus trailer. Into York, by the look of it, over.'

As we sped towards the outskirts of the city I saw the lights of the York ARV unit heading towards me – and then speeding right by.

Surely they hadn't missed us? No, they hadn't. In my rear-view mirror I saw the driver execute a perfect 180-degree skid turn and race up behind me. Time for me to back off and let him pass. To my surprise, he'd no sooner signalled the Mondeo to stop than the driver did just that, barely a hundred yards down the road.

I eased off and slowed down, drove on past the ARV guys and the Mondeo before pulling over a little way down the road. The last thing I wanted was to have my private car identified. If that got out on the bush telegraph I could look forward to all sorts of trouble. I left my car and walked the rest of the way back towards them.

They had the driver out on the verge and were taking his details. He was what I'd call gaunt, sort of skinny with narrow shoulders, lank hair and a thick lip. With his eyes narrowed and the blue lights flashing into his face he looked a pretty sorry figure. I now saw that his left eye was swollen and the cheek below it bruised and grazed. He was busy protesting his innocence. 'They made me do it,' he kept saying. 'They made me. They woulda killed me if I didn't.'

'Yeah well, you'll have plenty of time to explain everything back at the station,' the arresting officer said as they took him to their car. Then his partner turned to me. 'Pannett, isn't it?' he said.

'That's right.' I knew him vaguely, the way you do get to know a few faces from the beats that border your own. We'd met once or twice on various courses.

'Hardly recognised you in civvies,' he said. 'What was this, an undercover job or what?'

I shook my head, and watched his mate put the prisoner in the car. 'No,' I said, 'I was on my way home when I came across this lot.' He looked at me blankly. 'I'm off duty,' I said. 'I was just in the right place at the right time, and – well, call it a sixth sense.'

'What, and you gave chase in your own vehicle?'

'Nah – I followed them, that's all. And tipped off control. Not often you come across criminals in the act, is it?'

'S'pose not. Bloody good job mate. Well done.'

'Well,' I said, 'looks like you've got everything under control.' My only concern was that the Malton crew hadn't been able to find the pick-up, but circulations were out for both of the outstanding cars and another unit was on its way to Flaxton to attend the premises that had been broken into, with the key-holder on his way. 'I'll meet you in York,' I said. 'I'll have to give a statement, I guess. See you there.' I lit a cigarette and made my way slowly back to my car.

As I drove into York I had mixed feelings about the night's events. It was brilliant that we'd made the arrest and recovered the property intact, but we hadn't managed to pick up the other members of the gang. The guy we'd got looked like the weakest link, someone they'd roped in under duress. The main gang seemed to have got away, and would doubtless be at it again before long.

Fifteen minutes later I was walking into York police station and making my way to the custody area when I heard a familiar voice behind me.

'Mike, what on earth's going on?'

Ann was standing there in the corridor, gaping at me. 'Has something happened?'

'No, it's all right. I was on my way back from my mum's and I came across a trailer theft.'

'You did what?'

'Well, I was on my way home and I came across a team nicking a trailer, out Flaxton way, so I – well, I got after them. Your fellow officers from York collared them, and I've just come in to do my statement.' I looked at her and put on my most winning smile. 'Hey, any chance I can sit in your back office while I write it up?'

She shook her head and sighed. 'Can't let you out of my sight for two minutes, can I? You were supposed to be having a quiet night round at your mother's. Yeah, course you can use the office. Are you all right?'

'Yeah. Bit hairy at times, but – I'll tell you all about it later.'

'I'll put the kettle on. You'll find the statement forms in the drawers on the left. Hello – here they come.'

At that the door opened and the ARV crew appeared with the suspect. While Ann set about booking him in and sorting out a doctor to check his injuries I went and started on my statement. I hadn't been writing long when I spotted Ann's familiar pack-up box on a side table. The thought of those cheese and tomato sandwiches I'd lovingly prepared for her several hours previously was too much for me. I had a little peek, and sure enough there was one left. It would be a pity to see it go to waste.

'Don't even think about it!' Looking up, I saw Ann at the door. 'I was saving that for later. Here' – she threw me a half empty packet of custard creams – 'have these.'

The moon was setting when I made my way down the wooded drive that led to Keeper's Cottage, and I was flagging. You burn a lot of mental and nervous energy on a job such as that. Yes, you have that glow of satisfaction when it comes right, but in the end your body reminds you of the resources you've used up. All I could think about now was bed. Henry, though, had other ideas. He'd been on his own since early evening and assumed I was going to take him out.

'Come on, then,' I sighed, threading Walter's rope through his collar. 'Just down the lane and back.'

It was half-past three when I got into bed. I never heard Ann come in.

It was a few weeks after all this that a letter arrived from the chief superintendent, addressed to me. I remember looking at it for some time before opening it. I was thinking, Christ, now what? Letters from on high don't often land in your in-tray – and when they do they can spell trouble.

I needn't have worried. Our leader was writing to congratulate me on my display of initiative in chasing after the gang and whistling up support. A few days after that I got a second pat on the back, a congratulatory email from the chief constable. When I got home that night I couldn't wait to tell Ann about it. She listened patiently, then said, 'I've been thinking.'

'I thought you were listening.'

'I was. I have also been thinking. I am a girl, I can multitask, remember?'

'This sounds serious. Ominous, in fact.'

'Serious, yes. Ominous, no. Listen,' she said, putting her hand on mine, 'I think you're a fantastic copper.' She laughed. 'Unpredictable, slightly mad, but great at your job.'

'I like this. Is there more?'

'There is. I think you'd make a brilliant sergeant. I mean, look at some of the people you and I have seen promoted over the years. Some of them are fine and some—' She pulled a face. I knew what she meant. 'And when you think about the bad ones, you wonder how on earth they got where they are, am I right?'

'You can say that again.'

'And the good ones . . .'

'Cocksy, for example?'

'Yes, I'd rate him. But do you really think he brings anything to the job that you haven't got?'

I looked at her and thought for a moment. 'That's not for me to say.'

'I think it is, Mike. This is not the time for you to come over all modest,' she said. She smiled and looked me right in the eye. 'Come on, how do you rate yourself as a copper?'

'Blimey.' I had to think for a bit before answering. 'Well, now that you're asking I think I'm pretty bloody good at what I do. And I love the job.'

'That's more like it. And how about gelling with your fellow officers? Could you . . . lead them into battle, take the initiative, lead by example?'

'Yeah, sure I could.'

'And would you stop and consider your options, before going in all guns blazing?'

'Of course. You have to get people onside, don't you? All singing from the same hymn-sheet as they say. Y'know, what you were saying about good supervisors and bad ones – I've always reckoned it's a matter of picking out the good characteristics and weeding out the bad. I mean, if you were modelling yourself on them.'

'Right, so what I'm saying, Mike, is why don't you set aside a couple of days and go through those books I gave you at Christmas – about the sergeants' exams?'

I groaned. 'I knew there was a catch. I hate studying. It reminds me of school. Remember what I always say? I left school with two qualifications: one in the study of motorcycles and—'

'Yeah, I know – and one in girls.' Ann sighed. 'You have mentioned it once or twice. But this time, surely you can see there's a payoff. There's the increase in salary, and in your pension. I mean, how much longer do we want to keep renting this place?'

'Keeper's Cottage? I love it here, don't you? I mean, it's a great place to live. Character cottage with a bit of land, fantastic location. Secluded.'

'Yes, I know all that. We both love it here. But it's like pouring money down the drain isn't it, paying rent month after month.'

'Costs a hell of a lot to buy a place like this,' I said. 'To be honest, we've been spoiled living here, haven't we? Any place we moved on to – that we could afford – it'd be a step down, wouldn't it?'

'Right, so why don't we hit Algy boy with a proposal? Why don't we ask him how much he wants for Keeper's Cottage?'

'D'you reckon he'd sell it?'

'No idea. We'd need to ask him.'

'Well, Ann, that sounds like a plan. One that calls for a celebration.'

'We haven't bought it yet!'

'I know. But you've just agreed to get a mortgage with me. And that's a statement of intent, isn't it?'

'Only one trouble, Mike.'

'What's that?'

'You gave the last of the duty-free to Walter.'

Chapter 2

Sting in the Tail

'So how's the plans going then?'

'What's that you say, cock-bod?' Soapy's voice, emerging from the attic, was muffled, his tone just a little tetchy. Looking up through the tiny access, all I could see – apart from the seat of his worn jeans and the loose sole flapping off a cowboy boot – was the light of his torch, playing on the crooked beams that held up the rows of pantiles.

'Weren't you and Becky supposed to be getting married about now?'

'Hey, spare a thought, Mike lad. You don't send an expert to look for a hole in your roof and then start grilling him like a future mother-in-law. Bloody dangerous business, this. D'you want me putting a foot through your bedroom ceiling and suing you for neglect, or what?'

'Sorry, bud.'

'Aye, you just concentrate on holding them steps steady and leave a craftsman to his trade. I'm calling on twenty years of experience here, cock-bod. 'Tisn't a job for an amateur, this.'

I didn't answer. If Ann had taught me anything over the last couple of years it was that sometimes it pays to keep your mouth shut. And to be fair, this was a serious business. We'd spotted what looked like a damp patch right above our bed a week or two earlier and alerted our landlord, Algy. Now he'd sent his right-hand man, his Mr Fixit, who'd got halfway through an apprenticeship two decades ago and consequently thought he knew everything worth knowing about the building industry – and here he was giving the roof timbers the once-over, and loving every minute of it.

'Course, I've got City and Guilds in this, y'know. Years ago, like, but they were worth more then. All this dumbing down caper . . .' There was a muttered curse as Soapy dropped the torch and a dull thump as his head made contact with a beam, followed by a further outbreak of profanity. 'But y'know what they say, it's like riding a bike. Once learned never forgotten.'

From the bottom of the stepladder I peered up into the roof space. 'So, where's the rain getting in?'

'It isn't, cock-bod. You ask me, that yellow patch is just natural ageing. Maybe a spot of duff plaster. Previous tenant having a champagne breakfast. Or maybe you had a rat die up there and – you know, sort of oozed its vital juices out. Sommat like that. No, you don't want to worry about it.' He patted the timber that he'd just bumped his head on. 'See all them knots and that little kink in it? Shows how old this place is. All they did, them days, was find a nice straight branch and mek it fit. You take a good look at that roof and you'll see all little dips in it. Might let a bit of wind in now and then, but that's good for your attic. Gives it an airing. But rain? Listen to the expert, cock-bod. She's water-tight.' He paused for a moment, then lowered his voice. 'Hey, come up here and tek a look at this though.'

'What have you found?' I climbed to the top of the steps and hoisted myself partway through the tight rectangular hole. 'Oh – that's a good 'un.' It was a wasps' nest, the size of a football and beautifully patterned with whorls of darker and lighter brown, like hundreds of snail shells all clustered together. 'Not live, is it?'

He prodded it, dislodging a few flakes of the papery material. 'If this was live, cock-bod, tek it from me, they'd be active – nice spring morning like this with the sun on the roof. They'd be all over me like a rash.'

'You gonna remove it, or what?'

'Nah, they don't come back to an old nest.' Soapy prodded it again. 'Bloody marvellous, these, and solid too.' And just for luck he gave it another whack, harder this time – and dropped his torch as a cloud of wasps emerged from the wreckage and headed towards the light.

'Outa me way, for f***'s sake Mike!'

I jumped off the steps just as Soapy came flying down, trampling my knuckles and then slamming the hinged trap-door on the angry buzzing sound that filled the roof space.

'I thought you said it was dead!' I shouted, as the pair of us danced around the bedroom with wasps dive-bombing us from every direction. 'Downstairs, quick!' I led the way, arms flailing about my head, ran into the living room and, as he followed me, slammed the door behind us, shutting our attackers in the stairwell.

'Now what?' I gasped, pointing upwards with a grazed and bloody right hand. 'What we gonna do with that lot?'

'I'll tell you what we're gonna do, cock-bod. We're gonna put the kettle on, have a cuppa tea and when me heart's stopped thumping I'll maybe pop down to Yates's for some poison. Then I'll fettle 'em.'

'And what about the leak?'

'How many times do I have to tell you? There is no leak, Mike. That roof is sound as a bell. Trust me.'

'Yeah, I'll trust you – 'cos you know what you're talking about, don't you, Mr City and Guilds?'

By the time I'd mashed a pot of tea and stuck a couple of plasters on my hand, Soapy was perched on the log outside the back door, puffing serenely on a cigarette, eyes closed, head back as he soaked up the sunshine. Over by the gooseberry bushes Henry was lying in the rank grass, snapping half-heartedly at the odd wasp that drifted past him. Up on the roof they were flying in and out of the slenderest of gaps where one or two tiles were tilted upwards at a slight angle. Soapy saw me looking. 'Don't worry, cock-bod. They'll be all right,' he said. 'Won't bother you for a month or two yet. People don't understand wasps. They do a lot of good – early in t'year.'

'Is that right?' I was thinking about the angry, buzzing cloud we'd trapped in the stairwell. They certainly seemed bent on mischief, if not murder.

'Aye, quite handy in t'garden. They'll eat aphids and suchlike. Just later on, when they've got the next gener-ation up and running, they start feasting on your ripe fruit, your jam and suchlike. That's when you find 'em in your kitchen, being a nuisance.'

'So what you saying? We're going to leave them be?'

'I would. Why go spending your hard-earned on poisons? Not very eco-logical, is it?'

'No,' I said, handing him his tea. 'I suppose not.'

'Aye, they'll not do any harm.'

'Especially if I can resist the temptation to poke their nest with a sharp stick. No, I tell you what, let's get rid of 'em.' I said. He didn't answer, and I decided I'd get onto less controversial matters. 'So,' I ventured, 'question for you.'

'Go on.'

'The wedding.'

'Aye, that.' He placed his mug on the grass at his feet and turned down the corners of his mouth. 'But I've got a question for you first.'

'Let's have it.'

Soapy jerked a thumb towards the house. 'This place? You thinking of asking Algy to flog it to you?'

'How d'you know about that?'

Soapy touched the side of his nose with his forefinger. 'Ah well, that's for me to know and you to find out.'

'Well, yes, Ann and I were wondering what he'd want for it, so I asked him.'

Soapy nodded his head. 'That explains it then. He had one of his estate agent chums over for a drink last night. Lad from out Helmsley way. So what's he asking?'

'No idea, mate. Don't even know if he wants to sell. He said he'd come round later in the week to talk it over. Anyway, stop changing the subject, will you? Tell us about the wedding plans.'

Soapy lit another cigarette and studied the glowing tip,

his brow furrowed. I waited, looking down the lane at the stand of larch trees. Their needles hadn't been out long, and in the bright sunshine they were still a beautiful lime-green colour. May is my favourite month at Keeper's Cottage: the house sits in an oasis of green, and on a morning like this, with the sky a bright blue, it really is a little corner of heaven.

'Don't get me wrong, Mike. I mean, I've nowt against getting married. But what I say is, why not just pop along to the old registry office, sign on t'dotted line, and then get yourselves down the Spotted Cow with your savings? Eh? I mean, what's wrong with that?'

'Ah, well,' I said. 'That's not what it's about, is it? You know what these lasses are. They want an occasion. An excuse to dress up.'

'Me too, but no need to go overboard.'

'I see. Getting over-elaborate, is it?'

'Listen, Mike, I can cope with a spot of elaboration. You don't get married every day, and all that. And I know they don't come cheap, these modern frocks. Push the boat out, I say. Top hats and tails for t'leading men? Yeah, why not? Go for it. Algy says we can use one of his old cars, so that's not a problem. I mean, don't get me wrong, Mike. I'm not like old Walt there. I can splash the cash when it's called for. But she's got the bit between her teeth now. Wants the full monty. Church affair, choir, bridesmaids in matching dresses, full-on reception at t'Stone Trough, bloody fancy invitations and reply-paid envelopes, goody bags at the dinner table – one for every guest. Hey, and how many do you think she wants to invite?'

'Search me, mate.'

'A hundred and twenty. A hundred and frigging twenty. I ask you, Mike, could you name that many people in t'whole of t'North Riding? 'Cos I'm buggered if I can. I tell you, mate, it's getting out of hand. Latest thing is, she read this thing in t'*Yorkshire Post* where some footballer marries a model and they release a hundred white doves outside t'church. Ooh, she goes, that'd be nice. How much is that gonna set us back, eh? I told her we could mebbe shoot 'em and stick 'em in a pie.' He took a final drag of his cigarette and flicked it to the ground. 'Not amused, my friend, not amused. And then on top of that there's the bloody honeymoon.'

'Why, you want to go somewhere nice for that, don't you?'

'What would you say to Greece?'

'What, you and me? I never knew you thought that way . . .'

'Steady away, lad.'

'Sorry, mate. Yeah, Greece. Cracking spot. That's where we've just come back from. Hang about – no, it was Cyprus; but they speak the same lingo, don't they? Anyway, great grub, fabulous weather.'

'Well, it might be good enough for you and Ann, but it ain't good enough for her. So how about Spain, I said? She laughed at me. Italy then? Doesn't like the grub. South of France? No, you'll not catch her bathing topless on the old Côte d'Azur. So guess what she wants. Go on, have a guess.'

'Florida?'

He snapped his fingers. 'Just what I said. No, she goes,

and – get this – she said it's "obvious". Everyone goes to Florida, she reckons. It's too bloody "obvious". So I said to her, go on, I said, what you after, lass?' Soapy leaned forward, picked up a stone and hurled it down the drive. 'Mauritius, my friend. That's the place to be. Five-star luxury hotel, mini-cruise, the bloody lot.' He fell silent, stamping out the cigarette end with his boot, then scowling at the flapping sole. I'd never seen him look so glum.

'So, what's the damage likely to be?' I asked.

'Last time I totted it up it came out at eighteen grand.'

'Hell-fire.'

'Aye, and you know what she says?' He didn't wait for an answer, which was a good job, because I didn't have one. 'Oh,' she says, 'that's not bad at all. That's well below the national average – according to *Hello!*' He shook his head. 'Anyway, the long and short of it is, we're not getting married till next year now. 'Cos it'll tek that long to save up – if I can find enough work.'

'Isn't Algy keeping you busy?'

Soapy was on his feet and brushing himself down. 'Algy? All he cares about these days is that horse of his. Lord bloody Nelson.'

'Oh aye, how's he managing?'

Soapy snorted. 'Old Walter's lady friend asked the same question in t'Farmers the other night. "With great difficulty," he goes, "with great difficulty".'

'Doesn't surprise me,' I said. 'Remember how Ann had to help him off it at New Year's?'

'I do. And I'll tell you this much, Mike. He hasn't improved. And he's still on about following the hounds first chance he gets. Anyway' – he took out his keys and made his way towards his van – 'better get myself to town and get that insecticide. Then his lordship wants mucking out.'

'His lordship?'

Soapy pulled a face. 'The horse, mate. Not Algy.'

'So he gets a horse and you have to sweep up after it?'

'Don't worry, cock-bod. I'm making it worth me while. Where there's muck there's brass and all that, y'know what I mean?' I looked at him and he gave a sheepish grin. 'Hoss manure. They can't get enough at the allotments down in Norton.' He got in the van and started it up. 'Pound a bag? It's like pinching money, mate.'

I watched Soapy drive through the woods and then went into the house. One or two wasps had managed to get under the door and I swatted them with a rolled-up newspaper. What I wanted was to go upstairs. I was starting back on the night shift, so I still had the rest of the day to myself. Normally I'd try and grab an hour in bed, but today bed was out of bounds until we'd dealt with our visitors.

By the time Soapy had returned, rigged up his sprayer and sorted out the wasps indoors – then sat and drunk more tea and had another moan about the cost of the wedding – the day had more or less slipped away. Thankfully Ann had been up and out early, visiting her parents. She's not at her best after a night duty, and wouldn't have appreciated the afternoon's excitement. 'Oh well,' I said, when she returned home at teatime and I filled her in with the day's events, 'I'll survive. Get my second wind once I'm out on patrol.'

It always feels a bit odd being back at work, even after a short break. I'd only been off ten days or so, but as ever things had moved on, and it would take a bit of time to catch up. Some of the cases that were top priority when I worked my last shift were history, new ones had come up, and a lot of the chat in the parade room concerned characters and incidents I knew nothing about. But I needed to make a call to York and find out what had happened about my off-duty adventures with the trailer thieves.

The depressing news was, not a lot. York CID had interviewed the fellow with the beat-up face, the one who was pulling the trailer. His story made sense. He told them the other members of the gang had come round and told him he was going to have to do this job. He refused at first. With his record, he said, he'd wind up in prison. That cut no ice with the gang. They beat him up and told him he could expect worse if he didn't co-operate. If that wasn't enough on its own to persuade him, he had a drug habit and needed whatever they might pay him. So he was very much an outsider, and his claims that he knew nothing much about the gang had the ring of truth. He'd given nothing away as to the identity of the team involved, and it was plain that his fear of prison was less than his fear of what they might do to him if he did reveal any information about them. Sometimes you genuinely feel sorry for people like that. They're basically inadequate, probably unfortunate. They get into bad company at a young age and never really escape the criminal environment. A couple of months later he was to appear at York Crown Court and be sentenced to eighteen months in prison.

As for the rest of the gang, we drew a blank. We had no other evidence or forensics to make further arrests. All we could hope was that the intelligence we'd got from the vehicles involved would prove helpful in the future.

'So what's new?' I was back in the parade room, digesting the news, when Ed came in to wait for our briefing.

'Not a lot, buddy. Apart from your drama the other night it's been pretty quiet, really. Which suits me fine. I've been on duty ten days on the trot.'

'Overtime?'

He nodded. 'Thommo managed to get himself on the sick again.'

'Ed, I asked you what was new.'

'Yeah yeah yeah.'

'So what's he done to himself this time?'

'Use of Force training.'

'He went on that? Fatal, buddy. Fatal.'

'Yep. He's got himself properly fixed this time. Ended up with his arm in plaster. I mean, how does the man do it? How can anyone be that unlucky? It has to be deliberate.'

'No, it ain't deliberate. Just . . . predictable. My old dad had a phrase for blokes like Thommo. They have what he called "an excess of zeal". Too bloody keen. I've been on Use of Force training with our friend, and let me tell you, Ed, he gets stuck in.'

'With an excess of zeal, right?'

'Right.'

The Use of Force and shield-training used to be a regular thing for me, back in my Met days. When I was in the

TSG, or riot police as people like to call it, we attended the Hounslow training centre several days each year. We had to both keep ourselves in physical shape and sharpen our technique, as well as familiarising ourselves with new equipment as it was developed. They have a whole mocked-up town there – entire streets where you can carry out all kinds of exercises, from one-on-one combat to crowd control to handling a full-on civil insurrection. Sometimes we even had twenty or thirty police horses down there to practise tactics. It's quite a sight when the mounted branch are clattering along the street in full riot gear. And the noise – it's like the Charge of the Light Brigade. If you need an adrenaline rush, you've got it.

Normal uniformed cops train twice a year. Our sessions are held at Swinton sports centre, just down the road from us. It's a two-part affair, and both are compulsory. Without them you can't refresh your training records, which are what allow you to carry your handcuffs and your CS gas and use your baton.

It's physically demanding, more so as you get older. You practise bringing a subject to the ground, applying wristlocks and armlocks, handcuffing a target who's armed or aggressive – all the techniques you need to subdue someone and make a safe arrest without putting yourself or the subject in danger. People think it's a simple matter, slapping the handcuffs on someone. It is on TV, but what the public doesn't realise is that the new rigid cuffs, if applied incorrectly, can cause serious injury.

You also learn and practise karate chops, judo throws, and how to disable someone by finding the various pressure points around their body. And you practise it all in pairs. Having been through it with our mate Thommo, I had no problem imagining how he might end up with his arm in a pot. Thommo went into this sort of thing with an enthusiasm that he rarely displayed at work. 'Reminds me of my young days back in Glasgow,' he'd say as he waded in, grabbed you round the waist, hoisted you over his shoulder and thumped you down on the thin matting they have in the gym there. Of course you have to try to bring a semblance of reality to the training, but Thommo pushed it to the limit.

As for the instructors or PTIs, it's a bit like Dirty Harry meets the Terminator. Especially when they're all padded up with protective wear – what they call the 'angry man suits', with the whole of their body protected. It's real tough-guy stuff, the idea being that they attack you, either unarmed or with a dummy weapon. You have to fight back and defend yourself, and because they're padded you can use a fair bit of force, but those instructors are as hard as nails and wily with it. They'll try to catch you out with every trick in the book. It's a funny feeling being attacked by a fully protected man, six foot four tall, putting on a display of fake anger that would make Steven Seagal look like a teddy bear. If you get it wrong they take you down – right in front of all your colleagues. And no matter how fit you are, after a full day of seeing off a succession of assailants armed with plastic knives and fake guns, being kneed and elbowed, thrown and hand-cuffed time after time, you can expect to go home covered in bruises, and aching in muscles you never realised you possessed. So it was no real surprise that Thommo was on the sick.

Ed and I had a quiet start to the night. There wasn't much happening in town and by a little after midnight we were on our way round the villages. I was praying for action, mainly to keep me from nodding off.

'Stop yawning, will you?'

'Sorry, Ed.'

'Should hope so. You're just back off holiday. And you've had all day to sleep.'

'In theory, yes.' I wasn't going to go into details. Whenever I mentioned my home life he'd tell me what a lucky fellow I was and start on about his own domestic woes: too many kids, too much clutter, too many jobs to see to. No, I'd best steer clear of the subject. Ed was driving, and he'd pulled up in a gate-hole beside the road that runs through Hovingham. I wound the window down and took a deep breath of the night air. 'Smell that,' I said. Someone must have just cut the grass verge and the atmosphere was heavy with the scent of newly mown grass. 'Summer's on its way, old buddy. Summertime – and the living is easy,' I crooned. But Ed was sniffing his sandwich.

'Bloody corned beef,' he said. 'She knows I don't like it. D'you think she's trying to tell me something?'

'Course she is.'

'What? What's the message? I don't understand women.'

'Ed, mate, she's saying it's time you learned to make your own pack-up. At a rough guess, like.'

Ed grunted and took a bite. 'She knows if I'm hungry enough I'll eat anything.'

We sat in silence for a few minutes. The road was deserted. There was barely a light on in the entire village.

'I don't think I could stand the excitement,' Ed said, taking a last bite of his sandwich and hurling the crust out through the window.

'What do you mean?'

'Living in a place like Hovingham. I mean, when was the last time you had to deal with a crime out here?'

'Can't remember. I stopped some guys in a van one time, coming up to Christmas. I was sure they were stealing turkeys. Positive.'

'We all remember that. Turned out to be a bunch of silly pluckers, didn't they?'

'No, that was me, buddy. I was the silly one. Come on,' I said. 'Change of scene.'

Ed started up the car. We pulled out from our parking spot and drove slowly through the village, past the Worsley Arms towards Malton. A pair of headlights dazzled us on the sharp bend that takes you out of the village, but the driver quickly dipped them and sped past. I only caught a glimpse of the car. It was a Golf, purple with customised plates, some sort of high-performance thing.

'Flash bastard,' Ed muttered.

'Just 'cos he's got more money than you.'

'I shouldn't think he's got three kids and a mortgage. Nor a wife who tries to poison him with corned-beef sandwiches.'

Back in town we were all set to swing by the station when we got an emergency call.

'*Control to 1015, over.*'

'Go ahead, over.'

'*We've a report from Pickering, Mike. A young girl, semi-conscious. Sounds as though drink is involved.*

There's a friend with her, very concerned. Ambulance on its way, over.'

'OK, Julie. Show me en route. Over.'

'Tuesday,' Ed said as we sped around the roundabout and over the bypass. 'They never used to start this caper till a Friday. Now it's any night of the week.'

The roads were fairly clear at that time of night and with Ed getting his foot down we were there in six or seven minutes.

We found the girl lying on the pavement at the back of a pub. She looked pitifully young, and very sick. Semi-conscious at best. Her mate was crouched beside her. As soon as we approached, a couple of youths who'd been standing nearby sloped off into the shadows. The girl had put a coat over her friend's shoulders and was shaking her, but the only response was a low moan. I presumed she was drunk, but her friend was having none of it.

'She just started staggering about. Said she felt giddy.'

'Here,' I said, kneeling down and putting the girl's head to one side, 'let's check that her airways are clear.'

That's always one of the biggest worries, that they'll throw up and choke on their own vomit, or that their tongue is blocking their airway – and it happens, even though it's so easy to make sure that it doesn't. But in this case the girl was breathing perfectly well, and there was no sign that she'd been sick. I could smell a bit of alcohol on her, but it wasn't what you'd call overpowering.

'What's happened? Is it just drink, or is she poorly?' I asked.

Her friend seemed relatively sober – and very nervy.

'She's hardly had anything,' she said. 'Couple of glasses of wine. She wasn't drunk at all. Maybe – it must be food poisoning.'

I could tell the friend was trying to hide something. 'No, she's had something to be in this state,' I said. 'C'mon, what's she taken? You're going to have to tell the ambulance crew, otherwise they won't know how to treat her.'

The girl looked at the ground. 'She told me she'd had an ecstasy tablet.'

'Right,' I said. 'When did she take that?'

'I don't know. About half an hour ago?'

'Just the one tablet, you say?'

'As far as I know, yeah. Just one.'

'Have you taken anything?'

'No.'

I wasn't sure she was telling the truth but I let it go. The important thing right now was to get her mate seen to. 'And where did she get it from?' As I spoke I saw the lights of the ambulance flickering against the side wall of the pub. She didn't answer. 'And what's your and your friend's names? Addresses?'

I got their details and went to meet the paramedics as they got out of the ambulance. 'She's taken an ecstasy tablet,' I said, 'as far as we know.'

'OK,' was all I got as they bent down to attend to the girl.

'Believed to be just the one, about half an hour or so ago.'

'Yeah, cheers.' I left them to it and took the other girl aside. 'Your friend, does she live with her parents?'

'Yes.'

''Cos we need to contact them.' The girl looked pretty shaken. Her face was pale and she was shivering. She only had a thin dress on. 'You do realise how dangerous that stuff can be?' I said.

'People take it all the time,' she said, then added quickly, 'I don't, but . . .'

'Where they getting it from?'

'They used to go to Scarborough or York, but you can get it here now.'

'Who's "they"?'

'People. Lads. I don't know. They come round and they have it in their pockets.'

'And where are they getting it from?'

'Look, they just get it, OK?'

'Where did your friend here get it?'

'I never asked. We – she got it off a lad we know. I don't know his name.'

'Listen,' I said, 'you're running a huge risk taking this stuff. You don't know for sure what you're taking, or how your body will react.'

'She was drinking plenty of water, like.'

'Yeah, dehydration's a danger, we all know that. But you can take too much water as well. You know that?'

She didn't answer.

'You should be leaving this stuff alone. It might look like fun, but it'll mess you up in the long run.'

I've always been anti-drugs. I suppose I'm what you'd call a hardliner. I can't really see much difference between the so-called recreationals – cannabis, ecstasy, ampheta- mines – and the harder stuff, the heroin and crack cocaine.

Maybe it's because I grew up in an era when they just weren't around, at least not where I lived. And then I'd spent ten years in the Met, seeing the consequences of drug use: the ruined lives, the gang wars, the degradation of the addicts who turn to petty crime, prostitution, anything that'll pay for the next fix. Most experienced cops can spot a long-term heroin user a mile off just from their physical appearance; it's easy. They're like the living dead. One thing I'd made up my mind on when I moved back to North Yorkshire was that I'd do my level best to keep drugs out of the market towns. But already we'd started to come across people using heroin. We'd search someone suspected of shoplifting, for example, and find them in possession. There were one or two smackheads around town and we knew who they were. What we were finding now, though, were more casual users of recreational drugs, and while it shocked some of my colleagues, I have to say that more than anything else it annoyed me. I simply didn't want it on my beat. It was another case of 'not on my patch, lad'.

Even though we'd started becoming aware of more widespread recreational drug use, ecstasy was still quite rare at this stage, although there were rumours that it was becoming increasingly available. That did worry me. An awful lot of people seem to think that it's harmless. Perhaps it is for the majority. They go out, and instead of just having a few drinks and then getting tired and going home at two or three o'clock they can pop a few tablets during the course of the evening as well, and keep going, wide awake and partying hard, till the next morning. As far as I'm concerned, they're buying tickets in a lottery, and as I drove this young lass home I tried to tell her about the risks she and her friends might be running. Because the risks are huge. Is the drug clean, or has it been adulterated? Some dealers, I pointed out to her, will cut it to increase their profits. Sugar, powdered milk and baking powder are some of the milder additives; some dealers use much nastier substances, including other drugs such as cocaine, speed, heroin and so on, all of which give different effects, meaning that you can't be sure what you're taking. Then there's the matter of how strong each dose will be. Most users find out by trial and error. And errors can be fatal. Have they mixed what they're taking with alcohol, and if so are they aware of the possible outcomes? And how will the concoction affect their judgement, their behaviour, their long-term health? Will they be making themselves vulnerable to robbery, assault, rape? And after you've taken all these risks into account, there's the simple, inescapable fact that these substances are illegal. Ecstasy is a class A drug, which means that possessing it – and, more especially, dealing in it – carries a heavy sentence.

I dropped the girl back at home, partly to make sure she was OK and partly so that I could confirm where she lived. I told her I would be back to speak to her at some point. From there I had the horrible task of visiting the parents of the sick girl and delivering the news about their daughter. They immediately headed to the hospital, shocked and angry, struggling to come to terms with the fact that this was happening to their daughter.

When Ed and I got back to the station and mentioned to our colleagues that we'd had to pack this lass off to hospital, we learned that a number of them – Jayne, Fordy, even Thommo – had good reason to suspect that the use of ecstasy was on the increase. They all said they'd been finding it more than they used to, which was just about never. And over the next two or three weeks I came across further evidence that this was indeed the case. More than once I found young people in possession. The little white tabs looked innocent enough, with just some sort of identifying insignia or trademark to distinguish them. The most common type had what looked like the badge off a Mitsubishi car, another had the outline of a dove. The word was that someone in the market towns was supplying, and that he – or maybe it was a she – was a reliable source.

So we had a problem. I started to put word out to various contacts, people who were as keen as I was to see this nipped in the bud. Some of them had heard rumours, whispers that there were indeed one or two people in the area dealing in ecstasy. But so far nobody knew anything concrete.

The rest of that week was fairly quiet. I was looking forward to the weekend – well, not exactly looking forward, more that it was on my mind. After Ann's pep talk earlier in the week I'd been thinking about the business of working my way up to sergeant. Ever since Christmas, when I'd promised Ann I'd start thinking about putting in for the exams, I'd managed to sweep the whole business under the carpet. I still wasn't sure whether I wanted to go for promotion. I wasn't sure that it was for me. Did I really want to be a sergeant, or was I just responding to all the mickey-taking I'd had for being a kept man? In the end it was my mum who spurred me into action, as she had done so many times in the past. She talked to me about my dad, and asked me what he would have thought to see me idling in the slow lane when I was capable of so much more. She knew that would get through to me, because I'd always idolised my dad. He was an extremely clever man, and I always worried that he'd think I was a failure for not being as accomplished as my sister, for example, who'd studied hard and was a total whizz with figures; or my brother, who was a chief pilot on the Humber. My mother made me promise that I'd start working through those books, and that I'd report back to her before I called round again.

So, Saturday morning, after I'd finished my last night shift, and with a two-day break ahead of me, I brought the books out from the shelf behind the television and placed them purposefully on the coffee table before going up for a few hours in bed. I'd get stuck into them in the evening. But before that, in the afternoon, we had a date with our landlord.

Algy arrived in his 1934 Frazer Nash, a great beast of a car that roared up the drive raising a cloud of dust.

'Where's old Dobbin?' I asked, as he reached outside the driver's door and yanked on the handbrake.

He clambered out of the seat and removed his goggles. He was frowning. 'Dobbin?' he repeated. Then his face broke into a grin. 'Ah, you refer to the recalcitrant Horatio. The gallant Lord Nelson.'

'Aye, grand day like this I thought you'd fancy a ride out.'

'Between you and me, Michael old chap, I'm starting

to wonder whether I haven't bought a pig in a poke, as my late father would say. I'm no longer convinced that horsemanship is destined to be a feature of Algernon's CV. If the Birdsall Hunt is to engage my services it may have to be as a mere hanger-on, a camp follower, a supporting player. I can see myself mingling with the gallant hunters with a tray of sherry glasses held aloft and cheering them as they gallop off over hill and dale.'

'You're still struggling then?' I said.

'No longer, alas. I'm afraid the struggle has been suspended. I am on the point of unconditional surrender.'

'No, no, no,' I said. 'You can't give in now. You can do it. You just need a spot of tuition. And here's the very woman who'll put you right,' I added, as Ann came out to admire the car.

'That would indeed be a help. Any chance you could help a duffer like me get the hang of this riding lark, Sergeant Barker?'

'How long have you had him now?' she asked.

'Well, let's see, I must've had him a week or two before we went on our maiden voyage . . . That is, when we came around on New Year's Eve.'

'And have you made any progress at all? Been out practising?'

'Ah well, that's the point. I did find that first ride somewhat trying, so I sort of − well, I decided that the best policy was *quieta non movere*.'

'Quieta what?' I said. 'Algy, mate, are we talking the same language here?'

'No no, do excuse me. It's Latin. Roughly translated, it means let sleeping dogs lie.'

'Ah,' Ann said, 'so what you're saying is, you haven't been on his back since we sent you home that night?'

Algy looked as sheepish as it's possible for a man to look when he's wearing a deerstalker hat and a paisley cravat and has his hands encased in long leather gauntlets. 'No,' he said, 'I haven't.'

Ann gave a little sigh. It was probably too faint for Algy to hear, but I knew what it meant. It meant she'd be round as soon as possible to sort the daft bugger out.

'Right,' I said, 'd'you want to step inside and talk about house prices?'

A lot of people underestimate Algy. Because he talks in that colourful way of his, and has an eccentric lifestyle, they assume he's one or two bricks short of a full load. They're wrong. Yes, he inherited money, but he's invested it cleverly and built on his good fortune. He's a very shrewd businessman and he can drive a hard bargain. So he wasn't about to let Keeper's Cottage go at a knock-down price. He named a sum and stuck to it. And once Ann and I had had time to reflect on the sum he was asking, we realised we would struggle to pay it as things stood.

'Well,' I said, as Algy roared off down the lane, 'that's that. It's well out of our range.'

'Oh no it isn't,' Ann said.

'Well, how can we manage that on our salaries?'

'I'm not suggesting we can.' Ann stood there looking at me. Her face was set, her lips pursed, and her brow furrowed. If I had to guess I would've said she was looking . . . determined. 'We just have to . . . what's the phrase? Adjust our parameters.'

'Come again, love?'

She rubbed her thumb and first two fingers together. 'We need to make more money – which means that PC Pannett needs to crack on and pass his exams. If you were on a sergeant's pay we could probably match his asking price.'

'You're right,' I said. 'You usually are. OK, I'll give it a go – but I'll be relying on you to help me.'

'Help you?' she said. 'I'll be standing behind you ready to kick your rear end.'

Chapter 3

Snout and About

'Cubs, you say?' As one part of my brain concentrated on noting down what the man on the phone was telling me, the other part was frantically trying to dredge up what I knew about young badgers. Adults I'd had some dealings with, but the young? I'd never had much to do with them.

'Two of them. I see . . . And what sort of state are they in, sir?'

He said they seemed fine, but that they were obviously orphaned.

'So are you in a position to stay with them till I can get over?'

'No problem,' he said, 'I'm here all morning, making charcoal. Got a stack of timber to put in my kiln. They're not going anywhere.'

I looked at my watch. 'Fantastic,' I said. 'Look, I'll be there as soon as I can. Let's say eight thirty.'

I put the phone down and went to my locker to look for the notebooks I still had from my wildlife course. What the hell do you do with baby badgers? Had we covered that? For an awful moment I was reminded of Walt's tale about his dad, serving them up as a Sunday roast, wrapped in pastry. He'd be locked up today, of course – but that was back when times were hard, in the 1930s and if they could trap it, or shoot it, they'd eat it. I put the thought from my mind. Right now I was already more concerned about my personal safety. There was no way I wanted to handle a pair of adolescent badgers. Cubs are born in February, and they don't come out from underground until May time, and by then they're a fair size. If you find one in the open early in the year it's a fair bet someone has dug into the sett and killed the adults, and it was more than likely that that's what had happened in this case. What was troubling me was that these youngsters would be four months old now. No way would they come quietly. But even as I shuffled through the chaotic muddle of circulars, notebooks and copies of legislation in my trays, something was starting to nag at the fringes of my memory.

I went back to the front desk where Chris Cocks was stirring his tea and reading a case file I'd submitted the previous day. 'Sarge?'

'What is it, Mike?'

'Am I imagining it, or is there a lass they call the badger woman?'

'Lady,' he said. 'We call her the badger lady.'

'Thought so. I was sure I'd heard about her. Doesn't she take in waifs and strays and so on? Injured animals, like?'

'She'll take in anything. Pets, wild animals, birds . . . even been known to take in a thirsty copper and give him a drink of tea. Lives across the river in Norton. And it's your lucky day. I have her details right here.' He opened a drawer in a desktop cabinet and riffled through a stack of index cards. 'But her speciality, as you'd say, is badgers. No idea why. Ah, here you go.' He pulled out a card and inspected it.

'Thank God for that,' I said. 'Y'know, it's all very well being a wildlife officer, but . . .'

'But people expect you to know all about wildlife, right?' Chris didn't look up, just ripped a page out of the pad on the desk and scribbled the phone number down for me. 'You'd think they'd have more sense, wouldn't you?'

'What, to assume I know – yeah, thanks Sarge.'

'Pleasure. And let's just hope the lady's at home.' He looked at me then and asked, 'Got your tetanus shots up to date?'

'I'm not that daft, Sarge.'

I suppose it's the same with any kind of so-called expert, or specialist. You can't be expected to know everything; but you do need to know how to find things out, who to call on. That's the key to it. And in my line you rely on your contacts. Normally I'd have gone to one of my gamekeepers. They'd know what to do. But Nick had just taken off on an African safari, and my other reliable source of information was out on the moors all week on some sort of National Park survey. As I dialled the number Chris had given me I made a mental note to call on Rich, another of my gamekeeper contacts, next time I was through Hovingham.

The phone rang several times. I was just starting to wonder who the hell I was going to call next when the lady I was after picked it up. I explained what had happened. 'Where are they?' she asked.

'Howsham woods. There's a guy burning charcoal up there—'

'Oh, Phil somebody?'

'That's right. He found them this morning.'

'What's he done with them? Are they still running loose?'

'No, he's got them under a tub of some sort. Turned it over on them. He assures me they won't get away.'

'Where shall we meet?'

'Oh, you're happy to come out then?'

'No offence intended, but I wouldn't want them to fall into the hands of an amateur, however well-meaning.'

I took the main road out of town and headed west, dropped down to Kirkham, then climbed up the other side of the Derwent valley, swinging past the Stone Trough to hit the woods at the point where the road turns towards Westow. The badger lady was already there, rummaging about in the back of her estate car amidst a tangle of boxes, wellington boots, blankets, cages, pet carriers and leashes.

'Mike Pannett,' I said.

'Jean,' she said, holding out her hand. 'Jean Thorpe.' She pulled out a stout plastic crate with a hinged lid, and looked towards the woods. 'Can we get any closer? 'Cos there's two or three miles of track in there.' She handed me the crate. 'You don't want to be trailing along with this thing, do you now?'

'Not on a morning like this,' I said. It had started out bright enough, but now the sun had been obscured by a towering, white-topped cloud. There was hardly a breath of wind.

'I think I know where to find him,' I said. I'd got to

know the basic layout of these woods the previous year when I made a series of visits to Gerald, the naked cyclist. I remembered seeing one of Phil's metal kilns smouldering away, but I'd never met the man himself. 'Let's shove this in my old Puddle Hopper here and we'll go down together.'

We followed the rough road along the side of the corn-field, then into the woods proper, climbing a steep, rutted track.

'There he is. Or at least, there's his workings, d'you see?'

I was looking at a metal sectional kiln about six feet across and four feet high, beside which was a neat stack of logs, graded by thickness, and all about two feet long. A few yards away, standing by an earth bank, was our man, wearing khaki trousers and a black T-shirt. 'Now then,' he said. 'I see they've sent the A team. Which one of you's going to take them on?'

There was no need for an answer. Jean was already approaching the sett.

'Someone's been busy here,' she said. 'Look at it.'

You can tell a badger's hole by the great piles of soil they throw out. But there were several mounds of freshly dug earth around this one, and broken roots, upturned stones, trampled greenery. I knew what it meant: men with dogs, bent on tormenting an adult badger, had been attacking it with spades. All in the name of sport, and without a thought for the young, who could starve to death for all they cared.

'Animals,' I said.

'I'd rather you didn't call them that,' Jean said. 'They're

not worthy of the name.' Then she turned to Phil. 'So, where are these young 'uns?'

'Just over here.' A few yards away Phil'd got some kind of galvanised metal tub, turned over and weighed down with a large piece of wood.

Jean walked towards it and crouched down. She was wearing a pair of leather gauntlets that reached almost to her elbows. 'Let's have a look,' she said, wiping the sweat off her face before kneeling down and carefully lifting one edge of it a few inches clear of the leaf-mould and faded bluebells. A dark snout appeared, snuffling. She carefully lowered the tub. 'Right, Mike, can you hand us the crate?'

I set it down beside her and then stood well back. I've seen how badgers can behave and needed to give her some room to operate in. I was wondering what I would do if one came bolting out.

'Cute, aren't they?' Both of the cubs were snarling and flailing out with their sharp claws as Jean picked them up, one after the other, dropped them smartly into her crate and closed the grilled lid. Now that they were safely locked in I edged forward to have a closer look at them. They were indeed exquisite, with their luxuriant fur dark at the tips, paler underneath, their heads marked with the familiar black and white stripes, their eyes as bright as little jewels.

'Aye, they're cute enough, so long as you don't get into a fight with them,' Phil said.

'Oh yes, they know how to look after themselves.' Jean picked up the crate, which rocked in her hands as the two occupants hurled themselves at the lid, trying to find a way out. 'Until they come across a gang of men with dogs bred for the express purpose of killing. Well, thanks for calling us – and for watching over them.'

'What'll you do with them?' Phil asked.

'Feed them, water them, and when I think they're ready to fend for themselves I'll set them free, as near to this place as I can.'

Before we left I grabbed some police tape out of my vehicle and marked off the area around the disturbed sett. One thing they'd hammered into us on the wildlife course was that it was always worth getting the scene of crime officer in to examine a site like this. It might be a bit of a long shot, but there was always the chance that there might be some sort of forensic evidence: a fibre, some DNA material, perhaps just a footprint. The fact is, a crime had been committed – and, like any other, it deserved to be investigated. The SOCO would take and file photographs too. You never know what sort of incidents will come up in the future. And if you have a record, you can maybe establish links.

I followed Jean back to her house. I wanted to see what kind of set-up she had for looking after wild creatures. I was surprised, then, to find that she lived in an ordinary detached house on an estate on the edges of Norton. Even her garden wasn't that big, but it was a little wildlife haven. Just inside the gate was a large aviary, with creepers running up the sides and a large tree overshadowing it. As we walked around the side of the house a frog hopped across the path in front of us. There were kennels, nesting-boxes, a couple of small ponds, and in her garage a pair of stalls, carpeted with straw. She let the badger cubs into one, and put out some water and a bowl of dog food for them. 'So who's next door?' I asked, looking at the neighbouring stall. She laughed, and opened it up for me.

'Blooming mallards,' she said. 'They've got to be the world's worst parents. They lose their own young, collect a few off other birds, and then wander off into the rushes and leave 'em to their own devices.' She looked at the huddle of fluffy brown-and-yellow chicks, most of them fast asleep. They were a tangle of downy feathers, beaks and oversized feet, crammed into one corner as if they'd been washed up there by a tidal wave. 'And then the public, God bless them, bring them to me. I'd fifteen of them, last time I counted, and I think they came in four different lots.' She closed the door, pausing to lift the lid of a large chest freezer. Inside was a plastic tray full of frozen chicks, not unlike the ones we'd just seen sleeping peacefully. 'Day-olds,' she said. 'I get them from a poultry breeder. They've either died or aren't viable. I feed them to any ferrets I get in, or foxes. Or owls, or badgers. The list, as they say, is endless. Anybody around here finds anything, it's "Take it to Jean".'

'I thought you'd be in a farmhouse, with a couple of acres,' I said, as she showed me into her kitchen and filled the kettle. 'Somewhere out in the country.'

She emptied a large china pot and spooned some fresh tea into it. 'Grab a seat,' she said, moving aside a bowl of water with her foot. Three floppy little black-and-white puppies followed it, tumbling over each other and starting to chew on my trouser leg. Jean bent down, scooped them up and dropped them in a basket across the other side of the room. 'You'll find I'm not sentimental about animals.

What do they say about nature, that it's red in tooth and claw?' She filled the pot with boiling water. 'Well, it's not far off the mark, is it? So why do people go all mushy?'

She poured the tea and shoved a tin of biscuits towards me, then said, 'But to answer your question, about me living here – go on, help yourself – I would be out in the country, no question about it, if I'd had any idea I'd end up doing all this.' She picked up a computer printout and passed it across to me. 'Even have a website now. And you know, it all happened by accident.' She looked at her watch. 'How you doing for time? Because I don't want to keep you.'

'Don't worry,' I said. 'There's nowt spoiling.' I know my colleagues think I spend too long supping tea and chatting, but to my mind this was another recruit to my army of contacts, people who would help me out, pass on information, advise me, educate me. You can't learn if you don't make time to listen, and you can't listen if you're always dashing. I've said it before: you can't police 600 square miles effectively without getting the community behind you.

'It all started after my dad died. We went through his things, the way you do, deciding if there was any memento we wanted for ourselves. I picked out his binoculars, 'cos he liked to sit in the window and watch the birds. It was barely a month or so after we'd buried him. I was in this kitchen baking a pie. I'd just put it in the oven and for some reason I picked them up and looked out of the window, over towards Howe Hill.' She got up, and pointed. 'You can still see it, look, across the field. And I spotted three badgers, under a sycamore tree, young ones, looked as though they were playing. And out of curiosity I got a book out of the library and started learning about them.' She laughed. 'Next thing someone's rescued one from a trap and I'm hand-rearing it, then I'm giving talks to the W.I., and before you know it it's turned into a full-time job. I even get the odd little donation now – you know, people who read about me in the paper and slip a tenner through the door in an envelope.'

I looked around at the large sacks of feed, the shrink-wrapped stacks of dog food that lined one side of her kitchen. 'Looks like an expensive hobby.'

'It is. But . . .' She shrugged. 'Someone has to do it. And besides, it makes me happy.' She stood up. 'I should think you need to be getting along, don't you?'

'If there's no more tea to drink I reckon I'd better,' I said. 'But listen, I'm very glad to have got in touch with you. I do come across injured animals from time to time – or have people calling in, reporting them – and it's not always easy to raise someone who knows what to do for the best.'

'Well, make a note of my number. I'm on call twenty-four seven whether I like it or not. If you ever need any help, you know where I am. If you call me out at three in the morning it won't be the first time.'

There are times, and this had been one of them, when doing my job didn't seem like work, at all. In fact, as I drove back into town I found myself thinking how very lucky I was to have a job where no two days were the same, where you keep coming across new and interesting people – and learning things. That's the great thing. You're always learning. Never bored.

There didn't seem to be a lot happening that day, and by about lunchtime I decided I might as well go back to base and see whether Stuart the SOCO had come up with anything at the badger site.

'Not really,' he said. 'But here' – he showed me the photos he'd taken. 'Might be useful to have on file.'

'OK, matey. Fingers crossed, eh?' I only had an hour left of my shift, so I decided I might as well make a start on sorting out all my incidents and crimes on the computer. I'm not a big fan of modern technology. It certainly has its benefits, but when it comes to record keeping, for some reason it always seems to take twice as long as when we did it with a pen and paper. Ah well, I thought, maybe I'll go through my work trays instead. Looking for my notes from the wildlife course that morning had reminded me that they weren't exactly in apple-pie order. Being a bit of a hoarder, I didn't like throwing anything much away. Bulletins, monthly updates, magazines: you name it. It could all come in useful some time.

I used to have a mate who worked in the civil service. He said there were two ways of going about a major sort-out such as I was planning. Plan A was to go through every piece of paper and diligently read it, then decide where to file it – and grow old and grey in the process. Plan B was to decide that life really was too short, check the date on every item and if it's older than three months, bin it. Unfortunately, in the police Plan B is not an option. Very little can be just thrown away, and most things have to be filed on completion and kept for seven years. With my trays looking like an artist's impression of an explosion in a paper recycling plant, option C came to mind – to pop it all back in and tackle it another day.

Half an hour later I was back in the parade room, telling myself I really needed to set some serious time aside to sort out my paperwork once and for all. But right now I was more concerned with the handover. With a bit of luck the late-turn guys would be in shortly and we could begin. There's a sort of unwritten rule in the police force that you always show up a bit early for work, in order to let the previous shift get off on time. It also gives you time for the odd bit of banter. Thommo was the first to show up, and I was just going to start taking the mickey out of him about his right arm, which was now out of plaster, when my mobile rang.

'Mike?'

'Speaking.'

'It's Ronnie, mate. Ronnie Leach.'

'Now then, lad. What's on your mind?'

'Er – I've a bit of information, like.'

'Oh aye?'

'It's – well, it . . .' He sounded muffled, and the line wasn't the best. 'I just thought you'd want to know, like.'

'I might, Ronnie. Depends what it's about. Are we talking racing tips, or more important matters?'

'No, this is serious stuff, Mike. Can we – er, can we meet up somewhere?'

I looked at my watch. 'Listen, where are you? You in town?'

'Aye, I've just been visiting me mum. I'm in Wentworth Street.'

'Right. Well I'll be away from here in a bit. How about

Malton station café? You know the place? It's right on the platform there.'

'Station café? Aye, what time?'

'Make it a little after two. Say a quarter past.'

'See you then.'

I was slightly taken aback when he rang off so abruptly. Normally he likes to prolong our conversations, to the point where I have to cut him off. I was starting to have hopes for Ronnie. We'd known each other way back in primary schooldays. We lived less than a mile apart, but we'd taken very different paths in life. It was only a year or two since I'd had to arrest him for theft – and then there had been the little matter of the milk disappearing off doorsteps out at Wintringham – but as far as I was aware he'd stayed out of trouble the past couple of years. Like a lot of petty criminals, he wasn't bad – not bad at heart, as you might say. He was more what you'd call feckless, which I never really understood, because he was bright enough. Certainly did better than me at school, as a rule, without ever having to work at it. But he'd never had what you'd call a proper job. Always bits and pieces, seasonal work, driving, labouring, short-term engagements on the side for people who paid cash in hand. A few days here, a weekend there. And, not surprisingly, some of the people he'd got to know over the years, first as a stable lad and then as a jockey, later as a regular in the bookies in town, would occasionally operate on the wrong side of the law. But he was a man who, I was convinced, would never do anything with malice in his heart. And, when you think about it, that's more than you can say for some of our so-called law-abiding citizens.

I got to the café in plenty of time and ordered one of

their excellent homemade cakes to go with my coffee. The place was almost empty, just a couple with a child sitting near the door. I took a table as far from them as I could. The guy at the counter had a radio playing, so it was ideal for a confidential chat.

'Now then, Mike.' Ronnie had slipped in without me noticing and was standing there looking hesitant, as if he was waiting for permission to take a seat.

I motioned to the chair. 'Sit down,' I said. I put my hand in my pocket and took out my loose change. 'Cup of tea? Coffee?'

He looked at his watch. 'No,' he said, as he sat down. 'I haven't got long.'

'Right then, so what's on your mind?'

'Look, I've got some information that might help you. But' – he looked around the café – 'I don't want to get – I mean, no involvement, right?'

'Listen Ronnie, first things first. It's not something you're involved in is it?'

'No, no, nothing like that.'

'Are you in any bother?'

'No, Mike. I'm doing OK. The old straight and narrow, you know what I mean? In fact, I've even got myself a little part-time job in York.'

'What's that then?'

'Er – it's in the tourist industry, you might say.'

I could tell by his manner that he didn't want to discuss it there and then. Besides, we had more important things to talk about. 'OK,' I said, 'so why don't you let me know what's on your mind and then we can work out what's best to do about it.'

'OK then.' He put his elbows on the table, cast a look at the family across the other side of the café, and leaned forward. 'There's a lad . . .' he said, and paused.

'Go on, I'm listening.'

'He's dealing in them ecstasy tablets.'

'Go on mate, sounds interesting.'

'Well, this lad ain't the brightest pebble on the beach, right? I mean, he had a job selling papers on the streets of York once over, and he got the heave-ho from that. So I'm thinking there must be someone behind him. If he is dealing.'

'What sort of quantities is he knocking out?'

'That's the point. The word is, it's just a few, nothing big time. But I think he's just a frontman for somebody much bigger.'

'So this lad then. What do they call him?'

Ronnie held up his hands. 'Mike. No names, no pack-drill, right?'

'OK, fair enough. So what are you trying to tell me, Ronnie?'

'Well.' He tapped the side of his head. 'This is just me putting two and two together, like, and I could be all to cock . . . but there's a lad in town who's been away for a year or two. I think he was out in Spain, or maybe it was Greece. Bit of an operator. Never had a proper job. Not the type.' Ronnie gave a nervous sort of laugh. 'Bit like me, really. Except that he always had a few quid to spend. He's only twenty-six, twenty-seven, and suddenly he comes back and he's absolutely bloody loaded. I was in the Spotted Cow a few days ago and I saw him take his wallet out. Bulging, it was. Crammed with notes.'

'Might've been payday,' I said. 'Or maybe he got lucky on the horses.'

'Ah, but there's more to it than that.'

'Go on.'

'The car he drives. One of them VW Golfs. Not the standard model, but a VR6. Turbo-charged. Alloy wheels, customised plates. Twin chrome exhausts.' He paused, then added, 'Bright bloody purple. I mean . . . Isn't that what they call making a statement?'

I didn't tell him that Ed and I had spotted just such a car just a couple of weeks earlier. I was too busy reminding myself not to jump to conclusions. 'Anything to connect him with this mate of yours who's dealing?'

'He's not a mate. He's just someone I've been told about, that's all.'

'Fair enough.' I was pretty sure Ronnie was trying to protect someone. Maybe he was trying to stop whoever it was from getting into big trouble. 'So this guy in the purple VW,' I said. 'You got a name for him?'

'Aye, I have. They call him Baker. Jed Baker.'

'Where's he live?'

'No idea. But I don't think he's living in Malton.'

'What's he look like?'

'You'd know him if you saw him. Tanned – like he's been under a sun-lamp. And he's dyed his hair bright blond. Sort of spiky, it is. Otherwise he's pretty average. Medium height, medium build. Always has a nice clean shirt on. Not a cheap one either. Fancies himself with the ladies.'

'Ronnie,' I said, 'why are you telling me this? What's in it for you?'

Ronnie looked at me, kind of puzzled. 'Look, we've all done a bit of stuff in our time. Well, most of us anyway. But it was small-scale, people growing it on windowsills. It was what you did back then, and you moved on. But now . . .' He shook his head. 'Bloody drugs everywhere, and then you see these big-time operators moving in and you know sooner or later some poor kid's going to pay for it, maybe with his life. Besides, me-laddo's a flash twat.' He scraped his chair back. 'And us country lads, we don't like that, do we?'

I couldn't help grinning at that. 'You in a hurry?' I asked him.

He looked at his watch. 'Yeah. Two-forty Goodwood. I've got one running with most of my worldly wealth riding on him.'

'Ronnie, lad, there's only one winner in that game, and you know who it is, don't you?'

'Aye, but remember what old Mr Bridges used to say to us back in primary school?'

'Can't say I do, Ronnie.'

'Some people never learn. And when he said it, he always seemed to be looking at me.'

'Yeah,' I said, 'and it'd be a pity if you proved him wrong, wouldn't it? Go on then. We'll talk later, I dare say.'

In modern-day policing we have a number of ways of obtaining intelligence. They range from Crimestoppers and registered police informants to members of the public and simple, old-fashioned observation by coppers themselves. The days of meeting your snout down the pub and slipping them twenty quid have long gone, along with

The Sweeney and Gene Hunt. As soon as you get into police informants you're looking at reams and reams of policy documents and procedures that have to be followed. You not only have to have completed the official handling course, but you have to meet your informants in the company of another officer and log every conversation. The safeguards involved now are never-ending. But I was on safe ground with Ronnie. He was a casual acquaintance and wasn't seeking reward. However, I would need to keep Inspector Finch updated and make sure that Ronnie wasn't giving me information for some ulterior motive, such as revenge – or to set somebody up. If I found out this was the case our casual meetings would have to be formalised.

I left the café with Ronnie and watched him scuttle off towards town and the bookies. Then I drove home, watching the sky and hoping the weather would hold. I'd planned to spend the afternoon tidying up the garden, starting with the grass. Normally I leave it fairly coarse, partly because of Henry's tendency to dig holes everywhere, partly out of pure idleness, but Ann had been getting onto me – and, looking at it as I got out of the car, I could see what she meant. The buttercups were out in force, the dock leaves were flourishing, and the whole garden was dotted with dandelion clocks. The trouble was, the skies had been darkening since before I left work, and already a few large drops of rain were splattering against the windscreen, accompanied by a rumble of thunder over towards the Vale of York. Oh well, I thought, maybe this is a clue from above: time for me to get into those books and start out on the long road towards promotion.

I went into the house, grabbed a waterproof and took Henry for a quick stroll. It tends to calm him down. But we'd got no further than the end of the lane when the storm broke. Suddenly it was chucking it down, and Henry, who hates thunder and lightning rather more than he loves exercise, was quivering from head to tail. Back at the house he tried to slip in through the back door. 'Sorry,' I said. 'In the kennel with you.' Nothing I like less than the smell of wet dog around the house.

I dried my hair, picked up the books, took a large apple out of the fruit bowl, switched on the light and sat myself down in the old recliner that Ed had palmed off on us when we moved in. Shabby it may have been, but by heck it was comfortable. And despite Ann's threats to sneak it off to Oxfam, I'd managed to hang onto it. In fact, she'd used it as one of her bargaining points when she was trying to persuade me to take this promotion business seriously. 'Tell you what,' she said, 'if I come home and find you sitting in it with the telly off, and the books open, I'll reprieve it. Providing you're awake,' she added. She drives a hard bargain, does Ann.

I like a good book. Especially if it involves travel, fishing, warfare or football. And when Ann and I ever get a night off together, especially in the winter, we do like to sit by the fire reading for an hour or so, with a large glass of wine. Trouble is, after a long day at work I always – always – nod off after a couple of pages. Then when I wake up I have to start all over again. I picked up the books Ann had given me. Not much here in the way of escapist entertainment, I muttered to myself. Just solid, down-to-earth law and criminology. I flipped through the titles, fully aware that my pulse was not exactly racing. PACE, the Police and Criminal Evidence Act; the Codes of Practice; the Human Rights Act and – a subject guaranteed to have me snoring like a chainsaw – traffic law.

I'd only dozed for ten minutes or so when the sound of the rain lashing against the windows brought me back to consciousness. That and the cold water pitter-pattering onto my head and trickling down my neck.

'What the bloody . . .!'

I leapt out of the chair. The book on traffic law fell onto the floor, and as I looked up at the ceiling I saw a huge bulge that seemed to tremble under the weight of water inside it. As the lightning flashed outside I grabbed hold of my chair. I timed it to perfection, just managing to drag it out of the way before there was a crash of thunder that seemed to shake the cottage walls and trigger the inevitable bursting of the bubble. A cascade of murky water dropped to the floor, followed by a several lumps of sodden plaster – and the light-shade. As the tide lapped around my slippered feet I looked up at the ceiling, or rather the hole where the ceiling used to be. Water was trickling from splintered laths. A length of grey PVC cable was dangling from a beam. On the end of it was a naked hundred-watt bulb, flickering on and off before dying with a damp 'pop'. For a moment the room was plunged into semi-darkness, then another flash of lightning illuminated a stream of water that was running down the chimney-breast and forming a pool in the tiled hearth.

'Great,' I muttered as I sploshed my way to the

windowsill, picked up the phone and dialled Algy's number. 'Come on,' I said as it rang a third and a fourth time. 'You're surely not out in this.'

'Hello?'

'Algy, it's Mike.'

'Who did you say? I can hardly hear you, I'm afraid. Blasted thunder.'

'It's Mike!' I shouted. 'Keeper's Cottage. We've got a major, major problem here.'

'Lights gone, eh? Ours have too. Surprised the jolly old phone's working. I dare say they'll get 'em on again before too long though. Frightfully good, these electricity board chappies.'

'It's not as simple as that, Algy.'

'Really?'

'Really. You remember sending Soapy down to check for a leak in the roof?'

'Yes, he gave it a glowing report.'

'Well, he's got some bloody explaining to do. Me front-room ceiling's just collapsed and flooded the place. There's fresh rainwater running down the chimney-breast as I speak, our brand-new carpet's submerged, and I'm sodding wet through.' As I reeled off a catalogue of disasters I suddenly stopped and shuddered. Oh hell. I hadn't even looked upstairs yet. 'Algy,' I said, 'I'll call you back. Hang on though – why don't you get hold of Soapy and send him down. Then I can kill him with me bare hands.'

I abandoned my sodden slippers, splashed my way across the carpet, banging my right foot on the corner of the sideboard and all but ripping my little toe off. I hobbled, cursing, towards the foot of the stairs. The bedroom wasn't as bad as I'd feared. In fact, it was virtually undamaged. The water was mostly running down the wall, into the little cast-iron fireplace and disappearing around the back of it. The bed, by some miracle, was dry, but just to be on the safe side I dragged it to the far side of the room. Out of curiosity I tried the pull-cord – and hey presto. Light. So it was only downstairs that had gone; shorted out in all probability.

The phone was ringing. I galloped downstairs, pausing only to curse afresh as I whacked the little toe of my left foot on the sideboard. 'Yes!' I roared into the mouthpiece.

It was Soapy. 'You don't sound very happy, cock-bod.'

Have you ever noticed how, when you're really, really mad and just managing to control yourself, the thing most likely to push you over the edge is someone sounding like they haven't a care in the world?

'Lissen, you numpty, long-haired, idle, cack-handed pillock. Get yourself over here NOW! And bring your toothbrush and a fresh pair of underpants, because you ain't leaving here till you've sorted this lot out. Now then.'

'I was about to come, mate.' Down the phone I could hear him drawing on his cigarette. 'Just thought I'd wait till t'rain eased.'

'Till the bloody rain eases? Soapy, my friend, if you wanna salvage something from your worthless life you'd better get in that clapped-out motor of yours and get down here, with your tools, in record time. And you will enter this house on your knees, hands clasped, praying that I don't do what natural justice demands I do, and rip your bloody head off.'

There was a short silence, then a very subdued voice said, 'Right, cock-bod. I'm on my way.'

I put the phone down, looked around at the drenched carpet, the hole in the ceiling, the water coursing down the chimney-breast, at my little toes, one with the nail hanging off, the other weeping blood onto the floor – and laughed out loud. For some reason it made me feel a little bit better.

When Soapy showed up, about twenty minutes later, he was – there's no other word for it – abject in his apologies. 'Bloody hell, Mike, I'm sorry, mate. Honest I am.' He stood under the hole in the ceiling, poked at it with a long-handled screwdriver, then went outside. I followed him. The rain had stopped now, and the late afternoon sun was slanting through the linden trees. Steam was rising off the pantiles, and a solitary wasp was hovering above the little gap where we'd spotted the nest a few weeks previously. A couple of feet away from it, against the lead-lined gully that drained the water down towards the gutters, a tile had slipped, forming a sort of bridge.

'There's the source of our trouble,' Soapy said. 'T'water's come down that gully, struck the loose 'un, and got in – bloody hell, Mike, see that crack in the chimney?'

'Where's that?'

'Look, under where t'aerial's fixed to it. Runs right down to the base there. I make it that's two leaks you've got.' He shook his head. 'Tell you what, why don't you put t'kettle on, eh? Then start praying for a spell of fair weather, old lad, because this is gonna tek some time to fettle.'

Chapter 4

Going Dutch

Inspector Finch had a pencil in his hand. As he walked to and fro, waiting for us to settle, he held it as if it were a cigarette, flicking imaginary ash off it every few seconds. From a man who'd given up smoking a year earlier it wasn't a good sign. But I'd seen this all before. He was always like this when he had something on his mind – and a chief superintendent snapping at his ankles. He would have some sort of campaign to roll out. Either that or we were – jointly or individually – in for a rollicking. Because there was no doubt about it: he'd had one from higher up.

We were on the early turn, me and Fordy, Jayne and Ed, with Chris as duty sergeant. Let's hope for a quiet shift, I was thinking, because we're a man short. Thommo was rostered to be with us, but his missus had rung in to say he had a fever. Birdie went through a few routine matters.

'You may have seen that the government' he began, 'have introduced new league tables to measure our performance against other Police Basic Command Units – or BCUs for short. In a nutshell it means that nationally our performance will be judged against other, similar nicks in rural areas. The tables will be published for all to see. The chief superintendent has high hopes that we will do well.'

Ed nudged me and whispered, 'Thinks he's a bloody football manager now. Do you think we'll get some kind of sponsorship on our shirts Mike?'

'What was that, PC Cowan?'

'Nothing sir, just mentioned to Mike that we will do our best to hit the Premiership.'

'This is not football Ed, this comes from Whitehall. You'd do well to take it seriously.'

'Yes sir, of course sir.'

Birdie then got to the business that was clearly preying on his mind. 'We've talked about ecstasy a couple of times recently, and I know that one or two of you are worried that it's starting to be used more widely on our patch. So you'll be pleased – or alarmed, take your pick – to hear that the intelligence unit confirms what you suspected. There's been an explosion of its availability and use in the wider area around us. What we don't want is to start finding it on sale outside every pub and club. Our chief superintendent has been keeping an eye on the situation. She tells me she's very concerned about the problem and wants to know what we propose to do in order to get on top of it.'

Birdie paused, strolled to the window and looked out. It was a beautiful, sunny midsummer morning out there, with white puffy clouds sailing across a blue sky. It was hard to tell what was on his mind – whether he was awaiting a response from the floor, as it were – but we all sat and waited in silence. Nobody was going to say anything, not yet. Whenever the chief super got involved, Birdie jumped. And when Birdie jumped we knew that we too would soon be hopping.

'Now,' he said, turning to address us once more, 'all we have locally is your individual observations and reports. It's bits and pieces of information, arrests for possession, the collapse of that girl out at Pickering – and we've recently had Mike's tip-off about the lad in the VW with cash to burn. Rumours, word-of-mouth, and a general feeling that the drug is increasingly available, am I correct?'

We mumbled our agreement.

'The point is, we don't really know what's going on on the ground – not yet, at any rate. So what I'm proposing is a dedicated operation. Pannett.' He turned and faced me – as did Jayne, Fordy and Ed.

'Yes sir?'

'You ran an operation – Clean Sweep I think it was called – a couple years back, didn't you? Around the time you first joined us. Cannabis, am I right?'

'Yes sir.'

'And you got a decent result, I believe?'

'Myself and PC Cowans made twenty-seven arrests, sir, and a number of seizures.' I was going to add that I'd got a pat on the back from the former chief super, but decided not to push my luck.

'Right. I want you to mount a similar operation as soon as we can get it organised. First of all, we want to know what's out there. Ideally, we want a few leads on who's supplying it. You and PC Ford will double up on this.' Fordy looked surprised – as indeed I was. I'd presumed he'd team me up with Ed. Then I remembered that he was about to take off on his holidays. 'We'll make it a weekend op,' Birdie continued, 'and bring in a couple of Specials to keep the numbers up to strength. You will report to me.'

As he spoke, I saw Jayne pulling a face. She would love to have been in on this too, and to tell the truth I would happily have worked it with her, but I had no say in the matter. Fordy, on the other hand, was nudging me in the ribs and giving me the thumbs-up. He knew I would be up for this. And I knew he would give it everything. As the junior hand, he was new to this kind of operation, and keen as mustard. For him, it was a chance to learn; for me, it was going back to what I used to do on an almost daily basis.

When I was in the Met we dealt with drugs around the clock. Observation, surveillance, stop-searches: it was a never-ending process – and a more proactive kind of crime fighting. I'd seen most things on the drug scene down there, having arrested numerous cannabis, heroin and crack dealers. I'd also dealt with some nasty individuals – and shrewd operators. Having said that, ecstasy was something relatively new to me. Ryedale rarely saw any hard drugs, whereas London was plagued with users and dealers of class A drugs. They'd be on the streets from ten in the morning until the early hours, seven days a week. Which was why many nicks had a dedicated full-time drugs squad. Here in Ryedale, with cannabis, ecstasy and so on, what people call the recreational drugs, you were looking at a much more restricted spread of activity. People looking for 'something for the weekend', people who had jobs, who you never saw in the week, would be out in force on a Friday and Saturday evening, to a lesser extent on a Sunday. So it didn't take a genius to work out that we should launch our campaign over back-to-back late turns, on a Friday and Saturday. And Birdie agreed.

'This is all right, mate,' Fordy said as we made our way to Mennell Motors the next day. We were both in plain clothes, and we were on foot. 'Always fancied working undercover.' We'd come in to work a couple of hours early and plotted out what we were going to do. This would take the form of old-fashioned policing. We'd looked at the intelligence system locally for details of who had been arrested in possession, or reports on anybody who was thought to be involved in some way. Experience told me that the best chance of catching the low-level dealers was when they were moving their merchandise around from A to B, either on foot or by car, and generally before the punters hit the pubs. Our plan was to carry out as many stop and searches as possible and give the users and dealers a hard time, to cause them as much disruption as possible. We didn't need to hit the jackpot. Experience told me that the small finds can often give you the intelligence leads that point the way to the main players.

'Yeah,' I said, answering Fordy's earlier remark. 'It's hardly what I'd call undercover. But it makes a change, doesn't it?'

We were walking into the wire-fenced compound. They

had a number of white vans there, and a couple of fairly nondescript saloons – just the sort of thing we wanted for an operation like this that had a limited lifespan. Plenty of people – particularly the kinds of people we would be looking at – would be likely to recognise me and Fordy. They'd have seen us on patrol, in many cases got involved with us. So the anonymous hire-car, it gives you a head start. 'Once you start doing stop-and-searches,' I said, 'word's gonna get out, isn't it?'

'I suppose so. They'll be on their mobiles.'

'Right,' I said. 'The minute we start pulling people over, you mark my words, they'll be on to their mates in a flash. I reckon we'll do well to get one evening in Malton, another in Pickering and Helmsley, then we might as well shut up shop.'

'Sounds like we need to get lucky,' Fordy said.

'And soon,' I added.

We hired a Vauxhall Corsa, a nice, plain saloon car, several years old, the sort of thing that might belong to a student, a hairdresser, some pensioner who never went any further than the supermarket once a week. Unobtrusive. So when Fordy got in the car and whipped out a pair of mirrored sunglasses I had to give him the hard word. 'Gary, lad, this ain't *Miami Vice*, y'know.'

'I just thought it'd help. So they wouldn't recognise us.'

'Not recognise us? Fordy me old mucker, you might as well get a bloody great neon sign and stick it on top of the car. Police. Disguised as Ordinary Blokes. I mean, two fellers out together? Cruising the streets at twenty miles an hour and clocking everyone who looks a bit dodgy – and one of them is wearing shades?' I laughed – and even

Fordy could see the funny side now. 'Nah. Save 'em for the holidays, buddy. Besides,' I added, 'the sun's gone in.'

That Friday evening was near enough a total let-down. We made a number of stop-searches, and all we got for our trouble was a lot of abuse and aggravation. An operation such as this isn't as simple as it sounds. Just because you suspect that drugs are circulating it doesn't give you carte blanche to stop everyone you come across. Basically, you have to have reasonable grounds to suspect the person is in possession of drugs. However, I have long since learnt that you can go around and speak to whoever you want. There's no law against that, and experience does give you an idea of what to look out for: the fixed pupils, the smell of cannabis, the person's demeanour – and of course any intelligence or local knowledge. Obviously most people dislike being stopped and searched. It's intrusive and personal. People kick off because they have nothing on them and feel empowered to object, knowing they are clean. Others kick off because they *are* carrying something and want to deter you. My personal opinion is that it's an absolutely vital tool for the police to have. If you take away the power to stop and search – well, we may as well pack up and go home.

So we more or less drew a blank that night, although we did get one result when we chanced upon a group of lads on a bench outside the swimming pool. We might not have bothered had they not looked so startled when we drew alongside. They had a few spliffs between them, and we duly arrested them, took them back to the station and cautioned them. But it was a frustrating start. Not what we were after at all.

Fordy was properly downcast by the end of the shift. 'I was hoping for better than this,' he said, as he drove us back to base about half past midnight. 'I mean, how many stop-searches have we conducted?'

I flipped open my notebook. 'A dozen, just the four that were positive. Look on the bright side, Fordy. That's one in three – not a bad strike rate. I once did a street robbery operation in Croydon where we stop searched over 350 people and made forty-seven arrests in the week. What's that? About . . . Oh, I can't do the figures. Too bloody late at night.'

'One in seven, mate.'

'There you go then. Tonight's ratio isn't that bad.'

'Yeah, but not a sniff of the result we're after.'

'Well Fordy, as they probably told you when you joined up, it's not like on the telly. These things can take time – and a lot of luck.'

'Yeah, I suppose you're right. It's just frustrating.'

'Look,' I said. We were at the back of the police station now, and he was manoeuvring the Corsa into the far corner of the car park where it would be hidden away among the shrubs. 'This sort of operation is a bit like going fishing. You have to be patient. You have to wait for that little nibble. And you have to accept that some days you're going to go home with nothing to show for your trouble but a stiff back and frozen feet. I had far worse days in the Met. I remember sitting outside some guy's flat for ten hours waiting for him to come out – and then it turns out he moved house a week ago and no bugger's bothered to tell me. Patience, lad, that's the name of the game.'

It was always amusing, working with a young lad like Fordy. It made me feel like a real old hand. I found myself talking to him the way the old lags in Battersea had addressed me when I first started, fresh out of Hendon and full of it. So the pair of us went home feeling a little low – and I was about to feel even lower. I arrived at Keeper's Cottage to find Ann standing outside the back door shining a torch up at the roof and pulling a long face. There was a ladder propped against the wall, and a huge polythene sheet covering an expanse of roof where someone had stripped half the tiles off.

'Let's have it,' I said. 'What's the state of play?'

'Right,' she said, 'I've had Soapy. I think he spent the best part of the day here. Found him hard at it when I got in at teatime.'

'Hard at what? Supping tea and having a crafty fag?'

'No, he'll have heard me coming up the lane. By the time I got out of the car he'd managed to scoot up the ladder and raise a sweat.' She pointed at a stack of tiles up against the side of the cottage. 'As you can see, he's made a start. Next job is to replace the timbers – well, some of them. They're due to arrive some time in the next few days. Then he's putting us a layer of roofing felt on, because it's never had any, then they piece it all back together.'

'They?'

'He had some lad with him. Probably a blood relative working for peanuts.'

'Great. Just what we need. I mean, here we are, halfway through the year already, and I haven't even started on – well, you know what I'm talking about.'

'Preparing for your sergeant's exams?'

'Yeah, that.' I looked at my watch. 'Damn. They'll be closed, won't they?'

'The Farmers?'

'Aye. I could murder a pint right now. Can't remember the last time we got down there.' We trudged into the house. 'Oh well, guess we'll have to do without, eh?'

'Come on,' Ann said, 'there must be something in the drinks cabinet for a nightcap, surely?'

'Didn't know we had one of those.'

'OK, the sideboard.' We rummaged around and dug out half a bottle of cheap sherry left over from last year's New Year's Eve party, a bottle of very flat tonic water, a packet of Twiglets, and a dodgy-looking liqueur of some kind that neither of us could remember buying, let alone drinking.

'We should never have given Walter that ouzo,' I muttered.

'Relax.' Ann had reached deep into the top shelf and plucked out a bottle of rather expensive-looking malt whisky. 'Will this do?'

I took a look at it. 'Fifteen years old? I reckon it will.' I perched myself on my recliner, and kicked away a sheet of newspaper. We'd spread papers all over the floor to try and dry it up as much as possible. The carpet was still outside, draped over the logpile.

'There's one other thing,' Ann called out from the kitchen. 'Well, two. So shall I give you the bad news or the . . . interesting?'

'Go on,' I said. 'Hit me with the bad stuff.'

'The chimney has to be rebuilt. According to Soapy it's cracked and unstable.'

'That doesn't surprise me. So we're looking at builders trailing in and out and—' I clutched my head at the thought. 'I had this before, years ago. They park all over your lawn and chew your drive up. You end up eating cement dust with your grub. And you get Minster FM from dawn to dusk at about 110 decibels. Bloody marvellous.'

Ann came back through and handed me a glass. 'Cheers,' I said. 'Here's to sanity in the face of imminent calamity.'

Ann clinked hers against mine. 'And to our anonymous benefactor.'

'What d'you mean?'

'Well, you didn't buy this, did you?'

'No.'

'And I wouldn't spend that much on champagne, never mind Scotch.'

'We should have more parties,' I said, pointing towards the sideboard. 'Before we have to restock that.'

'I think you've got a point there.' Ann sat down on the arm of my chair. 'Anyway, I was going to tell you another piece of news.'

'And you said that this one wouldn't be as painful.'

She took a sip from her glass. 'Right,' she said. 'Algy was very apologetic about everything.'

'So he should be. It's a landlord's responsibility—'

Ann held up a hand. She had her 'Are you listening?' face on.

'Sorry.'

'Very well, then. I shall proceed. Algy is suddenly feeling bad about the price he quoted for us buying this place.'

'He actually said that?'

'No, he didn't utter those precise words, but I took the liberty of telling him that of course you and I had made a very shrewd decision.'

'About what?'

'About not buying a property that was in such a dangerous state of dilapidation. And he said he would have to – and I quote – reconsider his position.'

'Are you serious?'

'Yes. I opened the door and he walked right in. I'm a dab hand at negotiating, you know.'

'Looks as though living with me is rubbing off on you.'

'Mike, I'm my father's daughter. You ought to know that by now. Anyway, Algy also gave me the impression that, what with Lord Nelson taking so much of his attention, he really finds all this landlord business a bit of a faff.'

'Hmm,' I said, 'Lord Nelson. Thought you were going to straighten his lordship out?'

'Don't be changing the subject. The long and the short of it is, I think that your pal and mine is ready to see sense and consider a realistic price for this place.'

'Once he's fettled the roof, you mean?'

'Naturally. We wouldn't want to take on a burden like that, would we?' She clinked her glass against mine. 'Cheers.'

I was in high spirits when I breezed into work next day, and had put the disappointment of our first drug-investigation shift behind me. Things were looking up – at home, at least. The sun was shining, the carpet was drying – slowly – and Ann had raised the enticing prospect of Algy dropping his asking price.

'Another day of casting bread on the waters is upon us,' I told Fordy as we met up in the locker room. 'Anything is possible, my friend, anything.' All we had to do was run the gauntlet of the parade room, and the outgoing shift, putting their fingers to the lips with theatrical exaggeration when they spotted us.

'Well, who'd have guessed it? It's Pannett. And his side-kick. Never recognised you two in your . . . disguise. But hey, we won't say a word. 'Cos it's all hush-hush, isn't it?'

'Yeah yeah yeah, very funny, lads. Just you wait. When we haul the big fish in and you lot are standing to attention watching the big white chief patting us on the back, we'll see who's laughing then.'

Fordy never said a word at first. I think he'd taken it to heart, the previous day's apparent failure to seize any ecstasy, and I was waiting for him to get it off his chest.

'They get right up my nose,' he said, as we got our things together and prepared to hit the road. 'Bunch of pillocks.'

'It's only banter, Fordy lad,' I said. 'They're jealous to death that they're not getting a go at it. Out on the beat on a fine day like this, and we're on a special operation. Probably be a spate of domestics by teatime, just you see if there isn't. And here's us, free to wander wherever our feet take us. They hate it, that's what it's all about. Get used to it. There's always going to be a bit of shift rivalry, wherever you work.'

Fordy didn't answer. Jayne had come in, grinning like

a Cheshire cat. 'Why the long faces, lads? Thought you two was on a little jolly? North Yorkshire's own drug squad. Although from what I hear you haven't exactly nailed Mr Big yet.'

'Put it this way, Jayne,' I said. 'Our enquiries are ongoing. They are at an embryonic stage. When the break-through comes – when, not if – you will be among the first to know.'

'Meaning you ain't had a sniff of a result, yeah?'

'It's early days, lass, early days. We'll get there, you see if we don't.'

She shot a glance at Fordy. 'You should've 'ad me on the team, Mike.'

'Jayne,' I said, just before we slipped outside, 'if I'd been the chairman of selectors, you'd have been the first name on my team-sheet.'

'Is that right?' Fordy asked, opening the car door a few moments later. 'That you'd rather have her with you?'

'What am I gonna say? She's keen, same as you are. It's only natural she's disappointed,' I said. 'Listen, I don't mind who I work with, so long as they put a hundred per cent into it.' I got into the car beside him. 'Tell you what, though, I wish I felt as confident as I sound.'

'I s'pose it's a case of keeping the faith,' Fordy replied. 'That's what I was always told.'

'You're right, matey. Something'll show up. Has to.'

The thing with policing – especially the kind of policing we were now engaged in – is that you never know when you're going to get that break. What's important is, when something does come along, you have to be prepared to grab hold of it with both hands. And, being the optimist I am, I always expect my luck to change. Like that guy in Dickens – Mr Micawber. What did he say? 'Something will turn up.' Even so, I could hardly believe it when Fordy turned right at the traffic lights at Butcher Corner and there, passing us in the other direction, was the purple VW with the blond-haired fellow at the wheel.

'Hey, that looks like the lad I've had a tipoff about,' I said, craning my neck round to watch the car turn into Yorkersgate. 'He might be worth looking at.'

'Right.' Fordy was clutching the wheel and braking hard. For a moment I thought he was going to turn us round right there in the middle of Wheelgate.

'Steady on,' I said. 'Nip up the top and cut through the back of the cattle market. Plenty of traffic about. He shouldn't be far ahead of us.'

A minute or so later we were coming out by the war memorial, joining a stream of cars heading west, with our friend just eight or ten vehicles in front.

'So what's the SP on this bloke?' Fordy asked as we made our way towards the bypass.

'Basically that he's flashing a lot of money around, and he doesn't seem to have a job.'

'Any intelligence on the car?'

'No. I checked it on the PNC and it came back with nothing. Only odd thing was, it's registered in Pickering, to a female. Could be innocent enough, I suppose.'

'But on the other hand . . .' Fordy left the sentence

hanging, putting his foot down to pass a couple of slow-moving cars and keep the VW in sight.

When you're following someone in these circumstances you have to tread a fine line between not losing sight of the target and not getting so close that he becomes suspicious. The traffic was pretty heavy as we joined the bypass, with a solid line of cars snaking around the curves on the approach to Golden Hill. We were barely doing forty miles an hour, but as soon as we hit the dual carriageway we found ourselves doing seventy-five, and the VW was still threatening to get away.

'Bloody hell, Mike. Couldn't we have got something with a bit more poke?' Fordy had his foot flat down and was leaning forward, as if willing the Corsa to go faster.

'Relax,' I said. 'Soon as we get up to that Indian place he'll slow right down again.'

We could already see the Jinna restaurant, and the cars were all braking as the two carriageways merged into one.

'Wonder where he's heading,' Fordy said.

'Let's hope it's this side of York. Any further than that and we'll have to let him go. This is a local operation. If he heads off to Leeds or somewhere we're not set up to conduct a proper surveillance job.'

'Ah, but he isn't!' Fordy was braking sharply as the guy signalled right, slowed down, pulled into the forecourt of the Highwayman café and disappeared behind a couple of large trucks that were parked at the far side.

'Don't be following him in,' I said. 'Just drive by. We can turn around at the Hopgrove.'

It took us seven or eight minutes to get down to the big roundabout and back, and Fordy was getting edgy.

'Hope he's still here,' he said, peering over the wheel as he drove slowly between the rows of cars, the loose stones crunching and popping underneath us.

'He will be,' I said. Fordy nosed the car past the trucks. 'See?' I pointed to the VW, parked on its own, out of sight from the road.

'Now what? Do we park up where we can keep an eye on him or what?'

'Why not just go in and get a cuppa,' I said. 'Less suspicious than sitting in the car park, isn't it? Just act naturally. We're two guys on a trip to town, right?'

'Fair point. Maybe he's meeting someone, doing a spot of business.' Fordy unsnapped his seatbelt. 'Yeah, come on.'

Inside, the café was busy. Mostly it was families enjoying a snack and a drink with their children on their way to or from the coast, but there was a scattering of commercial drivers, most of them hunched over large plates of food, with newspapers unfolded in front of them. And there in the far corner was our man Baker, seated at a table and deep in conversation with a balding, middle-aged man wearing blue overalls.

We got ourselves a cup of tea apiece, Fordy picked up a newspaper from the rack by the counter, and we made our way towards a place that looked out onto the car park. It was as close as we dared get to Baker and his associate, perhaps ten or twelve feet away. I could just about see them out of the corner of my eye without turning my head.

If I say so myself, we put on quite an act. Fordy turned to the sports pages of his paper and started reading out bits of cricket news to me. I answered him in monosyllables, straining my ears to hear what was being said across the way. I couldn't catch much, because the two men were keeping their voices low, but what I did pick up – and Fordy noticed the same thing – was that the older guy had a pronounced foreign accent. Dutch, by the sound of it.

'Here we go, Fordy.' I nudged him under the table. They'd both got up from their seats and were heading for the door. As soon as they were through we shoved our mugs aside and followed them. The guy Baker went to his car and drove straight off, back towards Malton, while the man he'd been talking to got into an HGV.

'We gonna follow him, or what?' Fordy asked.

'No, we don't want to arouse suspicion,' I said as I scribbled down the registration number of the HGV. 'Thought so,' I added. 'Dutch.'

We made our way back to town at a leisurely pace. Fordy, at the wheel, didn't say anything for quite a while, not until we were climbing Whitwell Hill.

'Oh well. It's something, I suppose.' He sighed, as though he wasn't convinced we'd achieved much.

'Contact with a Dutch lorry-driver?' I said. 'I should say so. All these little bits of information, when we put them together, will start to form a picture. They may not add up to much yet, may not make much sense, but mark my words, if our man is dodgy – and he's got to be, hasn't he? – it'll all start to make sense before too long.'

Later that evening it became apparent that word had got out about our plain-clothes job and the fact that we were out and about doing stop-searches. Just as we expected, really. Quite a few of the people we stopped mentioned that we'd been seen out the night before; it seemed everyone was talking about it. This is what you get in small market towns, which is not a bad thing. Part of the objective was to raise our profile, so we couldn't complain. As I said to Fordy, the big success of the day was that we'd spotted our man Baker – and I was convinced he hadn't spotted us.

Inspector Finch was waiting for us when we wound the operation up that night. He invited us into his office and told us to sit down. He remained standing. He's one of those people who seem to think more clearly when they're on their feet, pacing the floor. It sets me right on edge. 'How have you two got on?' he asked. 'Have you made any progress?'

'Well, sir, we tried our level best. I'd say we achieved a bit of disruption. Word has already got out that we've gone proactive, but in terms of seizures we've basically drawn a blank.' I pulled out my notebook. 'Eighteen stop-searches, and we found four people in possession of cannabis.'

'Plus a couple of underage drinkers,' Fordy added. I could've kicked him.

Birdie looked at him. 'Hmm,' he said. 'Cannabis, you say? That all?'

'As a matter of fact we did uncover something that might be of interest, sir.' I told him about Baker, and the meeting with the Dutch lorry-driver. And I reminded him about the tipoff from my source.

He stood there, hands behind his back, rocking to and fro, lips pursed, eyes closed. 'Very good, Pannett. Yes, that's very interesting indeed.' I nudged Fordy. Maybe this would convince him we'd put in a decent weekend's work. Birdie sat down and was suddenly quite brisk and businesslike.

'When are you next on duty?' he asked me.

'Tuesday, sir.'

'Right then, when you come back I want you to dig up some intelligence. Talk to DC Carter, and bring in the crime analyst.'

I'd never really worked on a job like this with Amanda, but I had a fair appreciation of what she did. The one definite thing I knew about her – apart from the fact that she was a civilian employee, occupied a tiny office on the second floor and had information on just about every suspect individual throughout Ryedale and beyond – was that she would not tolerate being addressed as Mandy, as I'd found out to my cost the first time I'd gone to her for help. I was also aware that we had a mutual acquaintance in Walter, because her dad was none other than Ronny, one of Walt's Three Wise Monkeys, and bass player in the country and western band he'd put together.

However, I wouldn't be seeing her until Tuesday morning. Before that I had a few things to sort out on the home front. Somehow Ann and I needed to prepare ourselves for the imminent arrival of Soapy and his band of workers.

What I'd clean forgotten in all the excitement was that Walter had invited me and Ann for a day out in Scarborough, where Yorkshire had a limited-overs cricket match.

And we'd invited him over for a cooked breakfast beforehand.

We were in the middle of shovelling the wet newspaper outside when he showed up. In his best brogues and trousers, with his white V-necked sweater tied around his middle and his flat cap perched on his head, he looked like a village-green umpire. 'Oh heck,' he said, when he saw the mess. 'I heard you'd had a bit of rain getting in. Didn't realise it was this bad. Have we to abandon our plans?'

'Wouldn't even think of it,' I said. 'I know how much your cricket means to you, mate. But you'll have to go on your own, I'm afraid.'

Walt wasn't sure. He shoved his old hat back and ran his fingers through his hair. He looked like a man who was wrestling with his conscience. 'Why, you've a job on here, lad. You'll be needing all the help you can get.' He popped his head through the back door, looked into the kitchen and smacked his lips together. 'On the other hand . . . didn't you say sommat about breakfast?'

'Hey, give me a few minutes to get organised,' Ann said. 'Have you not noticed the hole in the roof? Go on, outside with you.'

'Aye, I'm off – but can I have me ball back first?' He plonked himself on the log, and chuckled like a naughty schoolboy before turning to me and saying, 'By heck, I wouldn't want to be in your shoes, lad.'

'What? You mean Ann?'

'No no no. Your Ann's all right. No . . .' He was looking up at the roof, where Soapy's tarp was flapping in the breeze. 'I mean with t'building works. If you need a hand, you know I'm not afraid of a bit of hard graft.' He held his hands out in front of him. They looked like a pair of shovels. 'Didn't get these by hiding out the road when there was work to be done.'

'Walt, I appreciate your offer, but you're forgetting one important thing. This isn't our place, it's Algy's. It's down to him to put it right. All Ann and I have to do is tidy up inside, bung a few dust-sheets over our furniture and await the builders. Algy's sending a team round first thing Monday morning. Just relax, enjoy your breakfast and then get yourself off to the match.' I sat myself down next to him. 'And if you ask Ann very nicely,' I said, cupping my hand to my mouth to make sure she could hear me through the open kitchen door, 'I'm sure she'll bring you a cup of tea while we're waiting for the fry-up.'

'And I s'pose you'll want one too,' she said, coming to the threshold and giving me the hard stare.

'Goes without saying, love.'

Walt loved his cricket, and of course like all Yorkshiremen he was convinced that our county was the only team worth watching – every bit as much as he believed this was the only place to live. He's one of those people you still meet from time to time who has never, in his entire life, been outside of Yorkshire. Never has, and doubtless never will. In fact, he claims only to have left North Yorkshire on one occasion and that was many many years ago when, as a youngster, he had to undergo surgery at Leeds General Infirmary. As he always says, it was against his better judgement and it caused him a lot of pain in a tender spot – so he made up his mind there and then that he wouldn't be going back. What this meant was that in order to see the finest cricket team

on the planet he always had to make a note of the
Scarborough dates as soon as the fixtures were
announced, and keep them clear of social engagements.
'Course,' he said, as he sat there on my log, tea in one
hand, flat cap in the other, his nose twitching as the smell
of smoked bacon wafted through the back door, 'if you
go back a few years we used to play at Middlesbrough.'
He thought for a moment, then sighed. 'Aye, I went there
a time or two.'

'But that's in blinking Cleveland,' I said.

Walt shook his head. 'Didn't used to be. Used to be
part of us, till them blooming politicians decided to
change t'map thirty forty years ago.'

'Oh, right. Like they got rid of Hull and so on.'

Walt sniffed. 'I dare say we can manage without Hull,'
he said.

'Right, well, looks like breakfast's ready. Time to put
the bad memories behind you and look ahead to brighter
times, eh?'

Walt cleared his plate, set off for the coast, and left
me and Ann to complete our preparations for the tidal
wave that was about to hit us. I mean Soapy and whoever
he'd persuaded to help him out. By the time Tuesday
morning came we'd got all our fragile and valuable assets
out of the way, and everything else covered in old sheets.
I went into work ready for a break – and keen to find
out what our crime analyst had come up with.

I didn't actually see Amanda first thing. There was a
note on her door saying she'd be back soon. So I sat down
with Fordy and logged on to the police intelligence crime
file. As a starting point we keyed in Baker's name – and

up it came, right away. 'Well,' I said. 'There's our man. Cautioned for "burglary other than a dwelling". Looks as though he was a bit of a tearaway as a kid, breaking into someone's outbuildings. Now then, what's this?' There was a second record, dating from only a year previously. It seemed our man had got into trouble after some kind of domestic incident involving a girlfriend. 'Not a very nice man,' Fordy said, as we read through the details. 'Harassment? Threatening phone calls?'

'Yeah, and see who dealt with it?'

'Thommo!'

'Say what you like about him, Fordy, he's thorough. Got it all logged. Good lad. Look at this: visited him at his address in Pickering and – yes! Mobile phone number.'

'What you thinking of doing with that?' Fordy asked, as I jotted it down on my pad.

'Just an idea,' I said. 'Sommat I picked up in the Met.'

An hour or so later I picked up the phone, dialled 141 to withhold my number, and called our man.

'Jed Baker?'

'Yeah, can I 'elp you?'

'Yeah, I'm a mate of . . .' I gave the name of someone we knew as a user of drugs.

'And?'

'He told me if I wanted some gear, you were the man, like.'

'Wass your name?'

I hesitated a moment. 'Nah, I don' wanna give it.'

'Right, well, I dunno what you're talking about, so f*** off and don't ring me again.'

I grinned at Fordy. He looked perplexed. 'Don't you

get it?' I said. 'Number one, we now know we've got his name right, and number two, we've got his number. It's still live. C'mon, let's go and see Amanda.'

Amanda greeted us like long-lost friends. 'Don't get a lot of visitors up here,' she said, shifting a pile of papers off a spare seat for me. 'Especially not PCs. Unless you're stuck, that is.'

'Well, we do take note,' I said. 'Trust me, we read all those intelligence reports and crime trends you bang out for our briefings with Chris. Anyway, I reckon we need your expert help with this one.' I filled her in on what we had so far. She said she would take it on board, search for any links between Baker and other known criminals or suspects, and see whether he fitted into the bigger picture. Amanda had access to what was going on all over the region, as well as being up to speed with national crime trends. Her work was invaluable in our fight against crime, both local and cross border. Day after day, all over the country, crime analysts painstakingly go through all the reports and make note of the methods the various suspects use when committing crimes. Amanda knew all the trademarks of our most proactive criminals; sometimes she would name you a suspect just by looking at how someone had gained entry to a house. She would also analyse the intelligence reports submitted on a daily basis by officers on patrol. She had an overview of what was going on, where it was happening and who had been seen out and about. Put this all together with her local knowledge, and she could quite often put you on to the person you needed to take a look at.

'Well,' I said, after I'd briefed her, 'what do you reckon?'

'It sounds interesting, Mike. And I tell you what, it'll make a change to get my teeth into a proper job again. I've spent the last few weeks providing statistical information for the senior management team for these new league tables.' She pulled a face.

'Yeah,' I said. 'I think I get the picture.'

'Anyway, the first thing I'll do is interrogate this phone number.' I could tell by her brisk manner that she was confident she could get something out of it. I knew that she'd use the phone number to find out who our friend had been calling, but it was a long and tedious process, and required permission from on high.

'Right,' I said as we left her little office, 'we'll leave it with you.'

Later that morning Fordy and I passed on the same information to Des, the CID man. And then we waited. If past experience was anything to go on, it would be a week or two before we heard anything.

Chapter 5

Occupational Hazards

'The thing with foxes,' Rich said, 'and let's be right about it: that's what lies at the centre of all this hunting ban malarkey — the thing about foxes is, aye, they're killers all right, but there's a sight worse killers out there. Plenty of 'em.'

We were sitting by the fire. It may have been early August, but it was a cool, breezy day with spits and spots of rain falling, and there wasn't much brightness penetrating the low-ceilinged house. I'd finished my pie and peas and had the empty plate on my lap and a cup of tea in my hand, with Rich's cocker spaniel Bracken slumped across my feet, snoring. Penny, Rich's wife, was in the kitchen cutting a slice of blackcurrant tart for my pudding. Lovely grub, I was thinking, but at the same time I was feeling sort of inhibited, because I'm the kind of person who talks a lot better if he can move around and wave his arms about. It helps me express myself. Not that I had much chance to say anything in this instance — which some people would tell you is a good thing – because Rich was on his favourite hobby-horse.

'Worse than a fox? Oh, cheers Penny.' I balanced the tea on the narrow wooden arm of the rocking chair as she took my empty plate and handed me the tart. 'How's that then?'

'Think on, lad, think on. A cat, for example . . .' Rich took a last drag on his cigarette and threw it into the fire. 'A cat is far worse. I mean, a fox is a menace, certain times of the year, don't get me wrong. But a cat – it'll kill anything it finds. Any place, any time. Don't kid yourself, Mike: foxes get blamed for a lot of things they aren't guilty of. And when it comes to pests, what about rabbits? When you're harvesting three tonnes of grain per acre and the buggers eat four, five acres – which they will do, if you don't keep 'em in check – that can be your profit for the year.'

'What d'you do with all the rabbits you kill?' I was thinking about the pie I'd just eaten. It sort of tasted like chicken, but I wasn't sure. Not that I mind rabbit. Or hare. Or anything, really. Like a lot of country people, I was raised to eat what was on the table. I just prefer to know what it is.

'We eat a few, but most of them' – he pointed at Bracken, still fast asleep and twitching, dreaming, no doubt, of chasing something to ground – 'most of them we freeze and feed to t'dogs.'

'Not that this one deserves it,' Penny said. 'She won't go out hunting. Never would. First time she heard a gun she started howling and ran back to the house. Proper little lapdog.'

'Don't you take any to market?' I asked. I was thinking about all the gamebirds and rabbits that hang outside the butcher's shop in Malton marketplace.

Penny pulled a face. 'Not worth the diesel,' she said. Then she glanced at Rich. 'Or the time. Is it?'

'Thirty, forty years ago,' he said, settling back into his easy chair and kicking his slippers off, 'we could get as much as a pound apiece for rabbits, which was worth having. 'Cos we were only lads then, looking to make a bit of pocket money. You know what you'd get now?' He sat there with his eyebrows arched, waiting for me to answer. I hadn't a clue. 'Fifty pence.' He nodded towards Penny. 'Like she says, not worth the effort. But it has to be done. Along with rats, magpies . . .' He sighed and stretched his arms out, working his shoulders. 'You never stop, mate.'

'I don't think most people realise you kill magpies,' I said.

'They wouldn't. 'Cos they're beautiful birds. But they're another of your corvids, and all corvids are classified as vermin. Rooks, crows, magpies, jays . . . We trap a lot of them, but mostly it's crows and magpies. They're the biggest nuisance. They'll take birds' eggs – and if they can get amongst t'young uns they'll have them too.'

I looked at my watch. It was nearly time I was on my way. I'd called on Rich for one simple reason, which was that I hadn't called on him in several months. I hadn't actually known him all that long, but the more I saw of him the better I liked him – and his wife, who couldn't half cook. He wasn't a local. Neither was she. They came from Barnsley. Well, that's not quite correct. They actually hailed from a South Yorkshire village called Fitzwilliam, the same place as Geoffrey Boycott. Rich started working on the Wentworth estate as an apprentice gamekeeper straight from school, and stayed ten years before going to work on the Nickerson estate at Rothwell, out on the Lincolnshire Wolds. The pair of them had moved to Hovingham quite a few years ago. It's a 3000-acre estate, combining arable land with mixed woodlands, and adjoins the land attached to Castle Howard.

Rich's job was, by his own reckoning, seven days a week. 'We never stop,' he said. 'That's why we always reckon to get abroad for us holidays – where they can't get hold of you. Job like this, you're always on call. Think you've spotted a poacher? They're on the phone. Injured animal? Call Rich – he'll know what to do. Why, one time some poor old lad went and hanged himself from a tree, and guess who had to guide t'rescue team in?'

'But' – he paused to light another cigarette, and I caught a twinkle in his eye – 'who else can they call on, eh? We're a dying breed, Mike. A dying breed.'

'How can you say that?' I asked him. 'They'll always need gamekeepers. Why, old Nick over by Rillington, he's training his lad up to step into his shoes.'

'Aye, they'll be called gamekeepers all right, but they won't be the real McCoy. They'll never know all what we know. Same as I'll never know what the old lads who taught me knew, things what've been handed down, generation to generation. Take me. I was taught by fellows who ought to have retired. Seventy years and older, some of them, and they told me things nobody would know now. They had' – he thought for a moment, as if grasping for the right word – 'they had infinite knowledge. They got it from a lifetime studying the wildlife in one little estate.'

He glanced at the clock, then said, 'I'll tell you an example, before you go – 'cos it'll soon be time for me to go back to work too. I was only a youngster, learning me trade, like. This was back in me time on the Wentworth estate. One day I caught a weasel. We'd had no end of trouble around the chicken run, so I was quite pleased wi' meself. Well, I made sure it were dead, and put it on top of t'trap, like. I'd come back for it later, to dispose of it sort of thing. And when I did, it were gone. Thought it were a bit odd, like, until I caught another one next day, put that on top – and same bloody thing. Well, I'm scratching me head now. Where are the buggers going? I told my head keeper it must be a tawny owl. He laughed. Said nowt. They were like that, them old timers. Left you to puzzle it out for yourself – which is one way of learning, I suppose. So I thought, he's taking the mickey. He's snaffled it away, like, just to confuse me. But no, when I challenged him he took me back to where t'trap had been and showed me. It was right there in the undergrowth a few yards away, buried under a pile of leaves and grass. "There, lad," he says, "now you know. Stoats – aye, and weasels too – they'll bury their dead".'

Rich flicked his ciggy into the grate and wagged his finger at me. 'Y'see, they knew which way was up, did them lads.' Then he laughed. 'By hell, they led me a dance – not that I didn't fight back. I remember how they used to wait while it were siling down, then send me out to fetch a load of kindling. And of course they'd complain 'cos it was wet. Or it'd be morning break time and they'd say, go fetch some eggs. Well, we had chickens running wild, just about, and every day I'd bring the head lad a load for t'pan and he'd say, "Is that all?" Right, you old bugger, I thought. I'll show you. So, next time he sends me – in the pissing rain, of course – I foraged. Under hedges, behind trees, in the long grass. Got meself soaked right through, I did, but what a pile of eggs! Must've been dozens, all covered with muck and bits of straw. Anyway, I hands him this basket, piled high. He looks at it and grunts – which was the nearest you ever got to a thank you. He's got all his bread sliced and buttered and stacked up, and he gets the old frying pan heated up, pops the dripping in, and starts cracking 'em. Well! Out they come. Old ones, addled ones, ones with half-grown chicks in 'em, dead chicks, the bloody lot.' Rich laughed and got out of his chair. 'He never asked me again. Right,' he said, putting his cap on. 'Work to do.' He picked up his jacket off the back of his chair and paused with it half on. 'Aye, and there's a thing. I'd never have been allowed to sit here in me shirt-sleeves. You wore a collar and tie to work, them days, and if you wanted to take your jacket off – even at your mealtime – you'd to ask permission of t'head man.' He clicked his tongue. 'Young lads today – why, they don't know they're born.'

I was thinking about young people as I drove back to town to meet up with Fordy – the kind of young people who buy drugs off older people who, if you want my opinion, are exploiting them. And I was thinking about this man Baker, wondering whether Amanda the crime analyst and Des the CID man had made any progress. It had been a full fortnight since we'd given them our bits and pieces of information. Surely they'd have come up with something by now.

'We have,' Amanda said half an hour later as we made ourselves comfortable in her cramped little office. Des had joined us, so there wasn't a lot of room. 'Firstly,' she continued, 'we identified this man Baker's phone as active, which was good news. We then had to jump through the usual hoops to get all the reams of paperwork completed and signed off by the superintendent. Then we had to wait for the phone company to turn it all around.' She shrugged her shoulders. 'Ah well, you know what that's like – but, I can tell you, it was worth it.'

Des pulled out a sheaf of papers stapled together. 'It certainly was. We've got a list of all his calls, in and out, going back several months. Haven't started working on the names yet. But soon as I looked at it I recognised a few players, so . . . very interesting.'

'That's one thing,' Amanda said. 'Then there's this. His vehicle has been sighted in the northeast. More than once. And there are addresses attached to the report, as well as street locations.'

'That's promising,' Fordy said.

'Oh, it's promising all right. It may not lead to anything – yet – but it helps build the picture.' She rearranged her papers and pulled out a single printed sheet. 'Now we come to something much more illuminating. Jeremy James Baker. He owns two premises in Pickering. One of them is the house he lives in, which is modest enough. As is the other one. Here.' She showed us a photograph of a terraced house with a small forecourt garden. 'Two bedrooms. For which he paid £90,000 . . .' She paused. 'Paid up in full, no mortgage involved.'

'Bloody hell!' I said. 'Where'd you get this from?'

'The estate agent. If a deal strikes them as extraordinary they'll let us know.'

I nodded. I'd come across this sort of thing a few times before. I was thinking about where Baker got his money. I was reminding myself that we shouldn't be jumping to conclusions, that it could just be a case of a fellow having rich parents – not that that would necessarily explain him buying a house for cash. I opened my mouth to speak, but Amanda held her hand up. 'Now, before you say anything, we had a similar call from a travel agent last week – and this is backed up by CCTV images of the transaction.'

'What transaction?' Fordy asked.

'He walked into the travel agents and booked a top-of-the-range holiday in a luxury Spanish resort, for two people. All-inclusive premier resort. Four thousand three hundred pounds – and he paid cash – used notes. The travel agent let us know because they thought it was unusual.'

I sat back in my chair and let out a long sigh. 'And do we know what he does for a living?'

'No,' said Des. 'But you won't be surprised to learn he doesn't appear to have a job. He's not paying tax and he's not signing on. That's not to say he isn't working, but . . .'

'It all points to him being into something pretty bloody lucrative,' I said. 'I mean, to be walking around with that much cash. Strewth.'

'Question is,' Fordy said, 'what do we do now? Could we mount a surveillance operation?'

'Well, Fordy lad.' Des stretched his arms out and rested his hands on the back of his head. 'At this moment in time, we don't have enough intelligence to even consider involving the surveillance team.'

Fordy cleared his throat. 'What about applying for a warrant to search his house?' he said.

Amanda shook her head. 'The first question we'll be asked is, is there enough to go on? I mean, evidence? It's all speculation so far. The man has a lot of cash. It's not against the law. Given what we've got at the moment Inspector Finch, as keen as he is, wouldn't grant you permission to apply for one.'

'What about going to that financial investigation team at the tax office?'

'Possibly, Fordy, but that's a last resort. We want to see what he's up to first.' Des turned to me. 'You know how it is Mike. We need to build a clearer picture and start gathering evidence to see what we're on with.'

We sat there in silence for a few moments, all four of us. Des was tapping his pen on his pad. Fordy was looking at me as if he thought I was going to come up with the answer. Amanda was leaning forward and idly scrolling through something on her computer screen. For some reason my mind wandered back to a case I'd worked on in London, quite a few years earlier.

A fellow officer – his name was Pat Dunne – was shot dead on duty, in Clapham. It was an awful case, absolutely dreadful, and it wasn't actually resolved until years later. When the killing took place I'd recently left Battersea, where I'd been on the robbery squad, and joined the TSG, or riot police. I still knew a lot of locals on my old South London patch and I had a lot of live contacts among the black community. The detective superintendent who was put in charge of the murder investigation had headed up Operation Trident, an attempt to take out the Yardie gangs who were infesting our part of the capital – and maybe this was what made me think about the old days, because one of the techniques he'd employed suddenly seemed relevant to what we were dealing with right now.

'Listen,' I said, 'there's a system for dealing with this. I learned it back in London, on a murder investigation.'

'Go on,' Des said.

'What we need is an Anacapa chart.'

'Anacapa? I've heard of it,' Amanda said. 'Never used it though.'

I grinned at her. 'Well,' I said, 'you see – you start mingling with humble PCs and you never know what you're going to learn.'

The Anacapa chart is simply a diagrammatic representation of all the lines that connect a central figure – in this case our friend Mr Baker – with his associates. You take a sheet of paper, or a whiteboard, or an entire wall if you have one to spare, and you stick your main suspect at the centre – that is, put his name in a bubble. Then you draw lines outward, like a spider's web, connecting him to all the people he deals with. Then, as more intelligence comes in, you are able to plot connections between people within that network. And slowly, it starts to make sense: where the main activity is, who the main players are, what are the most regular lines of communication, and so on. The pattern of communication. That's the theory of it, at any rate.

'We could start with Baker's telephone bills,' I said.

'Right, research who his contacts are and who they're calling. I get it.' Des was into this straight away, and so was Amanda. She was already on her feet, pulling posters off the wall in front of her. 'I'll stick a chart up here,' she said. 'Yep, leave it with me. The good thing is, Inspector Finch has agreed that Des and I should spend some time on this. We'll get together towards the end of the week, shall we?'

'Yeah, sounds like a plan. Just one more thing,' I said. 'While you two are on with that, shall I get him flagged?'

'If you could, it'd save me a job.'

'Right then, me and Fordy will get on with it. I'll make sure none of the regional teams are already looking at him. I'll also get a marker on him at all ports. Might as well get Customs involved, what with his meeting with the Dutch lorry-driver. By the way, did we get anything back on that lorry?'

'Nothing untoward,' Des said.

The meeting broke up with us all feeling a little spark of optimism – at least, that's how Fordy and I felt. And all the way home I was thinking about the case. What if this guy Baker was the dealer we were seeking? As I drove up the lane I had a feeling that maybe, just maybe, we were starting to get somewhere. So arriving at Keeper's Cottage was a little like being put under a cold shower. Soapy and his mate had made quite an impression on the house, but as far as I could see they were going backwards rather than forwards.

'What the hell are you up to?' I shouted as I got out of the car. Soapy was on the roof, sitting astride the topmost timber, stacking up ridge tiles. There was a scaffold tower against the side of the house, the lawn was littered with bits of old laths and broken tiles, and there, on my log, the one that Nick and I had hauled out of the wood, the one that Ann and I liked to sit on at the end of a long day to hold hands and wind down, sat a skinny youth with a tea-cosy hat on his head and an iPod in his hands, his head bobbing to the beat of his music. 'Oi!' I said, marching towards him, 'how about letting a man have a sitdown when he comes home from a hard day's work?'

No answer. He was completely oblivious to my presence.

'Give 'im a little tap with one of them laths, cock-bod!' Soapy was grinning at me from his rooftop perch.

I was about to take him at his word when the youth spotted me, stood up and started rearranging the mess on the lawn.

'All right?' I asked.

He grunted something and carried on trying to look busy.

'Nearly there!' Soapy shouted.

'Where?' I answered. 'Nearly where?'

'Stripping t'old roof, cock-bod. Next up we'll attack your chimney. Gotta take her down brick by brick and put her back together again. It's that bloody great crack we found.' He paused to light a cigarette, then slapped a hand against the pale brickwork. 'Time I've finished, you won't recognise her.'

'That's what I'm worried about,' I said. 'Just you make sure it ends up the same shape as it started out, that's all.' I approached the back door, then called up to him, 'I'll be inside. Studying.'

'You go and enjoy yourself, Mike. I'm telling you, this job couldn't be in better hands.'

I sat in the reclining chair and opened the first of my revision books. Before I started I checked the time. Half-past two. Right, I'd give it an hour, take Henry for a walk, then give it another half-hour. Then I'd see about getting some tea ready for when Ann came home. No point over-doing it. You can only take in so much.

As I've said before, I've never been much of a student. Spent most of my schooldays larking about. Bikes and girls, that was me. I excelled at both, and, as the teachers liked to tell my parents, I had the potential to go on to A-levels. They just wished I'd apply myself to maths and English with as much enthusiasm as I did the other stuff. My problem was that I just couldn't concentrate for any length of time. It was the sitting still that did for me. I'm talking about academic subjects now, not girls and bikes. I always have to be up and doing something, or I get distracted by what's going on outside – in this case the rhythmic tapping of Soapy's footsteps as he hopped up and down the roof with the ridge tiles.

I yawned, looked at my watch and saw that the second hand had completed one full revolution. Only fifty-nine minutes and I could get out with Henry. And suddenly I was aware of him whining from his kennel. That's another problem I have: I'm always aware of what's going on around me rather than what I'm reading. Where the hell is a decent pair of earplugs when you need them, I was thinking.

I was just, finally, getting my teeth into a section entitled 'The Duties of a Sergeant' when the peace was shattered by the sound of music. If you'd call it that. Whoever was singing was seriously ticked off about something, and wanted the world to know about it. I slung my book on the floor, got out of my chair and headed for the door. That lad was about to discover what anger really sounded like.

But the lad was nowhere to be seen. Instead I found Soapy, leaning against the chimney, eyes closed, neckerchief over his head, with a great chunky CD player blasting out some sort of gangsta rap.

I picked up a small lump of lime mortar and lobbed it up at him. As it hit the chimney and broke into fragments, he opened his eyes and reached out a hand to stop himself sliding down the roof. 'Soapy!' I shouted. 'Gimme a flaming break, will you? I'm trying to read in there.'

'Sorry, cock-bod.' He turned it down. 'That better?'

'Marginally,' I said. 'Where's your lad?'

'Santa's little helper?' he said. 'I've sent 'im home, mate. Shan't need 'im while we start mixing cement.'

Back in the house I sat down and re-opened the book. 'The Duties of a Sergeant', I read again. Then I put it back down. I was thirsty. Maybe if I had a cup of tea . . . But that would mean whistling Soapy up. You can't go mashing tea and leaving out the workers, and the last thing I wanted was a half-hour break. So I went to the kitchen, poured myself a glass of water and started all over again. When I got to the end of the first section I checked the time. Only forty-five minutes to go. I was dimly aware of a chip-chipping noise out there, a noise with a bit of a ringing to it, like someone hitting a cold chisel with a lump hammer. Every so often I'd hear a bit of mortar bounce down the roof, then a pause before it pinged off the scaffolding. Now and then a few grains of sand or lime sifted their way down the chimney. I was just starting to wonder whether Soapy ought to have sealed off the fireplace when there was a dull rumble from up on the roof, and a hideous grating sound that gathered momentum until a shower of soot, mortar, and broken bits of fire cement burst into the hearth and spilled out over the floor. There followed a cloud of dust, then a solitary brick. Finally, a cold chisel clanged off the fender and landed at my feet.

'For God's sake, Soapy! What next?' I was up from my chair and outside, snarling, ready to do him some serious damage.

The trouble with people like Soapy is that they always, somehow, disarm you. Sometimes they appeal to your better instincts. Sometimes they do it by being so completely hapless that you take pity on them. Sometimes they make you laugh. Looking up I could see that Soapy had had a narrow escape. He'd got his upper half wedged down the chimney and could easily have followed all that dust and rubble down the flue and into the sitting room. Only his legs were visible, and his rear end, complete with traditional builder's cleavage. His feet were flailing helplessly at the air, and as I stood there, not quite believing what I was seeing, I heard a muffled, plaintive voice.

'Mike, where are you mate?'

'Hold steady!' I shouted. I climbed up the scaffolding, onto the roof, and worked my way uncertainly up the roof-ladder to where he'd built a wooden platform around the chimney.

'Right,' I said. 'I'm gonna grab your legs and pull, yeah?'

'Aye, go on.'

I wrapped my arms around his legs and heaved. It was like pulling a cork out of a bottle. Out he came, his face blackened, his knuckles bleeding, and his red bandanna up around his ears. He plonked himself down on the platform, reached in his pocket for a cigarette, and wiped a piece of grit out of his eye. 'Tell you what,' he said, 'it's no bloody wonder old Santa Claus only comes round once a year.'

I did manage to get some studying done that day, but only after Soapy and I had cleaned up in the front room, sealed off the fireplace, and steadied our nerves with a cup of strong tea. But it wasn't long before Ann came home, tired and hungry and wanting an update on what was for tea – and an update on the work in progress.

Soapy, having got the chimney dismantled and roped a polythene sheet over it, told us he was going missing for a couple of days. He had another job to see to, and would start on the rebuilding the following week. 'That suits me fine,' I told him. 'I've three night shifts coming up. I can't be having all this noise and banging about when I'm trying to sleep.'

'Aye,' he said. 'Gets a bit hairy at times, doesn't it? Life in the fast lane. Rock and roll.'

'Get yourself home,' I said. Then I turned to Ann. 'Just let me put some clean clothes on,' I said, 'then I'll treat you to a meal at the Jolly Farmers.'

The pub was quiet that evening. Maybe it was because they'd had the quiz the night before. Maybe it was the weather, which was cool and breezy. Back-endish, in fact. Either way, it suited me. I'd had enough excitement for one day.

'So,' Ann said, as we waited for our food to arrive, 'any thoughts on what we were talking about the other day? About going back to Algy and seeing whether he's ready to reconsider.'

I laughed. 'Do we really want to buy a house that's falling to bits?'

She shook her head, as if she despaired of me. 'You don't get it, do you? What better time to talk business? Keeper's Cottage is a thorn in Algy's flesh. Every time Soapy goes back and reports a fresh disaster it'll be more so. I'd be willing to bet he'll be falling over himself to get rid of it.'

'I thought he was emotionally attached to it. Wasn't it part of his inheritance? Been in the family for generations and all that?'

'No. He bought it about ten years ago. Thought he was going to make a pile on it. He just timed it wrong, that's all. Bought at the top of a boom. In his own inimitable words, it was "a frightful clanger".'

'How d'you know all this?'

'He told me.'

'When?'

'When I was round there trying to teach him to ride that

blasted horse of his.' She took a sip from her wine glass, and smiled a very knowing smile. 'Take a tip from me. If ever you want to loosen someone's tongue, wait until they're perched on top of a frisky seventeen-hand horse with their feet stuck in the stirrups. Works like a charm.'

'You crafty young . . . Anyway, where does this leave us? And what would we do about the roof? I mean, that's not going to be cheap, is it?'

'Why should it cost so much? You've got a bungling amateur on the job, and a hapless kid to carry his tools for him part-time – and the only material costs'll be the mortar.'

'Plus a few roof timbers,' I said.

'Yes, one or two. OK, there are a few costs, but basically they're taking it apart and putting it back together.' She leaned back in her chair. The food was arriving. 'How about,' she began, 'how about telling Algy we'll assume the cost of the work and deduct that from the price we're offering. We buy whatever materials Soapy needs and pay him by the hour.'

'Not sure about that,' I said. 'I mean, he spends half his time supping tea and nattering. How will we know what he's up to when we're not around?'

'We'll put him on a bonus then. So much if he completes to deadline.'

'Right, and supposing he dashes through it, takes the money and then we find out he's made a pig's ear of it?'

'Hmm. You've got a point there.' She turned her attention to her steak. Neither of us spoke for a few minutes.

'Now then.' I'd suddenly had an idea. 'He's getting married, right?' Ann nodded. 'And remember when I told you how he was going on to me about the costs mounting up, and the date being put back?'

'I'm listening.'

'So, how about we barter with him? He does the job, and we sort out – I dunno, the catering, or the photographer? Payment in kind.'

'I like it, my dear. But he's not getting married for months.'

'It's next spring. By which time we'll have had a full winter to test out the roof.'

'Genius!' Ann said.

We clinked glasses. 'I'll put it to him,' I said. 'Then you can get Algy back up on Lord Nelson and explain why he has no choice but to accept our generous offer.'

As we walked back home that night I was already looking forward to a nice quiet day to follow. No rubble coming down the chimney, and no rescuing hapless builders off the roof. A nice mid-afternoon nap, and off to work at half nine.

Chapter 6

Night Rider

I've probably said it before, but it's worth saying it again. I do not like bullies. Never have, and never will. Even when I was a child, I wouldn't let anyone try it on with me. I'd always stand up for anyone who was having a hard time at the hands of someone bigger and older. My mother loves to remind me of an incident that took place when I was a little lad – very little; before I'd even started school. I can't say I really remember it, although I've heard the story so many times that it feels as if I do, if that makes sense.

I had a little tricycle, and I was pedalling it up and down the lane outside our house when a big boy came along and demanded a ride. I refused, and even when he punched me I stood my ground. So he punched me again, but I still wouldn't give in, and in the end he went away. As my mum loves to recall, 'You just wouldn't give that trike up, Michael.' Well, as I say, the memory is indistinct, but it rings true. I had a lot of my mother in me, and she's always been a tough one herself. As was my dad, in his own way. He couldn't stand bullies either. He always said, 'The bigger they are the harder they fall. But remember, Michael, you have to get them to fall in the first place.'

As well as having a stubborn streak I also had a sense of what was right and what was wrong. I hated injustice. I still do. So it wasn't long before I was taking on the bigger kids, not so much to defend myself as to protect whichever little kid was in trouble. Later on, when I went to what was quite a tough secondary school – Joseph Rowntree, in York – I found that the city boys all wanted to pick on us country lads. They thought they were hard, and were going to prove it to us – and, I suppose, show off to their mates. Once or twice I saw young lads who lived near us being chased home by these supposed tough nuts, and I stepped in. Next thing I got a bit of a reputation as being someone who could be looked to to protect youngsters who were being bullied. People started coming to me for help. I think the difference in me was, yes, I was frightened of these big lads, but that never stopped me from getting involved. And maybe too I had a tough streak, or anyway some kind of inner strength that meant I just wouldn't back down. Either that or I was plain stubborn. I didn't like to fight and I certainly didn't want to get hurt; but none of that seemed to matter to me when I was dealing with bullies. I had a burning sense that it simply wasn't right for the nasty aggressive types to get the upper hand. It's one of the reasons I joined the police: to right wrongs, to protect the vulnerable against aggressors.

I don't know why this was on my mind when I drove

in for my night shift. Maybe I'd half heard something on the telly before I came out. Ann had been watching a film set in an American high school as I put my pack-up together in the kitchen. Those places look like jungles to me and kids always seem to be ganging up on each other. Or maybe the memory had just popped into my mind because I was relaxed, well rested after a day spent between the recliner, working on my revision, and the sofa, where I'd had a nice nap mid-afternoon.

The other thing that was on my mind as I drove down to town was the chat Fordy and I had had with Des and Amanda. I was wondering when we'd get some kind of result from them. That case mattered a great deal to me. As I saw it, the dealers who exploit their young customers are no more than a type of bully anyway – so maybe there was a theme there in the way I responded to this case. But the CID lad didn't work the same shifts as us, and neither did the crime analyst; they tended to work office hours, and with the weekend coming up it would be a few days before Fordy and I could get together with them and receive an update. So I knew I'd have to be patient.

It seemed pretty quiet as I came through town – quiet for a Friday, at least – and when I got to the station and met with the late-turn officers at briefing they said they'd had a pretty steady shift so far. Maybe it was the weather; it had been threatening rain all evening and it was still very cool for the time of year. Here we were, halfway through the summer and we really hadn't had a lot of what you'd call holiday weather yet. It was a real shame for all the schoolkids, mooching around the streets, hoping for a nice day on the beach at Scarborough or Filey. A lot of people had given up hope already, and were talking up the prospects of an Indian summer. As far as I was concerned, though, they were clutching at straws.

So with not a lot going on in town, we did the usual tour around the time the pubs were turning out, then made our way back to the station. The usual thing on a weekend, if you had time, was to pop back in around midnight before heading back out for the finish-off – the late licences, discos and the like. The plan was to grab a quick drink before you got involved in jobs that could easily tie you up for the rest of the night. We had the full complement on duty, and I'd been paired up with Jayne. I'd been quizzing her about her revision, partly because I genuinely wanted to see her do well, partly because, to put it bluntly, I was worried that she'd outshine me. Either that or she'd beat me to the first sergeant's vacancy that came up, always assuming that she wanted to remain in the North Yorkshire area. So when she said she was finding it tough going, and was struggling to make time to do all the work, I was, I'll admit it, slightly relieved. It wasn't just me finding it hard, then.

It got to past midnight, and nothing much had happened. I was getting fidgety. Some coppers love it when there's nothing doing, but I'm one of those who would far rather be busy. Not only does the time drag when you've not much on, but, as my grandmother always used to tell us, the devil finds work for idle hands. Which is why I always ended up in the CCTV control room with my cup of tea, looking at the various images that were being beamed in from the cameras around our patch.

During the day, or the evening, I'd often wander in and have a chat to our shift operator, Phil. He was a Malton lad, born and bred, and knew a lot of the locals. Sitting with him looking at the TV screens you got a sort of overview of what was going on – at least in Malton and Pickering, which is where the cameras were sited. And you got to see some pretty odd things. Most people are unaware that they're being filmed, but some are more savvy. So from time to time you'd get a hen party putting on a show for the cameras. It could get . . . interesting, let's say. Other times you just got a general sense of the mood on a particular evening. You could have an instant overview of how many groups were out, how drunk and rowdy they were, what kind of spirits they were in, even what the weather was like. It may sound daft but the weather has quite an effect on our job. Rain, for example, will – literally – put a damper on the evening and send people scuttling off home early, which is why we refer to PC Rain. So, as I say, I liked to keep an eye on what the cameras were feeding us, and I liked chatting with Phil. He was full of stories about the things he'd seen captured on-screen. He loved to tell about the night he was using the cameras to keep an eye on a drunken man as he staggered along Yorkersgate to the traffic lights and then started weaving his way down towards the station. By carefully twiddling his controls and altering the angle, and switching from one camera to the next, Phil had just about managed to keep the guy in view while he passed on directions to one of the cars coming in from the other side of town. It was all going fine until the drunk went off-camera, somewhere down towards the river, causing a major panic. With cars now approaching the areas from three separate directions, Phil sat there twiddling away like a man possessed. He had a camera down on Railway Street, and after panning it round to its full extent, left and right, he swivelled it downwards. There, right underneath it, was the drunken lad, propped up against the post and sleeping like a baby.

Spending as much time as I did in Phil's control room, and being the kind of person I am – namely, someone who cannot resist fiddling with things – I soon learned how things worked. Not only that but I'd got Phil to give me the password to get into the system. He wasn't strictly supposed to let me have it, but, like a lot of people, he found it was easier to give in to me than to argue. I can be very persistent. Besides, he would usually go home after two o'clock, and as I said to him at the time, it made sense to have someone about the place who could manipulate the cameras. This particular night he hadn't actually gone off duty but, with Chris Cocks being busy, he'd taken a call from a member of the public and was listening to an apparently endless complaint. I'd grabbed his seat and was flicking idly from one camera to another, through a series of quiet street scenes, when something – or rather someone – caught my eye.

I spotted a young lad, eighteen or nineteen years old, walking along Wheelgate, one foot in the road, the other on the pavement. I recognised him right away. It was his hair, all long and frizzy, and his build. He was a good six feet tall but I doubt he weighed more than nine and a half stone. I knew him because he lived in Easingwold, and I'd had occasion, a year or two previously, to talk to his parents about underage drinking. He wasn't a bad lad at all, and had accepted the talking-to in the spirit in which I intended it, since when, as far as I was aware, he'd kept out of trouble. Anyway, here he was, in Malton, obviously drunk, at just gone midnight, which made me curious. I panned the camera and followed him up the road as he made his way towards the bank opposite the Gate Inn. He stopped at the hole in the wall, reached into his hip pocket and took out a card. When someone who's a bit worse for wear is standing at a cashpoint they can be quite vulnerable, so I swung the camera round to take in a bit more of the street. There, walking along the opposite pavement, were two other lads I recognised.

In London, as much as I patrolled the streets for ten years and got to know a lot of people, it was quite rare for me to bump into someone I knew. If I did, it was often a case of 'fancy seeing you here!' Not only is the population huge, but it's constantly shifting, and there are always people visiting or passing through. Transient, you might say. Everyone is a stranger, it seems. But in a small town like Malton, and a thinly populated area like Ryedale, it's different. You get to be on first-name terms with people on your beat. Certain characters, particularly your loudmouths and bullies, they stand out. And they show up time and again, especially at the weekend when they're fuelled with drink. And that's precisely what these two characters were, crossing the street now and heading towards the unsuspecting lad from Easingwold.

One was known as Big John. He was a mechanic of some sort; I think he worked on agricultural machinery. He would be in his late twenties, and he'd got himself a reputation around Malton as something of a hard case. He'd come to notice with monotonous regularity. Time after time you'd go to a fracas outside the Milton Rooms, or one of the pubs, and he'd be among the crowd, pushing and shoving, shouting the odds and puffing out his chest, spoiling for a fight. He was someone who, if you met them in the street and he was stone cold sober, you'd move out of the way and give plenty of room. He gave out a strongly aggressive vibe. And to be fair, he was well made. He had what you'd call a blacksmith's hands, and huge biceps.

If Big John was, as his name suggests, on the large side – although a lot of his bulk was due to his intake of beer – his mate, Shaun, was a man mountain. If I say he was close to seven feet tall it'd sound as though I was exaggerating. I'm not. I have had the dubious pleasure of leading him by the hand – well, he had cuffs on at the time, and I was escorting him to the big van – and he made me feel like that seven-stone weakling you used to see in the adverts for Charles Atlas's bodybuilding courses. Shaun was a woodman, or forester. He was a mate of an individual I'd dubbed Tango Man, who'd got himself arrested on his own stag night a year or so previously and almost missed his wedding. Shaun was not a fighter, as such. Not in the way Big John was. But when he'd had a drink he tended to be a bit mouthy, abusive even. He'd push his luck, but by and large he knew just how far to go. It was rarely enough for you to feel justified in bringing him in, but he was always pushing things as far as he could, keeping you on edge.

By now the young lad from Easingwold – Will, his

name was, had got his cash and was walking, no, weaving his way across to the takeaway. He was clearly well under the influence. And between him and the kebab place were Shaun and Big John. Even as I stood there, leaning over the screen, I felt myself tense up. It was one of those horrible situations where you just knew what was going to happen, but there wasn't a damned thing you could do about it.

The lad Will staggered to one side of the pavement, and then back again, right into the path of Shaun. As the young lad's shoulder met Shaun's midriff, Big John leaned across and eyeballed him. Here we go, I thought. 'Jayne,' I shouted, 'get ready. There's gonna be trouble here.'

I hesitated for a moment. Was it going to blow over? Would it be just a bit of argy-bargy? A spot of banter? I could now see Will remonstrating with both of them. He was pointing at them while staggering about. No, I was thinking, don't try it, lad. Walk away. He had about as much chance as a Jack Russell pup taking on a pair of Rottweilers. I knew Will was going to get hit, but I was quite unprepared for the ferocity of the assault. Jayne came rushing into the room, but we could only stand and watch as Big John swung a giant fist and hit the lad smack in the face, catapulting him across the pavement. He fell flat on his back and lay there, half in the road and quite motionless, while the two hard cases – the two bullies, I should say – strode off as if they'd done nothing out of the ordinary.

'Phil, get off the phone, keep an eye on Big John and his mate. He's just smacked somebody.' I shouted.

Then I sent out an active message. 'Big John Simmonds has just assaulted a youth in Yorkersgate and is now making his way to the marketplace. We're going to need an ambulance and someone to back up. Show me dealing.'

'All received Mike, can I have a unit to back up?'

Ed came straight in, 'Yes, control, show me and Fordy backing up.'

'Received. For information just getting on to ambulance control now.'

In the corridor Ed was dashing out with Fordy. 'C'mon,' I said, 'it might take four of us to square these two up.'

Jayne and I got into our car, put on the blue lights, raced down to the traffic lights and crossed into Yorkersgate. We were just pulling up at the takeaway when we got the message from Phil on the CCTV.

'Ambulance just coming down Commercial Street, Mike. Be with you in two minutes. Big John and his mate are still in the marketplace.'

'Thanks Phil, We're just going to check on the casualty then we're going to get hold of them.'

Young Will had been moved out of the gutter and was now sitting against the wall of the kebab place with three or four youths standing over him. As we approached him I could see that he was conscious, but looking very groggy. Behind us Fordy and Ed got out of their car and set about moving the onlookers out of the way.

'Christ.' Jayne was as shocked as I was at the state of Will's face. His nose looked all out of alignment, and was spilling blood down his mouth and onto his T-shirt. Both his lips were split. I slipped a pair of plastic gloves on and gently moved his lips to check on the extent of the damage. I could see that his two front teeth were literally hanging out. He was in a right mess; this was a serious assault. The lad was barely conscious and needed to be taken to hospital as soon as possible. I was very relieved to hear the ambulance approaching from the direction of the train station.

'Right,' I said to Jayne as the ambulance arrived and the paramedics took over. 'Let's go and round up Big John.'

'We'd better come with you,' Ed said. He'd got names and addresses from the witnesses and would sort out the statements later.

Jayne and I got in the car and drove towards the marketplace. 'This sort of thing makes me angry,' I said. 'We need to bring this Big John character in.'

'Yeah we do,' she said.

'The guy's a thug and a bully. I doubt he'll come quietly.'

When you witness something that affects your emotions and floods your system with adrenaline the way this assault had, that's when you really have to be on your mettle. The challenge is to maintain a professional approach and not let your feelings take over. At the same time, you know someone like Big John will attack you as soon as look at you. You have to be prepared to get in quick and restrain him before he gets any ideas.

'*Malton control to 1015, over.*'

'Go ahead.'

'*Suspect heading across the marketplace towards the Royal Oak, over.*'

'Yeah, received. About a minute away. Stand by.'

'I mean, there's no bloody need for it, is there?' I said

to Jayne as I swung into the marketplace. 'Poor lad, probably on his way home and taking out a few quid for some supper and he ends up in hospital. Yes, he's had a drink and he decided to stand his ground, but they knew he was no threat. No threat whatsoever. You didn't see it, but I'm telling you he could've killed him, a blow like that. Specially if he'd hit his head on the pavement.'

'Yeah, but the good thing is, it's all recorded on CCTV.'

'True.' We were outside the Royal Oak now. The two men were crossing the road right in front of us and making their way across the car park. 'Here we go. Jayne. Let's not go wading in; keep them at a distance.' I swung the car around them, then pulled up just in front of them and got out.

I didn't wait for them to speak. I got straight to the point. 'John,' I said, 'I've got to tell you that I just witnessed you assault somebody in Yorkersgate outside the takeaway. Just stay where you are and stand still.'

He took half a step back, then stepped forward, staring me right in the eye. 'What the f*** you on about?'

'I'm telling you now, I saw it happen. You are under arrest for assault.' I could immediately see him tense up and clench his fists. 'No, no way are you f***ing arresting me,' he snarled.

At the back of my mind I was remembering a conversation I'd had with Thommo about Big John. 'Whatever you do Mike, don't CS gas him, because it doesnae work. It just enrages him.' Strange as it may seem, some people do seem to have a tolerance to CS gas, and in my experience I'd say it tends to be people with some kind of inner strength – or mental-health issues. I was looking at Big John, wondering what was the best approach here, when, just for a second, he was distracted as Ed and Fordy's car pulled up behind him. He had a quick look over his shoulder, then turned back towards me and started coming my way.

It's in situations like this that I'm glad of the experience I gained in the TSG. Over the years I have faced everything from rampaging football fans to major-league pub free-for-alls and full-scale riots in Trafalgar Square. And you don't come through that lot without picking up a few tricks. When you're dealing with someone twice your size you have to summon up every ounce of strength you possess, and one way of doing that, I've found, is to remind yourself that you're going to get just one chance – and it has to work. I looked at Big John and told myself, he's coming in. End of story. Crouching low on one knee, I drew my right leg back, took aim, and let fly, scything my way through Big John's legs.

I gave it everything I had, and more. Down he went, a look of utter shock on his face as he hit the ground. In an instant Jayne was on his back, pressing his face into the pavement with her knee. As he scrabbled at the ground to try and heave her off, young Fordy landed on the back of his legs.

'Shaun, mate, where are you?' Big John was struggling for breath. I looked up and saw his mate coming towards me, his arms spread wide as if he planned to wrap them around me. I cracked my Asp open, and held it back over my shoulder in a strike position 'Keep back, or you're coming in too!' I shouted. That was enough to change his mind. I'd dealt with him before in similar situations. He was all mouth until it came to actual confrontation.

As Shaun took a step back, hands in the air as if to say, 'Who, me?', Ed, Fordy and Jayne struggled to keep Big John restrained. 'I'll f***ing have the lot of you,' he spluttered as he writhed and kicked out and threatened us all with death and destruction. 'One at a time, I'll take you.'

I added my weight to the pile of bodies, Asp in one hand, cuff in the other. Slowly, gradually, I got a set on his left wrist, Jayne got hers on his right, and we used a third set to join the two together. Not exactly textbook stuff, but it worked.

In situations like this you're aware that the suspect can be causing himself quite a bit of harm, struggling on the hard pavement. But you can't apply the handcuffs until you have him under control.

The marketplace was now illuminated by flashing blue lights as Chris Cocks arrived with the van. Shaun was now lurking in the shadows, but Big John, restrained as he was, was still mouthing off, and I was the target of his venom. 'You might have the cuffs on me now,' he shouted, his bloodshot eyes staring right at me, 'but you f***ing wait till I see you're off duty. You're a bastard and you're gonna get what's coming to you.' He never let up, not even as Chris, Jayne and I manhandled him into the van. Suddenly I decided I'd had enough of his foul-mouthed tirade.

'I'll tell you what you are, my friend' – and I remember looking him right in the eye as I said it – 'you're nothing but a piece of scum.' I had my hand on his shirt and I could feel the sweat coming through the thin fabric as I pushed him into the van. 'Now get in there. You don't frighten us.'

For a second or two everything went quiet. Then as we closed the doors on him he erupted into a fury, kicking the panels, pressing his face to the grille and screaming at me.

'No f***er calls me that. I'll 'ave you, you piece of shit!'

Ed was looking at me. 'Scum?' He glanced at the back of the van where Big John was still ranting, and shrugged. 'Sounds about right to me, buddy.'

Back at the station we had a reception committee waiting. When you've taken a man like that into custody you always try to make sure there are plenty of bodies on hand to stop him from running amok and causing any damage – to himself as much as anything else. There was Jayne, Ed and Fordy, plus a couple of the late-shift lads who hadn't got away yet, all stood there around the back of the van as Chris unlocked it. I kept well out of the way. If Big John caught sight of me he might kick off again. He would be booked in, put in a cell and dealt with the next morning when, no doubt, he'd be a bit more biddable. Then he'd be interviewed, quite probably by the CID because this was most likely a case of serious assault.

It takes a while to calm down after a confrontation like that – not that you always have time. As it happened, things went pretty quiet for the next hour or two, enabling me to write up my statement. By the time I'd done that I felt it was time to call York District Hospital, where the ambulance crew had taken the boy from Easingwold. I was in luck. He'd already been attended to in the A & E department. He'd lost three teeth, had several stitches to his lip, and had to have his nose straightened, but had suffered no other physical damage. Mind, they told me, he would take a time to recover from the shock of the assault. Yes, I thought, and he'll most likely think twice about coming into Malton for a night out, certainly on his own. But overall he'd been lucky, I suppose. He could easily have had his jaw broken, or his cheek, or had his skull fractured in the fall to the ground. He could have died. It happens.

I went home that morning assuming that was that. There would, I hoped, be a court case, and a serious punishment, perhaps even a custodial sentence. I certainly wouldn't have shed any tears over that, because it really seemed to me that this man, once he got a few drinks inside him, was a menace to the public.

I really, really, hoped it would have a satisfactory outcome. Justice, in other words. As a police officer you try not to dwell on these things. Your job, after all, is enforcement of the law. Any trial, and sentencing, is out of your jurisdiction. And besides, you've no sooner dealt with one miscreant than a stack of other things are on your plate.

One such – and I kept coming back to it – was this Jed Baker business. He was on my mind all the time now. As soon as I'd finished nights I made a point of going to see the crime analyst. Had she or Des come up with anything?

'Yes,' was the short answer to my question. Amanda showed me the chart she'd pieced together on her wall. It must have been four or five feet square and was made up of several sheets of paper taped together. 'Here's your man, slap bang in the middle' she said, tapping at the red-circled name with her magic marker, 'and here are his main contacts, in blue.'

'There's enough of them,' I said, peering at the lines radiating from the middle of the chart to the dozens of names dotted around the periphery, and the criss-crossing of connections between them. 'Who are they all?'

'All manner of people,' she said, 'but there are a number of doormen working at nightclubs, in some cases managers.'

'Right. It all starts to add up, doesn't it? And are these all local? Can't be, can they?'

She shook her head. 'Most of them aren't from around here at all. They're all over the northeast – Newcastle, Sunderland, Middlesbrough – but they extend right down to Sheffield, even Derby. This man has quite a little network.'

'Starting to look as though he could be a main player,' I said.

'Well, I wouldn't get carried away just yet. There could be all sorts of reasons why someone might have a list of contacts like this.' She sat down and put her marker back in its tray. The tray, like her desk, and the rest of her little den, was amazingly neat and organised. 'But yes,' she said, 'I would have to say that it looks promising.'

'Anything I should be doing?'

'I don't think so, Mike.' She pointed at the chart. 'This is just the beginning. We need to circulate this man's details. I need to make some enquiries with my counterparts in other areas, see what we can find out about his contacts. Des has already checked on a couple.'

'And?'

'And he's found they're linked to the drugs scene.'

The frustrating part of our job is the waiting. Part of me wanted to rush out now and apprehend this guy Baker. He was surely up to his neck in the drugs business and needed to be taken out of circulation. When you gather information on an individual such as him, information that points to him being 'a wrong 'un', as they used to say in *Dixon of Dock Green*, all your instincts are to go round to his house and haul him in. But of course you have to tread much more carefully than that. It's one thing convincing yourself that you've identified a miscreant, but you need good evidence, evidence that will stand up in court. And you have to be prepared to show that that evidence has been gathered by legitimate means. If you're going to go to court with a suspect, you need to be quite, quite sure of your facts. Because the bigger the fish, the sharper and more devious his lawyers are likely to be. And they can make a monkey of you, given half a chance. So, much as it goes against the grain, you sometimes have to hang back, knowing that an individual is going to carry right on with his business – in this case, I was ninety-nine per cent certain, dealing in a Class A drug right under our noses. I've never been the most patient person, at least, not by nature, although I have learned over the years to temper my enthusiasm. Still, as it turned out, we didn't have long to wait before we ran into Mr Baker again.

It was a week or so later, and I was back on the night shift with Ed. We'd done our usual tour of town, had a quick break and were about to have a look out in the

villages and along the 'crime corridor', or A64. It must
have been about one o'clock. I was driving, and for some
reason I decided to drop down through the marketplace,
go by the bus station and along Blackboards Road. Then
we'd run through Norton, past the bacon factory and out
towards Scagglethorpe. You try to alternate your routes
out and back as much as possible, partly for variety's
sake, partly to reassure the public by your visible presence
– not that many of them are up and about at that time
of night to watch you drive by – but also to keep any
watching villains on their toes.

We were just approaching the level crossing, where
Blackboards makes a junction with County Bridge, when
a pushbike passed us, heading the other way.

'Who's that, this time of night?' Ed half-turned in his
seat to watch the guy ride by. I didn't. I knew right away
who it was.

I didn't say anything but turned out across the railway
tracks, swung quickly right into Welham Road and made
a swift U-turn round the bollards before pulling up in the
garage forecourt. 'The man on the bike, my friend, is
none other than Jeremy James Baker. He's the guy me
and Fordy are looking into at the moment. Possibly dealing
in ecstasy.'

Ed was fully turned on now. 'Well well well,' he said.
'Wonder what he's doing out on a bike at this time of
night.'

'Good question.' I was on the radio right away. '1015
to control, over.'

'*Go ahead, Mike.*'

'Yeah, Julie, I've just spotted a guy who's of interest to

us. Jed Baker. Out on his pushbike, would you believe? He's just gone down Blackboards, heading towards the bus station. Can you get someone at Malton to pick him up on camera?'

'*Stand by Mike. Chris Cocks is in Malton. I'll see if he can log on.*'

Chris was on the radio within sixty seconds. '*Yeah, got him, Mike. Fair-haired fellow, on a mountain bike?*'

'That'll be him.'

'*Just coming up past Yates's hardware.*'

'Tell you what, Sarge, can you keep an eye on him. I don't want to spook him, but I'm interested in where he's off to – or who he's meeting.'

There was a pause, then, '*He's turned up Yorkersgate. Heading towards the war memorial – and puffing a bit, by the look of him. I'm afraid he's gonna be out of range once he gets past there.*'

'OK, Sarge. Thanks for that. But just – can you keep your eyes peeled in case he doubles back into town?'

'*Will do, Mike.*'

'What's your plan?' Ed asked.

'Yeah . . . good question.' I drummed my fingers on the steering wheel for a moment before setting off along Blackboards and up towards Yates's. 'We want to be after him, but we wanna stay out of sight. Trouble is, if he's heading up past the war memorial he could be . . .' I swung out into Yorkersgate. As far ahead as we could see, the road was deserted.

'Any one of three ways, yeah?'

'That's the trouble. Which one? You feeling lucky?'

'Oh no,' Ed said. 'It's your call, buddy.'

I pulled up by the memorial. Was it to be the A64 to York, back into town around the Mount, or might he have set off on the Castle Howard road?

'Gut instinct, Ed. Always trust it.' I turned right towards Castle Howard, and kept to a steady thirty.

'What do you think he's up to then?'

'Not sure buddy. But you've got to say it's a very odd time of night to be heading out of town, and on a pushbike.' I drove on towards the edge of town. 'The other thing is, what's he doing in Malton? My intel says he lives out Pickering way.'

'Maybe he's off to do a deal.'

'Yeah, but at this time of night I can't see that it would make sense. Riding a bike, he sticks out like a sore thumb. Surely it would be easier to blend in during the day when there's people around.'

'What we going to do if we find him? Are we stopping him or what?'

'Good question Ed. What's on our side is he certainly doesn't know who I am. So if we just happen to come across him on patrol then we might just get the opportunity to speak to him without spooking him. You never know, we might just get the break we need.'

We were almost out in the country now, approaching the bridge that crosses the bypass, and there was no sign of our lone cyclist. Ed was ready to give it up. 'I mean, if he came this way we'd surely have caught up with him by now.'

'Hmm. Maybe.' I carried on across the bridge and went another mile or so. 'Nah,' I said. 'He's not up here. Bugger!'

I swung the car round, paused to let my lights shine down the wooded lane that leads to Broughton, and headed back towards the bridge. This was really frustrating. But just as we got to the other side, something caught my eye. I put my foot on the brake. 'See that, Ed?'

'What?'

'Not sure. Looked like one of those plastic reflectors.' I stopped the car and backed up fifty yards or so. There, against a tree, tucked away almost out of sight, was a bicycle.

'That the one matey was riding?' Ed said.

'Has to be. But where . . .?' I glanced around, wondering if we might see another bike, or a parked car. 'Wonder if he's met up with someone,' I said. I had a really strange feeling. Something was going on, and not far away, but we couldn't see it. Were we looking in the right place?

'How about back through town and out onto the bypass?' I said. But before Ed had answered I'd made up my mind. As I set off that way I got on the radio. 'Yeah, 1015 to control, over.'

'*Go ahead, Mike.*'

'We've found the pushbike hidden by a tree on the Castle Howard Road, near to the bridge which crosses the A64. We're going down to take a run along the bypass, see if we can see anything.'

'*Echo Tango 18 to 1015, over.*' A traffic car had been listening in.

'Go ahead.'

'*Yeah, we're just on the bypass now heading towards Scarborough. What have you got?*'

Ed explained briefly what we had going on and I pulled

over. If there was a rendezvous taking place on the bypass then we should maybe hold back just in case Baker returned to his bike.

'That was handy,' Ed said. We couldn't see the bypass from where we were parked up, but we could hear it – or could've done if there had been anything moving. But it was dead quiet. With the window wound down all we could hear was the murmur of our own engine, a rustling sound as a light breeze stirred the foliage above us, and the screech of a barn owl out hunting somewhere across the fields.

'What the hell do you think he's up to?'

'No idea, Ed. But the more we find out about this character the more dodgy he seems.'

'And why's he not in his car?'

'You tell me.'

'*1015, receiving.*' It was the traffic car.

'1015 go ahead.'

'*Yeah, I'm just approaching the bridge now. There's a fairly new-looking black 5 series BMW pulled over – right under the bridge.*'

'There is? Right, I think I need a word with the driver. Can you turn around and make sure he doesn't go anywhere?'

'*Too late, mate. He's off.*'

'Bloody typical. Are you in a position to try and catch him up?'

'*Will do. But we'll have to go up to the A169 interchange to turn around.*'

Exasperated, I set off for the bypass. But to be honest I was caught in two minds. Was it better to get down there when the traffic car had as much chance as we had of catching up with the BMW, or would it be better to go back to where we'd been and see whether we could catch Baker picking up the bike? I pulled up at the war memorial.

'Hobson's choice Ed. Has he dropped off or picked up? And which one has the gear – Baker or the BMW driver?'

'We can't tell,' Ed said. 'But we've a far better chance of nabbing our cyclist chummy.'

I agreed. The only fly in the ointment was, when we got to the bridge the bike had gone.

'Damn it!' I got on the radio to Jayne and Fordy, and Chris Cocks on the CCTV. 'We need to find this man,' I said. 'I'm sure he's just pulled off a drugs deal. So he's surely carrying the merchandise or the cash, one or the other.'

I turned to Ed. 'Let's retrace our steps. I don't think he realises we're about. He's no reason not to go back the way he came, don't you reckon?'

'Worth a chance. Yeah.'

Back in Malton I shot down Yorkersgate, turned down past Yates's and across the river. There was nobody on the streets. Not a soul.

We'd just entered Blackboards again when Chris came on the radio. *'Mike, I've got him on camera. He's—'*

'Yep. Me too. Ta.' There he was right in front of us, pedalling along towards the crossing, wobbling slightly as he flicked a cigarette end into the river.

We were almost level with the signal-box when I got myself alongside, eased ahead, and pulled up, right in front of him. I was straight out of the car. 'Can I have a word please?'

You learn what to expect over the years. And you're rarely disappointed. Cheap villains will come quietly, most of the time. They haven't the experience, or the sheer nerve, to try to wrong-foot you. But the more determined types, the serious crooks, are inclined to be much more confrontational. They know that if they come on strong, especially with a young or inexperienced officer, it'll most likely throw them off.

'What the f*** do you want?'

I wasn't going to fall for that. We were playing a long game with this character, and the less he knew – the less he thought we knew – the better. If he had me down as some officious little copper stopping to check his lights to rack up a few points on my report card, well, all the better. I was happy to play it that way in the interests of achieving the ultimate goal.

'Mike Pannett,' I said. 'North Yorkshire police. Seems an odd time to be going for a bike ride. Can you tell us what's going on?'

'Whatever it was, matey, it's f*** all to do with you.' He looked me up and down with a sort of sneer on his face. 'So piss off, yeah?'

'There's no need for any of that, mate. Now, are you going to answer my question?'

'Am I hell!' He was off his saddle now, straddling the machine and trying to give me the hard stare. There wasn't a lot of him. He was maybe five foot seven, and slightly built. Take away his bleached hair and there wasn't much to make him stand out in a crowd. 'Have

you got a bloody reason for stopping me? 'Cos otherwise I'm off.'

'Well, firstly you've got no lights on your bike, mate.'

He puffed his chest out and started to come towards
me. He reminded me of a little bantam cockerel. 'Oh for
f***'s sake. You really are a f***ing joke.'

I took off my glasses and slowly, deliberately, put them
on the bonnet of the car. Small as he was, I had a feeling
that this could easily turn nasty. At the same time, I was
sending him a clear signal that I wasn't going to back
down, even if he decided to get violent. Ed came and
stood beside me. He was reading the situation the same
way I was. This guy was showing all the signs of someone
who was about to kick off. His chin was jutting forward,
his fists were clenched and he'd leant the bike against the
wall that separated the road from the river.

'Right,' I said, 'I suggest you calm down, right now, or
I may have to arrest you under the Public Order Act for
using foul and abusive language and threatening
behaviour.'

It had the desired effect. Blondie now came up with
what he thought was a reasonable explanation as to why
he was out and about at this time. 'Look, I've just had a
falling out with my girlfriend, right? I'm just out to cool
off and get some fresh air. I don't need this crap.'

Nice try, I thought. 'Right, well the quicker we get this
sorted, the quicker you'll be on your way. Now, I'm going
to search you. Just stand still and show me the palms of
your hands . . .'

I had every right to search him. He might have been
carrying a weapon, stolen goods, drugs, anything. But he

didn't like it. They never do. The only thing with this guy was, he was cocksure of himself. As he had every right to be, because he was clean. Clean as a bloody whistle. I managed to hide my disappointment. He made no attempt to disguise his anger.

'What did you think you'd find, you bloody Nazi? Can't a bloke ride his bike around town these days without being harassed? Eh? Wass your frigging problem? I could sue you, y'know.'

'Well, everything seems to be in order, mate.' I wasn't going to rise to the bait. I was a simple country copper looking for brownie points, remember? 'If I could just make a note of your name and address,' I said. I wondered whether seeing the traffic car turn around on the bypass had stopped him completing a deal. Was that what was needling him? Or had they completed a transaction? If so, where was the merchandise, or the money? Not only was he carrying no cash whatsoever, he didn't even have a mobile phone with him. That struck me as very suspect. Who ever goes out at night without a phone and some cash? As I noted down his details, his manner changed.

'Well,' he sneered, 'at least you've got some paperwork to show the boss, eh? Make you feel you've earned your corn for the night, does it? You wanna get a proper job, you do. Or aren't you bright enough?' He tapped his head and pulled a sort of monkey face. This was good. As far as he was concerned, he'd got one over on me. But in the broader context of our ongoing investigation, we'd learned a little bit more about him, pieced together another bit of the jigsaw – especially if the traffic officer got that car's number and we were able to trace it. Baker, on the other hand, was still unaware of what we were doing. As far as he was concerned he'd been stopped and scarched by a village plod. He'd given away nothing, and was going to be laughing all the way home.

I have to say I was gutted when I got back to base and found that the traffic car had drawn a complete blank on the BMW. They'd never seen it again, let alone got its number. I felt as if we'd almost gone backwards, but I was reassured when we had our next meeting with Birdie. We reviewed the information we'd managed to gather. It was now quite plain that this man was a bigger operator than we'd first thought. Birdie told us he was alerting the chief superintendent to take the case to the next area meeting, where they would discuss the possibility of bringing in the Regional Crime Squad and setting up some kind of surveillance operation.

The net wasn't exactly closing, but it was certainly being laid out very carefully, and it was covering a wider and wider area. Sooner or later Baker would get himself caught up in it.

Chapter 7

Good Cop, Bad Cop

'You've got the place as good as new,' I said. It had been an absolute age since I was up at Baz and Jackie's place. 'Last time I was here there was still muck and rubbish everywhere you looked.'

'Aye, there was. Thanks to them bloody fire-raisers.'

I looked around the yard. It was more or less empty, apart from a stack of pallets piled neatly against the side of the old machinery shed where the combine-harvester stood ready. Baz had been cleaning it, and water was still dripping from its yellow bodywork. The whole place looked remarkably spick and span. The collection of used car batteries and worn tyres, which, for as long as I'd known Baz, had been hurled in an unruly heap against the side of the big barn, were all tidied away in a corner next to his vintage Land Rover. A length of plastic hose was coiled under the standpipe, and a pair of old pot sinks outside the house were overflowing with blue and red petunias.

'Took us a time, but we've got her lookin' sommat

like.' He nodded towards the barn. 'The insurance company stood us a new roof on that, so I s'pose some good came out of it in the end.'

'Wasn't fun while it was happening though, was it?'

I followed Baz back towards the house. As we kicked our boots off at the back door he shouted out, 'You got that kettle on, lass?' Baz knew I was after a brew as well as a bit of a catch-up.

'Tell you the truth, I was surprised to find you home,' I said. 'I only popped by on the off-chance.'

'You're lucky to find me in, lad. I was going to go to town – market day, like. But' – he slung his jacket on the hook behind the door – 'things are flat just now.'

Baz sat himself down and pointed to a chair in the corner of the room. 'Help yourself,' he said, 'and never mind that lazy old thing. Never caught a mouse in its life.' I tipped the cat off, pulled the chair over to the table and joined him, just as Jackie came in.

'Hello, stranger,' she said. 'We were starting to wonder whether we'd ever see you again.'

'Been busy, Jackie. You know what it's like in my job: you're here there and everywhere. And we've had a bit of excitement ourselves.'

'Who? You and Ann?'

'Had a crack in the chimney. Didn't find out till the rain came in. Brought the ceiling down and now the whole roof's to replace.'

'It's a good job it's not your house, eh?'

'That's another story,' I said. 'I tell you what, though – blooming builders, you have to watch 'em like a hawk.'

'Aye.' Baz was unfolding his *Yorkshire Post* and looking

at me over the top of his glasses. 'They'll sit in your kitchen all bloody day if you let 'em. And eat you out of house and home. Nearly as bad as policemen.'

Jackie laughed. 'Don't listen to him, Mike.'

'I never do, miserable old . . .' I sniffed the air and rubbed my hands together. 'Am I imagining it, or has something just come out of the oven?'

'See what I mean?' Baz said from behind the paper.

'How did you guess?' Jackie said. 'Redcurrant muffins. Trayloads of them. We had more currants than we knew what to do with this year.'

'And guess who had to pick the buggers?' Baz said.

'Now Barry, you know how you've been moping about this last week or two. You needed something to keep you busy. You said so yourself.'

'I thought this was your busy time,' I said. 'Reckoned you'd be out harvesting by now.'

'You'd think so, wouldn't you? First week in August, like.' Baz shook his head. 'But it's been a funny old year, you know. Cold spring, then that warm spell, and then the wet. What's happened is, the corn came through and started ripening, then there was another growth spurt. We've all new shoots that's still green in amongst them that's ready.'

'Oh,' I said. 'Never heard of that before. So what do you do about it?'

'Why, we do the best we can. Been spraying wi' Roundup.'

'Roundup? I thought that wiped out everything it touched.'

'Green stuff, aye. That's the point. You kill off the new growth and harvest what's ripe.'

I shook my head. 'Tell you what, Baz, I'd rather have my job than yours.'

'Course you would, lad.' Jackie had just placed a mug of tea and a plate of warm muffins on the table, and was gesturing to me to get stuck in. 'All you do is drive around in that vehicle of yours and sup tea all day.'

I tapped the side of my head. 'Hey, I might look like I'm taking it easy, but this thing, mate, it's always ticking over. Always on the go, that's me. People think I'm lozicking, but what I'm really doing is intelligence-gathering.'

'Well, you gather your intelligence while you can, Mike' – Baz leaned forward and helped himself from the plate – ''cos I reckon you've got some stormy weather up ahead, your lot.'

'How's that, Baz?' I mumbled, my mouth full of muffin. 'By heck, these are good, Jackie.'

'Thanks, Mike. I'll maybe wrap some up for you to take home.'

'So you haven't heard about the rally?'

'What rally's that, Baz? Not another vintage car job, is it?'

'He means the Countryside Alliance,' Jackie said.

'Aye, they're planning a big march down in London. I'm off, and I know one or two others that's going. They reckon to be lobbying parliament. They're talking about getting a coach, some of 'em.'

'This is all about the hunting ban, I take it.'

'Aye. Bloody politicians.'

'Still, that's in London,' I said. 'Won't affect us, I shouldn't think.'

Baz put his paper down and finished off his tea. 'That's where you're wrong, Mike lad. Them politicians, I'm telling you, they've made an error of judgement on this. A serious one. And what I reckon is, there's going to be more protests all over t'country.'

I was about to interrupt, but he stopped me. 'Aye, and don't be surprised if you see a bit of bother on your own doorstep. You ask me, I'd say some of the hunts are going to go out regardless of what t'law says.'

'Yeah,' I said, 'but it isn't the law yet. It's still got to go through parliament.'

'It'll go through all right,' said Baz. 'You see if it doesn't. Majority such as they have there's nobody to oppose it. And once it does, and once people decide to defy it . . .'

I groaned. 'So we'll be having pro-hunt, anti-hunt . . .'

'Aye, and more of them sabotage merchants.' Baz shook his head. 'You could be in for a lively time, lad. You see if I'm not right.'

I thought about Baz's warning as I made my way back to town. He was probably right. The feeling I'd encountered among the people on my beat was that the government was taking on something bigger than they realised. Not everyone in the countryside was a supporter of the hunt, and only a minority were actually involved in it, but it seemed to me that there was a resentment building up that went much deeper than the single issue of hunting with dogs. People who had no particular interest in it were seeing this as an attack on a way of life – their way of life. It was a case of city people, perhaps not very well-informed of how the countryside works, trying to change a culture that had deep,

deep roots going back through the centuries. It had all the makings of a classic them-against-us situation.

I drove up onto the top of the wolds before I headed back towards town. I went by way of Wharram Percy, along the single-track, unfenced road that takes you towards the brow and gives that fantastic view across the Vale of Pickering to the moors. To one side of me they were harvesting wheat, the combine thrumming its way to and fro in a cloud of dust, with bits of chaff flying in the breeze. I pulled up and watched as the driver poured his load into a bright-red trailer, silhouetted against a blue sky dotted with puffy white clouds. I thought about what it must be like to be a farmer, and after all the ups and downs of the year, the good weather and the bad, to see those mounds of golden ripe corn going into the bins and to know that it had all come to fruition. Not a bad life, surely?

The field to the other side had already been stripped clean, and the plough had just started work on the barley stubble, which glowed a warm golden yellow in the sunlight. It reminded me that the poachers would soon be out in force, making the most of the stubble-fields before they were ploughed under. Another few weeks and the next crop would be in and then everything would soon come bright green again, but for now there was just a single ribbon of dark damp earth, slicked by the ploughshare and flecked with chalk, with the usual flock of seagulls wheeling above it.

I was in a reflective sort of mood when I drove into the yard in Old Maltongate. It was about one o'clock and I'd be going home shortly. I wasn't downbeat or anything, just . . . thoughtful. I suppose it was seeing the harvesters at work and realising that the year was, in a sense, already starting to wind down. There are things to delight in all year round in the countryside, it's just that they always seem to come round sooner than you expect. One minute it's midsummer and you're sitting out in broad daylight till half-ten and eleven o'clock, then before you know it you're having to come inside at half-past eight and the grass is soaked in dew on a morning. My old grandad used to say the years went faster and faster as you got older, and I was starting to see what he meant.

'Now then, Mike.' I was back at the station, still meditating on the passage of time, when Chris Cocks called out to me from the desk.

'What is it, Sarge?'

He hesitated, looking a little awkward, as though he was about to say, 'I don't know how to put this, but . . .'

'Inspector Finch wants to see you, matey; in his office, now.'

'Oh. Righto then. Any idea what it's about?'

Chris just shook his head. He knew all right, but wasn't going to say. I went straight to his office and tapped on the door.

'Ah, Michael.' It was never a good sign when the inspector called you by your proper name. Usually it was 'Mike' or, if he had something serious to say, 'Pannett'. I stood there and waited while he fished a slim folder out from one of his document trays.

'This man' – he had the folder open and was running

his finger down the top sheet of paper – 'this man Simmonds.'

'Big John,' I said.

'Ye-es, Big John Simmonds.' Birdie looked up. 'Er, do take a seat.' I sat myself down. I didn't like the look of this.

Birdie shut the folder and looked right at me. 'He's lodged a formal complaint against you.'

'Against me, sir? For what?'

'He says you verbally abused him, that you called him, and I quote, a piece of scum. Is it true?'

'Yes, sir.'

'Heat of the moment, was it?'

I didn't answer right away. I was thinking back to the incident, trying to remember. Had I lost my cool? Had I said something really stupid? No, I didn't think I had. The guy had been under arrest, in handcuffs, job done. I'd looked him up and down, thought about what he'd done to a poor lad half his weight, and told him, quite calmly, what I actually thought. Maybe it was unnecessary, but was it cause for a formal complaint?

'No, sir,' I said. 'It wasn't a heat of the moment thing at all. I was fully aware of what I was saying. I've known this guy for some time. When he has a drink he can behave like – well, like I said, a piece of scum, sir.'

'Well, that might be the case, Mike, but do you not think it would have been best to keep it to yourself?'

I paused for a moment. I was thinking back to my Met days and the old sweats who always told you to say nothing. 'I don't think I want to expand on the subject at this time, sir,' I said.

'Well, Mike, you know how it is these days. I have of course had to refer it to the complaints department. I dare say you expected as much.'

'To tell you the truth, sir, I didn't.' I was actually quite taken aback, and not at all happy about the prospect of being investigated by the complaints team. I'd had my share of dealings with them in the Met. Down in London, you expect complaints. You arrest anyone and they're straight on to a solicitor claiming wrongful arrest. Or that you've abused them, either verbally or physically, or planted something on them. Anything they think they can get away with, usually just to be difficult and to try and cloud the issue when they know bloody well you've got 'em bang to rights. Basically they put you on the back foot, and you have to satisfy the enquiry team that you didn't do whatever they've accused you of. Partly as a consequence of this culture, a lot of modern-day policing is, to put it bluntly, about 'covering your arse'. That's why we have custody suites wired for sound and vision, CCTV fitted to cars and vans, and have a system that ensures all telephone calls and radio communications to control rooms are taped. It's why we have 'black boxes' fitted to police vehicles, procedures for not having single officers in situations such as searching where all sorts of accusations could be made. It's all about lessening the likelihood of a complaint being made, and to strengthen our hand in terms of refuting it when one is made. It's a tedious and expensive business, and not always simple. More often than not it still boils down to your word against theirs, and the outcome is never certain. It's not something you like to have hanging over your head, but these days it's an occupational hazard.

'I would think the complaints department will be in touch shortly, Mike,' the inspector said. 'I'll be serving the formal notice on you fairly soon.'

There wasn't anything much else to say, really. I thanked Birdie, left his office and got ready to leave.

Ann was in when I got home, thank goodness. As soon as I was in the back door – before I'd even got my shoes off – I was telling her what had happened. 'You couldn't make it up,' I said. I was seething by now. 'A bloke like that, built like a brick outhouse, picks on a ten-stone weakling, no real provocation, and sends him to hospital. Lucky he didn't crack his skull. We make a swift clean arrest, get him off the streets before he does any more damage, and now I'm the one in trouble. How does that work, eh?' I kicked my shoes into the corner and went into the sitting room.

'What exactly is he saying you called him?' Ann asked.

'I said he was "scum". No, I correct myself, I said he was "a piece of scum". Which he is. God, if I'd said what I was really thinking I'd be in real trouble, I can tell you.'

I sat down in my recliner. 'So,' I said, 'it looks as though I've got myself well and truly in the mire. Me and my big mouth, eh?'

'Mike, stop being so dramatic. You're not well and truly in the mire. It's hardly the crime of the century, certainly not in the Gene Hunt school of policing. But'– Ann sighed and came to sit on the arm of the chair – 'you could really do without it now, couldn't you?'

'You mean there's a good time to be accused of abusing a prisoner?'

'No, I mean you could find yourself on a promotion interview board before very much longer.'

'Yeah, I suppose I could. So now what do I do? '

'Hmm.' Ann got up and went to stand by the hearth. She didn't say anything for a few moments, just plucked a few dead flowers off a bunch I'd bought her at the weekend. That's one of the things I really like about her. Where I've always got something to say for myself, and occasionally speak before I've thought my answer through, she will chew a thing over for some time before she comes up with a response.

As I waited, Henry came and put his head on my knee. It's funny how a dog sometimes knows you're unhappy. 'All right for you,' I said. 'Eat, sleep, walk, eat. You don't know how lucky you are.'

'Where's that dictionary?' Ann was looking behind the TV. 'You moved it?'

'Yeah, it's over there with my books,' I said. 'On the sideboard. I was using it for my exam preparation – till the bloody builders moved in.'

'Another week or two and they'll be done,' she said. 'If you believe Soapy.' She went and picked up the dictionary. It wasn't a massive one, not like the one my dad had when we were growing up. It was more the sort you could get in your pocket if you had to. 'Right.' Ann had done her thinking and was now into action mode. She started flipping through the pages. 'Scum,' she said, 'scum scum scum – where are you? We've got script reader, scuffle, sculpture – ah, here we go: scum.' She furrowed her brow, walked over to the window where the light was better, and read aloud. "A film or layer of foul or extraneous matter" . . . ye-es. "Refuse" . . . ye-es. Ah, this is what we want.' She turned to face me, holding the book in her two hands. 'Are you ready for this? Are you sitting comfortably?'

'Go on, let's have it.'

'Right then. "A low, worthless or evil person; a person of little or no consequence; riffraff or rabble".'

'Hey, I like it,' I said. 'Low, worthless and . . . say that last bit again, will you?'

'A person of little or no consequence—'

'That's him! Yeah, that's John Simmonds to a T. But how does that help me?'

Ann put the dictionary down on the coffee table and went to the sideboard drawer to get a notepad. 'It's the main prop of your defence,' she said. 'We'll copy this down, verbatim. In fact, I know what we'll do: we'll type it up and print it out. And while we're at it let's make a note of the actual dictionary we're quoting from. What edition it is and everything. Let's show them you know what you're talking about. Not a man to bandy words about without knowing what they mean, eh?' She grinned and tapped me on the knee. She was loving this. 'They'll be impressed by that, you see if they aren't.'

'You don't think I didn't know what it meant when I said it, do you? 'Cos I did.'

Ann raised an eyebrow. 'Of course you did, but now you know for sure.' She tapped her pen against the notepad. 'Documentary evidence. Now listen, you know how they work. What about your tray, your paperwork, your locker? What sort of state are they in? They'll see this as an opportunity to give you a full MOT. If they can't get you on one thing, they'll be looking for another. You know how they are.'

'Well, the only thing they'll find is a few wildlife magazines and a pair of dirty wellies,' I said. 'Y'know, I always remember what I was told as a young copper. That honesty is the main thing. If you've made a mistake, you own up to it. If you try and hide something and act dishonestly, then you're going to find yourself out of a job.'

'Yep, you're right there. That's what I was always told too. You know, if I hadn't transferred back up here from London I was going to go into the complaints department. I was seriously thinking about it, at any rate.'

'Me too. I was looking to join their surveillance wing. Quite a few of my old team have joined them since I came up north.'

'For me it was the next step towards promotion. A few of my old inspectors were on it. They actually invited me to join.'

'Strange the way things turn out, eh? Anyway, let's just hope they don't take too long. I've had these things drag on for weeks – months. Gets you down.'

As it happened it was only a day or two later when Birdie called me into his office again. This time he had me sat down straight away. And he called me Mike.

'The formal complaint has been lodged,' he said, 'and I have to serve this Regulation Nine notice on you.' He read the details of the complaint to me from the standard Reg 9 form. 'Would you like to say anything in response?'

I gave him the standard answer. 'Nothing to say at this stage, sir.'

Birdie copied down what I'd said verbatim on the duplicated forms, before asking me to read and sign it, confirming my response and receipt of the notification. He then handed me a copy and said, 'Sorry about that Mike. It's not a part of the job I like, but it's out of my hands now. From this point on, Complaints will be dealing with it.'

I wondered how Birdie expected me to react to this formal notification. I remember how unhappy I was the first time I had a complaint lodged against me – in fact, I was well and truly rattled – but that was many years ago now. I was particularly upset about it, because I felt it was unjustified. But I remember my sergeant at the time saying to me, 'Listen, it's normal. You've got to learn to expect them. It's part of the job. If you go through a full year without getting one it'll be assumed – I'll assume – that you aren't doing your job properly.' The thing was, people were a lot more confrontational down in the Smoke. They never actually said 'It's a fair cop' and came quietly. That's strictly for black-and-white films. It was always 'Get your f***ing hands off me; I know my rights', followed by 'I want to speak to a solicitor'. And fair enough. You could understand it, even if it was a pain in the backside. It became the norm. There were times when I had two or three complaints outstanding against me, and after a while they stopped bothering me – except when they were claiming I'd assaulted or physically abused them, that is, because I never did. Ever. Apart from the fact that it wasn't in my nature, I was only too well aware that you could lose your job and end up in prison if one of the more serious allegations against you was upheld. But since I'd moved back up north it had been a different story. I simply hardly ever got one. This was my first in three, maybe four years. I don't think young Fordy or Jayne had ever had one. Among thirty-eight Ryedale officers there might be one or two with complaints ongoing at any one time, sometimes none. North Yorkshire criminals tend not to bleat when they get caught, and they tend to mistrust solicitors.

I had a good idea what to expect as the procedure ran its course. I knew that I could expect a call to a formal interview with the C & D – that is, Complaints and Discipline, variously known to us humble coppers as the Leather Heel squad or simply the SS. At the time I left London it was the Met's fastest-growing department. How things change. When I first started the majority of everyday complaints would have been dealt with in-house, by your local inspector. More serious matters were passed to the small complaints team based at Tintagel House. There was clearly a need for a degree of impartiality, so they started bringing in small dedicated teams, and they just mushroomed. There's no point denying that a small minority of cops have stepped over the line, and perhaps the fact that every such case is very well publicised in the media reflects their comparative rarity. But of course, it only takes a couple of high-profile cases and suddenly every cop is tarred with the same brush, giving the public the impression that there are in fact far greater problems than there really are. Nobody likes a bent cop, least of all me, but in my opinion the police response has been over the top. Suddenly we had hundreds and hundreds of officers working on this kind of thing full-time. Integrity officers, they called them, plain-clothes outfits with under-cover and surveillance officers actually policing the police. It's a bit like the Americans and their Internal Affairs, I suppose. We were all, every one of us, wary of them. And we felt we were right to be wary, that they were out to get you. Word would soon get round when they were conducting integrity tests. An undercover complaints officer might, for example, hand in a wallet at a station front desk, pretending to be a member of the public who'd had just found it in the back of a taxi. A short time later the station officer would have a visit from a member of the complaints department, who would want to see the wallet to ensure that the contents were still intact and properly recorded. We soon figured out what was going on and of course the practical jokers latched onto it. You would find a pound coin left on a canteen table in the refreshments room. Nearby would be a handwritten note saying 'integrity test', and the pound coin would be left to gather dust for months. Every time a contractor was working in the station, repairing ceiling tiles or fitting new lights and so on, we would talk noisily about covert cameras and sound systems to see whether we could embarrass them. I actually remember seeing an overalled workman up a ladder in among the suspended ceiling tiles in the canteen at a central London police station one day. It was only when I recognised him as a police officer from a another station, a guy I'd worked with previously, that I realised he was probably now in Complaints and was rigging up some sort of covert equipment. I was, to put it mildly, taken aback, but I didn't say anything. The unwritten rule is, if you see a cop under cover you don't let on, just let them carry on as if you'd seen nothing. I tended to laugh about it – we all did – but in truth it made me feel sad that we needed to go to these lengths. It did seem to me that around that time morale amongst us beat bobbies dropped. We couldn't even have the usual team banter, the sort of jokes that kept everyone bonded together. We were worried that some of our comments might be considered politically incorrect and would be taken out of context and held against us. We always felt 'they' were plotting to get 'us' to incriminate ourselves, and we ended up asking ourselves, whose side are they on anyway? In theory, of course, they were neutral. And we soon came to the conclusion that they were: they treated everyone with the same degree of suspicion and condescension, regardless of rank. Amongst the humble beat coppers, the policy was to say as little as possible to them. Even here in North Yorkshire they'd just intro-duced a hotline to complaints for staff to use if they wanted to pass on any information without anyone else knowing.

Despite all of that, however, I was confident that I could handle what was coming. I really did feel that I'd done nothing worse than express an honest opinion to a man who deserved to be told that his behaviour was unaccept-able. And the worst-case scenario? Well, it wasn't as if I'd physically assaulted someone. That would have cost me my job. No, the most I had to fear was a reprimand or a fine. But I'd already made up my mind about that: I would contest the validity of the complaint every inch of the way.

The hard part of this sort of thing is the waiting, but mercifully it wasn't too long before things started to move.

Perhaps two weeks had passed when news came that Simmonds had been to the magistrates' court. The outcome, as far as I was concerned, was satisfactory. He'd received a six-month prison sentence, suspended for two years. If that didn't steady him down, nothing would, short of his being locked up. It was a sword of Damocles hanging over his head for the next two years, and if he ignored it, well, he knew what to expect. As far as I was concerned it should have been case closed, were it not for the complaint.

They came for me a few days after Simmonds' court appearance, two officers in plain clothes. One was an older, grizzled-looking guy, overweight in a rumpled suit, the other much younger and smarter, in a blazer and grey trousers. I wondered whether they were going to pull the old 'good cop, bad cop' routine. We went into the interview room, sat down, and the younger guy set up the tape recorder. That's never a nice feeling, watching someone press RECORD. You know that from that moment on you have to think about every word you utter. No throwaway lines, no flippant remarks, nothing that could ever be held against you at a later date. And no unnecessary detail. Just straight factual answers, and keep them as short as possible. I tried hard to keep in my mind how Ann would handle it. Think, think some more, then deliver your answer, nice and slow. I could have had a 'friend' present – which basically meant a member of our union, the Police Federation, or a colleague – but I didn't see the necessity. No, I felt well prepared. Ann and I had gone through what the best course of action was and I was ready.

From the off, the atmosphere was very formal. The two

officers who'd come to interview me sat forward in their seats staring me straight in the face while they formally cautioned me. They know it rattles you, and that's their intention. There's no denying that it's not a nice feeling. You dish out cautions in the line of duty on a regular basis, but to be on the receiving end – no, I didn't like it one little bit. It felt bloody awful.

From the word go I felt I was being treated as if I was a criminal. An officer with less experience than I had could have found it really intimidating and could easily have slipped up.

'PC Pannett, were you on duty on . . .?' They gave the date, the time and the place of the incident.

'Yes I was, sir.'

'Did you arrest John Simmonds?'

'Yes sir, I did.'

Then I suddenly thought, hang about, what am I doing here? I am guilty of nothing. I had arrested a violent man, and told him the truth about himself. Why was I being put under the spotlight? I decided I could save everybody a lot of time if I took the initiative.

'Excuse me,' I said, 'can I just stop you for a moment? There's something I want to say.'

'Go on,' said the senior man. He was an inspector, his mate a sergeant.

'Look,' I said, 'from the tone of your questions I get the impression you're expecting me to deny the allegation.'

They looked at each other. 'Carry on,' the inspector said. He wasn't giving anything away.

'I have got this right, haven't I? That he's taken exception to me calling him a piece of scum?'

'That's the sum and substance of the complaint, yes.'

'Well, I'm not denying it.' I looked at them, wondering whether they would respond. But they said nothing, so I carried on. 'The point is, I did call him a piece of scum. I admit it, and I'm standing by what I said. I mean, let's be clear about this: I chose my words very carefully.' They looked at me and still didn't respond. 'And when I got home, just to be on the safe side, I checked in here.'

I paused, and produced the dictionary from my jacket pocket. Ann had put one of those fluorescent sticky tags at the relevant place so that I didn't have to fanny about looking for the right page.

'Here we are,' I said, opening it up. '"Scum."' I couldn't resist stealing a glance at my inquisitors. I don't think they'd ever come across anything quite like this before and were, I suspect, bemused. '"Scum,"' I repeated, and ran through the definitions Ann had found, laying particular emphasis on 'a person of little or no consequence' before closing the book and replacing it in my pocket. 'This man,' I said, 'this Simmonds character – he fitted that description perfectly. All I was doing was reminding him of the fact.'

To tell the truth, I was surprised how quickly they wrapped things up after that. I could only assume that they'd come to Malton expecting me to deny everything. That that was what they'd prepared for. And I'd taken the wind right out of their sails.

I couldn't wait to get out of the room now. I didn't like being on the wrong side of the table. I'd interviewed enough villains, sat them in this exact chair. I felt tainted.

But my inquisitors hadn't finished yet.

'So,' the older guy said, 'one more question to deal with. Are you prepared – or are you willing – to apologise to the man for what you called him? Even though you claim it was appropriate.'

'Apologise?' I replied. 'Absolutely not. No, not in a million years. I stand by it, one hundred per cent.'

'How about agreeing to a meeting with him?' the sergeant asked.

'I beg your pardon?'

'A meeting. To come to an informal resolution. A sort of olive branch.'

I could see where he was going with this, but I wasn't having it. 'If I have a choice,' I said, 'my answer is no.' I was on a kind of high after the way they'd folded. Why yield ground now? Apart from which, I found the very idea of meeting up with Simmonds – what shall I say – distasteful.

They called it a day after that. They said they would go to Simmonds, or rather to his solicitor, and relay my response to him. Rather to my surprise, they called back the next day to say Simmonds had decided he didn't want to proceed. I wasn't surprised, to tell the truth. I think he realised that he'd been well out of line, both in the assault and in the way he reacted to me. Maybe he was even starting to see that I had a point. When it came down to it, Simmonds wasn't a complete tearaway. He had a job, and I believe he had a steady girlfriend. It was another case of 'He's fine until he gets a few beers inside him'. How many times do we hear that?

As things turned out, this was a good example of how effective a suspended sentence can be. I actually ran into

Big John a few months later in town. I was off duty, but he recognised me right away. He approached me, asked if he could have a word, and told me that his family, and his girlfriend, had given him a seriously hard time about what he'd done and that he felt this might have been a turning point in his life, a wake-up call.

After the dust had settled on the whole business, I occasionally thought back to the events that night in the marketplace. I asked myself whether I'd been out of order in saying what I'd said to him. The acid test in these things is, would you advise a young copper to do what you did? And the answer, I suppose, was no. I should have kept my mouth shut. But I would defy anyone to witness the sheer ferocity of Big John's attack on young Will from Easingwold – not to mention the verbal abuse he threw our way – and not to react. We're all human, after all.

Ann was pleased, and relieved, at the way things had turned out. I think she felt responsible, in the sense that she'd suggested how I should deal with the interview. I would never have thought of going to the dictionary, and I told her so. 'Maybe that's why you're a sergeant and I'm not,' I said as we sat outside on the log, the evening after my final discussion with the Leather Heel squad, and enjoyed a glass of chilled white wine. The sun was just going down over the meadow and the old fox was trotting across from the neighbouring field to the rabbit warren in search of his family's supper. He and his mate had had two cubs that year and we'd sighted them more than once, frolicking about in the long grass.

'The only reason you're not a sergeant,' Ann said, 'is because you haven't decided it's time to be one. You're perfectly capable of doing the job. You're just too happy being a PC if you ask me.'

'Funny you should mention that,' I said. 'Cocksy's on holiday in a couple of weeks and they're looking for someone to act up in his place.'

'Perfect.' Ann dug me in the ribs with her elbow. 'You want to get in there. Be a valuable experience.'

'Maybe,' I said. 'Maybe.'

Back at work the next day I was all set to approach Chris and ask him what the chances were, when he handed me his phone. 'Call for you,' he said. 'Customs and Excise, Dover.'

'Wonder what the hell they want,' I said as I took the receiver from him. 'Hello? Mike Pannett here.'

By the time I'd heard what the C & E man had to tell me I was grinning from ear to ear and punching the air in delight. You don't always get a satisfactory outcome in our job, but just once in a while everything comes together – and this was one such case.

It seemed that our man Jed Baker had driven down to the Kent coast and taken a ferry to France. Calais, I think it was. Since we'd flagged him up as being of interest to us, it automatically showed up on the Immigration computer. Baker arrived at the ferry terminal in the company of the lad Ronnie Leach had mentioned to me that time we met up in the station café, the one he'd described as not the brightest pebble on the beach. Using CCTV cameras, officers at Dover had watched Baker embark on the ferry, and noted that he didn't associate with the other fellow at any point. They had decided the best option was to let them run and pick them on the return journey.

They returned just twenty-four hours later. They came off the boat separately. From the moment they were recognised they were under close surveillance. They went through passport control, then were seen going to the same car together and getting in. Before they could leave the parking area customs officers had pounced, searched the two men's luggage and found a case containing some 5000 ecstasy tablets with a street value of around £50,000. Both men had been detained in custody pending a court appearance. This was, for North Yorkshire, a fantastic seizure. It would stem the supply to the street and hopefully put Baker and his mate behind bars. I couldn't wait to find Fordy and tell him the news.

'Good old-fashioned policing and intel gathering,' I said when I caught up with him. 'You can't beat it. Mind you, mate, it would have been even better if we'd nailed him up here. But I guess it's teamwork, isn't it? The bigger picture and all that.'

'It's a hell of a result,' Fordy said. 'What do you think they'll get?'

'No idea, mate. But I tell you what, it'll send out a message, loud and clear.'

'How d'you mean?'

'I mean to anybody who fancies dealing on our patch. Intelligence, mate, that's what it's all been about. Gathering intelligence and piecing the jigsaw together.'

'And teamwork,' Fordy said. 'You know – crime analysis, Customs and Excise.'

'Definitely. Even my initial informant, who shall remain

nameless. No, we can all take credit for this one, matey. Isn't it amazing how things turn around? Couple of days ago I was sweating cobs, getting ready to face the Spanish Inquisition there . . .'

'The who?'

'The Leather Heel squad, buddy; the C & D. Complaints and Discipline.'

'Oh, right.'

A few days later Birdie called us all up – me, Fordy, Amanda and Des – for a pat on the back. The chief superintendent, he told us, was over the moon. All of the intelligence we'd gathered was going to be extremely helpful in future operations in the region.

If I felt good that afternoon, I felt even better a month or so later when Baker and his mate went to the Crown Court and received a sentence that genuinely sent a shock wave through the rural community. He went down for seven years. And that, as I said to Fordy, was a result.

Chapter 8

Testing Times

My shift had just ended, I'd got changed out of my uniform and I was all set for home, and Birdie wanted to see me. Again. And once more, Cocksy wasn't giving any clues as to what it was about. Well, I thought, I've done nowt wrong, so I've nothing to fear. I made my way across to his office. It was always an odd sort of feeling when you visited the wendy house. It was occupied by the senior officers on our area and their civilian support staff, the HR people and so on. For security reasons we weren't allowed the door code and so you had to stand there like a lemon, rain or shine, waiting to be let in. As I stubbed my cigarette out and waited on the porch I had a little chuckle, thinking about the current management buzzword: 'my door is always open'.

It was now, and the chief superintendent's secretary was there to greet me. 'Hi Mike, back again so soon?'

'You know me, Carol. I keep turning up – like the proverbial bad penny.'

'What is it this time? Good news or bad?' she asked with a wry smile.

'Well, you're the one at the hub of this little universe. You tell me.'

'I could, but that would spoil the fun of watching you squirm.' She looked down and pulled a face. 'Have you seen the state of those?'

I followed her gaze. 'Muddy boots? Standard uniform for rural officers.'

She laughed and let me in. I made my way to Birdie's ground-floor room. I suppose you'd call it compact, if you were an estate agent. In the wendy house the office size was in direct correlation to the rank of the occupant. If I ever got a move over there, I was thinking, they'd have to find me a broom cupboard.

'You wanted to see me, sir?'

'Yes, Mike. Have a seat. Cup of tea?'

'Oh, thank you very much sir.' Tea was the last thing I wanted at that particular moment – I'd just come from Rich the gamekeeper's place out at Hovingham – but you never turn down a hospitable gesture from your senior officer.

'Help yourself to a biscuit.'

I was starting to feel uneasy. Something was in the air.

Birdie leaned forward, rested an elbow on his desk and rubbed his chin. 'I understand you've been studying for the sergeant's exams.'

'Yes, sir. Thought it was time to have a look at it. I mean, who knows? One day . . .'

Thankfully he cut me short. 'How are you getting on?'

'To tell the truth, sir, I'm struggling. To find time, I mean. Bookwork's never been my strong point. There's always something I'd rather be doing.'

'Hmm – more of a hands-on sort of person, eh?'

'Yes, you could say that – sir. Prefer to crack on with the job, learn it as I go along.'

'Right then.' He sat back in his chair, clasped his hands together and cracked his knuckles. 'Sergeant Cocks is about to start two weeks' annual leave. How d'you feel about standing in – acting sergeant?' Before I could answer – not that I was sure what I was going to say – he carried on. 'We've looked at finding cover and the fact is there aren't many options. Scarborough are stretched to the limit, and it's all hands to the pump over at York just now. Plus all the usual shortages with annual leave, sickness, officers attending courses. You know how it is. So, unless we draft someone in from outside the area, which would bring its own difficulties . . .' He tailed off, then just as I was thinking it was my turn to say something he carried on again. 'But I don't see why you shouldn't grab the chance to get some experience. Might help you make sense of all that book learning that you find so difficult.'

'OK,' I said. 'I mean yes, sir. No, I think you're right. I'll give it my best shot.' To tell the truth, he'd caught me on the hop. But this was an opportunity I wasn't going to miss.

'Good. I'm sure the rest of your shift will pull with you.' He glanced up at the wall-chart where he had all the shifts marked up. 'It's a full fortnight straddling the Bank Holiday weekend.' He took a biscuit and sat there for a moment with it in one hand, dabbing crumbs off his desk with the forefinger of the other. Then he looked up and said, 'If you really are serious about going for promotion this'll do you a lot of good. Open your eyes to what a sergeant actually does. I suspect there's more to it than you think.'

I felt strangely unsettled as I drove home. The fact was, I'd said yes without really giving it too much thought. It was starting to dawn on me what I was letting myself in for. You carry a lot of responsibility as a shift sergeant, particularly at a rural station where you're often the sole supervisor on duty in that area – especially at night. Still, Ann was coming off an early shift too, and I would talk it over with her. Last night's weather forecast had promised us the first fair day in a week or more and we'd planned to go for a walk.

We drove out in the direction of Pocklington and parked where the Wolds Way long-distance footpath crosses the Roman road. There's a lovely gentle walk that takes you down a typical dry valley, gently curving between steep grassy hills, and nothing to disturb the tranquillity beyond the bleating of a few sheep and the twittering of skylarks – although on this particular occasion we had Henry's strangulated gasps as he tugged on the new chainlink lead we'd finally bought him. The path winds downhill for a couple of miles, then levels out before bringing you onto the road at the top end of Thixendale village, just a few minutes' walk from the Cross Keys where we planned to have a pint and a meal.

I didn't raise the subject of my conversation with Birdie till we were on our way, skirting Thixendale Grange and starting to enter the valley proper. 'He kind of threw it at me out of left field,' I said. 'And I never really thought it over. I sort of heard myself saying yes.

And straight away I wished I hadn't. It's got me fretting a bit.'

'That's only to be expected,' Ann said. 'It's new, isn't it? It's the added responsibility. If you weren't apprehensive there'd be something wrong with you, don't you reckon?'

'You're probably right. It's just . . . I started thinking about it on the way home. You know, wondering what kind of sergeant I'd be. Who to model yourself on. I mean, you start thinking about all the ones you've worked with over the years, and they all have their own particular style, don't they?'

'Well, when I got promoted I thought of the ones I'd known and drew up a list of their good points and bad points. Then I tried to imagine an ideal, how to combine all the best features.' She laughed, and added, 'Mission impossible. I ripped it up and decided to be myself.'

'Sounds like good advice. But it still won't stop me quaking in my boots, first day on the job.'

'What do you mean quaking in your boots? You're an experienced PC.'

'Yeah, but you know me – things have a tendency to happen when I'm around.'

'It's only two weeks. I'm sure you'll be fine. I was nervous as anything, but you know what you're doing. Look, Mike, it's a hell of an opportunity for you. And it'll look good on your CV.' She stopped, right in front of me. We were walking single file along a sheep path, a thin line of bare earth worn into the cropped grass, and I almost crashed into the back of her as she turned and asked me, 'You have got a CV, I take it?'

'Course I . . . haven't.'

'You what?'

'What do I want a CV for? I'm not applying for a job as such.'

'What about when you applied to come up here? Didn't you write one then?'

'Yeah, but that was on the application form. I never kept a copy. I only knocked it up on a piece of scrap paper, then filled in the form and away it went.'

'But what about all the courses you've done, major cases, assignments, secondments? Haven't you kept a list?'

I tapped my head. 'It's all in here, love.'

'I bet it isn't. Listen, you'd better sit yourself down one of these nights and get it all on record. You think you'll be able to remember it, but trust me, you won't – not without some serious thought.'

'Whatever,' I said. The thought of yet more paperwork did not appeal. 'Now come on, let's get down to Thix. I'm starving.'

'Thirsty, you mean.'

'Thirsty goes without saying. But I am also hungry.'

My fortnight as acting sergeant got off to a steady enough start, which was the way I wanted it. There was a lot to get used to. Firstly, I had to come in earlier than the other officers, get the heads-up from the outgoing sergeant and make sure I was aware of all the ongoing cases and 'live' situations. It felt strange setting up in the sergeants' office and being on first-name terms with the very people I'd addressed as Sarge for the last couple of years.

The office was next door to the parade room. It was spacious and had a great view of the trees and gardens that surrounded the building. As I took it in a squirrel scampered up the side of the old beech tree. I had a look around the room that was to be my base for the next fortnight. It was like something out of a stately home, with its high ceiling, ornate coving and ceiling rose. There was an old painted bookshelf along one wall, crammed full of law and reference books collected over the years. Stacked up in one corner was the door-forcing equipment and a couple of riot shields for emergency use. In another corner was a walk-in cupboard, containing all sorts of booty – stocks of CS gas, spare radios, pens, batteries, pocket books, Sellotape and all kinds of stationery. I never even knew we possessed such things – staplers, Post-it notes, ring binders, document cases – and here I was entrusted with the sergeants' keys, which were not only for this cupboard, but for the entire station. There was a set for the large old drugs safe, another for the custody area and cells, another for the property store and a couple of offices that were normally kept locked when not occupied. I couldn't wait for my first night duty when I could have a proper root around the station and work out which key opened which door.

For my first shift, as I'd expected, there was only one inspector available in the Ryedale area – our man Birdie – and he was working in the daytime only. It felt really strange being his number two. Even stranger was the realisation that once he went home I would be expected to handle the entire Ryedale area, although I could call on our neighbouring supervision over at Scarborough or Hambleton if necessary.

To prepare for the shift briefing, I had to keep an eye

on all incoming intelligence and jobs on the computer and prepare to pass on any relevant information to the officers on my shift. I then had to look at the roster and decide who would work the separate beat areas, who would double up on the night shift, when they would come in for refreshment breaks and what areas needed to be targeted from the current intelligence. When I'd got on top of this lot I could look forward to briefing Fordy, Jayne, Ed – and Thommo, who'd been drafted in as cover.

It was an odd feeling, walking into the parade room with all my mates sitting round the table waiting to be told what to do. And the fact that one of them was twenty years my senior was odder still. I was glad when he broke the ice. 'My God, it's Acting Sergeant Pannett.' Thommo looked around at the rest of them and rolled his eyes. 'Is this the state of British policing today?'

'Ah, PC Thomson, glad you could make it. You've just volunteered for the worst outstanding job of the day award.' With that the rest of my crew started laughing – and took the wind out of Thommo's sails. He sat back in his seat and raised a conciliatory hand. 'Aye laddie,' he replied, 'it's a fair cop.'

The first shift was always going to be the most awkward. When you are acting up to a more senior rank, you're always aware that it's a temporary position and that you'll soon be back to your normal rank and working alongside the people that you've been supervising. The service is based on a rank structure and everybody knows that at the end of the day you call the shots and they do as you tell them. The important thing is how you go about it. People like Thommo and Ed were brilliant to have on the team because they were experienced and were on hand to help me out as and when. It's more difficult in some respects to act up with a team that you know and work with, so it was important that I made it clear that I intended to do a proper job. But I did make it plain that I looked to them to play their part in making things work.

Once the officers had gone out on patrol I was on my own, by and large. There was Phil covering the front office and the CCTV cameras, and from time to time one of the crews would come in for their meal break. There were also regular phone calls from Julie and Brian in the control room over at Northallerton, updating me on jobs I needed to know about, or asking what I wanted to do about particular situations as they occurred. I think Brian and Julie were both pleased that I was acting up, and they offered all the support I needed. Unlike Chris Cocks, I didn't have to sort out the duties for the entire area, so I was not as deskbound as he had been. This meant that I could take out the supervisor's marked car when I had some downtime. Other times I could check the computer, make sure that the incidents were updated correctly, finalise the completed crimes, write updates of ongoing cases, check case files for submission to the Crown Prosecution Service, and so on. Occasionally I'd receive a phone call or enquiry at the front desk from a member of the public that required a supervisor, or which the front office support staff needed advice on. You also got other area-based officers – traffic, dog section or ARV teams – dropping in for a brew.

Whenever one of our own PCs came in it was, 'Got yourself a good job there, Mike. Steady away.'

'Hey, don't kid yourself,' I'd reply. 'It only looks easy because I make it look easy. You've got a top man on the job here. Cool under pressure.'

The truth was that during the first week or so I wasn't finding it too hard at all. There really wasn't anything unusual to deal with. If I didn't know better I would've been tempted to ask what all the fuss was about – or, more pertinently, why had I been so reticent about the idea of putting in for promotion? It was all run-of-the-mill stuff: petty thefts, minor accidents and the odd dispute between neighbours. It was steady, very steady. And so the doubts remained: would I be up to the job when the going got tough – because sooner or later, surely, it would blow up in my face. It was bound to. How would I manage then? At one level, of course, I was happy not to have been tested. Another few days and I'd be done, back on the beat. I would have survived. On the other hand, a part of me really was wanting a challenge. You don't join the police for an easy ride, and you don't volunteer to step up to the sergeant's job so that you can coast. At least, I didn't. I wanted to stretch myself, see what I was made of.

What do they say? Be careful what you wish for.

I'd come in at half-past one for a late turn. It was Bank Holiday Monday. Everyone was on double time – nice for us, but with staffing levels at the bare minimum in order to cut costs I was well aware that if things kicked off we'd all earn our enhancement, every penny of it. The thing with bank holidays is that it can go one way or the other. That's part of the problem with working in a tourist area like Ryedale: the massive influx of people during weekends and holidays. I had one traffic officer and three PCs, plus

Thommo. He came in all smiles, happy to get 'a bit of plus', as he liked to call it, and I was glad to see him. He was the kind of old-style copper you wanted on your side if things got spicy, if only for his experience. He'd seen it all and wasn't one to get rattled.

The outgoing duty sergeant hadn't much to report. A few cattle had got out on the road over at Birdsall, and there had been a minor accident on the road leading up to Flamingoland. But it had all been sorted by the time I took over. Otherwise it was a typical summer Monday, with the warm weather bringing out the motorists in their thousands – and the traffic was already causing problems, particularly along the coast roads.

So everyone went out on patrol in pretty relaxed mood. In the station it was quieter than ever. No calls, no reports, little radio traffic. When it's like that you always wonder, is it the lull before the storm? It got to about three thirty and I was just flicking through the last of my paperwork when the call came in, the voice jagged with urgency.

'*Control to any units. We've got a head-on collision – Golden Hill, car versus lorry. Units to deal, please?*'

I was on my feet in an instant. I remember hearing myself say, 'This is it.' A serious accident requires the presence of a supervisory officer, and today there was only one of those in the whole of Ryedale: namely myself. I grabbed my hat, radio and jacket and headed for the door, my heart thumping. Fortunately we had the one traffic officer on duty in the district, and he called immediately to say he was making his way over from Helmsley. I could also hear Thommo on the radio. '*Aye, on my way from Ganton.*' So he could be fifteen, twenty minutes. I knew Ed was way over the other side of Pickering. He'd be struggling with the traffic coming out of Flamingoland. And Fordy was out West Heslerton way with Jayne, so they'd probably get snarled up on the A64.

I was in the supervisor's marked car, and driving fast. A lot of things were going through my mind. How bad was this going to be? Would I be first there? How easy would it be to get through once I hit the A64? I'd already had reports of traffic building up in both directions. Some people were making their way to the coast for an evening out, more were coming the other way, trying to beat the rush home. But there was nothing I could do about that. Not a thing. Besides, my head was already grappling with the question you always ask yourself as you head towards the scene of a road traffic accident. What would I find? I realised I was swallowing hard as images from accidents I'd attended in the past flooded my mind. There are things you'd rather not remember, but they're always there, just below the surface, and I needed to keep a clear head as I sped away from town, two-tones blaring and lights flashing, the line of cars ahead pulling over to the left-hand verge to let me by. So far we'd had no further information, but a head-on on a main road wasn't going to be good, especially right there on Golden Hill, a notorious black-spot where people were always travelling too fast, despite the warnings.

'*Control to 1015.*'

'Go ahead, over.'

'*Yes Sarge. We've taken several further calls on this. Apparently we have people trapped. Fire brigade en route.*'

'All received. I'm about two to three minutes away.'

I shot past the BMW dealer and out towards the bypass. Various things were going through my mind. I was aware that I was going to be first on scene and that the preservation of life was my top priority. The severity of the accident would then determine how I should deal with it. It had to be handled properly, and that was mainly down to me. I was the one in charge, the supervisory officer. They'd all be looking to me: especially the younger officers, Fordy and Jayne. Ultimately I'd be relying on specialist officers, but at the outset I would need to organise the staff available and implement the correct procedures.

I was about to join the main road now, easing onto the slip-lane where the old road merges with the bypass. Ahead of me the traffic was at a standstill. I didn't need to be told this was serious: as I drove west on the eastbound side of the road, past the queue of stationary cars, there was nothing, not a single vehicle, coming towards me. Whatever was up ahead had stopped the job completely.

I swung past the Low Hutton turn-off and started climbing. As the crest of the hill came into view I could see people out of their cars, some standing in the road, some on the verges, mobile phones clasped to their ears, pointing and directing me to the top of the hill.

Suddenly it was there right in front of me. In the middle of the road was the cab of an HGV. It was dark green. Above the windscreen, which was perfectly intact, was a bank of spotlights. Below it was the haulier's name spelled out in red lettering with a black border. The trailer was angled across the road behind it, its white curtains barely disturbed by the impact. Embedded in the tractor unit, smack bang in the radiator, was a grey Nissan Micra. When

I say it was embedded I mean just that. The rear end was undamaged. The front end was unrecognisable. It had all but disappeared into the front end of the truck. Sometimes it's as if your body knows what to expect before you do: my heart was racing.

'Control to 1015. Fire brigade and ambulance just leaving Malton. Should be with you in five minutes, over.'

Thank God I wouldn't be on my own. Not for long, at any rate. '1015 to control, just arriving at the scene now. We've got the road completely blocked. It's not looking good. Stand by for details on casualties.'

I pulled up about thirty yards short of the wreckage. Several people were out of their vehicles and standing nearby. A large man in shorts and flip-flops, his chest bare, was right up against the flattened Micra, bending forward to peer inside. A woman – she might have been his partner – was pulling him away, covering her mouth with her hands. I left the blue lights on and the engine running, got out of the car and ran towards them.

'Stand back, please!' I shouted. 'Will you stand back from the car?' I began to brace myself for what I was about to confront. It doesn't matter how many times you see people seriously injured or dead, it never gets any easier. Behind me I could hear two people sobbing and another whimpering. Somebody was jabbering into her mobile. 'They just went straight into it – oh Christ, you could see – you could see it was gonna happen.' Somebody else had a radio on playing music, really loud. As I ran past they wound their car window up.

There was a man in clean, dark-green overalls, crouched down with his head in his hands by the crushed car. Big fellow, broad chest. Insignia sewn on his top pocket that matched the name on the lorry. You notice these little things. He had to be the driver. I ran towards him as the man in shorts moved away and put his arm round his partner.

'I think they're both gone, mate. Elderly couple. I think they're both . . .' He tailed off. His voice wasn't the voice of a big man at all.

This was it now. I knew I had to look in the car to see what we were dealing with and check for vital signs. There was nobody else around to do it. Already I was trying to put my fear of death and the dead out of my mind, fighting my instinct, which was to recoil, close my eyes, run. It's always been with me, and always will. Ann once said it was a healthy fear. It makes sense that you're scared, she said. None of us wants to die.

Liquid from the lorry's radiator was dripping onto the concertina'd metal that had once been the car's roof, and trickling down the side of what had been the door. The sun-roof was all crushed, the glass twisted and crazed, a strip of black rubber beading wafting lazily in the breeze. I went to the passenger side. Looking through the buckled frame I could see a lady, maybe in her sixties or seventies. It wouldn't be right to describe her injuries, even if I could. In any case, what I saw put me into shock. There was no doubt that she was dead, no doubt at all.

I walked round to the other side, steadying myself with a hand on the tailgate. From the trees I could hear the sound of a pigeon cooing. A man wearing dark glasses was approaching me and looking at his watch. 'Any idea how long this'll take?' he asked, ''cos I've got a flight to catch.'

'If you'd just return to your car, sir, while we deal with the casualties.' I put my hand up to stop him coming any closer. 'Please.' You get people like that. You learn not to judge. I don't think they can help it, half of them.

The driver of the Micra was a man, same sort of age as the dead passenger, probably her husband. The vehicle was badly crushed around him. Mercifully, he wasn't conscious. His mouth, from what I could see, was closed. I managed to get my hand through the wreckage and held my fingers on his neck. I was shocked to feel a very faint pulse. I realised I was helpless. I couldn't get in to do anything for him, but there was no way I could get him out.

'Is he breathing?' The paramedics had arrived.

'Just.' I backed off and let them reach in with their gloved hands. 'Thank Christ you're here,' I said. In the distance I could hear another police car approaching. Looking up I could see it nipping along the side of the queue in the vacant offside lane. Barely a hundred yards behind it was a fire engine, headlights blazing.

'She's gone,' I heard one of the paramedics say. 'As for the other poor sod, I think he's about to go.'

Behind me a bystander gasped. 'D'you hear that?'

'If you could just return to your car,' I said. 'Let the emergency vehicles through, thank you.'

'What's the situation? What do you want us to do?' Fordy was there. He'd left his car alongside mine, a few yards away. Jayne got out, and came to stand beside him. They were both looking at me. That's when it hits you, that you're in charge. There are two dead or dying people in a car, the road is blocked in both directions, peak time on a bank holiday, the news media will be descending any time now, and the entire situation is yours. You have to stay strong, alert, decisive, and sort it out.

'Right, Jayne. The lorry-driver's sat over there on the verge. Will you just go and check he's OK and keep an eye on him until the traffic unit gets here.' She was looking at me, her eyes questioning. I nodded. 'It's a fatal.'

'OK Mike. Will do.' I could see Jayne take a quick glance into the vehicle as she walked past.

'Fordy, just go and speak to the first few cars and see if any of them witnessed what happened.'

'Will do, Mike.'

'1015 to control, update.'

'Go ahead Mike.'

'I can confirm it's proved fatal. We've got car versus lorry. Female passenger of car has proved fatal, and male driver is likely to. Both elderly. Could you let the duty SIO know and also contact the AIU? I'm going to seal the road off, so can you contact Highways. We'll need diversions putting in place.'

'That's all received.'

In a case like this you're glad of the procedures that you're required to adopt. They save you having to think too hard. I knew I now needed to treat this as a crime scene so that evidence could be preserved for the investigation team. The AIU or Accident Investigation Unit are a dedicated team of officers who specialise in serious road traffic accidents. They piece together all the evidence and establish what caused the accident. They would work with the SIO or senior investigating officer, an experienced traffic officer who is trained to oversee or lead the investigation.

There were still one or two people homing in on the crushed Micra, tentatively but purposefully. One looked shocked, another was frankly gawping. One was holding out a blanket, trying to be helpful.

'If you could please stay back and let the ambulance crew do their job,' I said, stationing myself between them and the wreckage with my arms out wide. 'I don't think there's anything you can do to help, so please return to your vehicles. Meanwhile, there's a fire engine coming right now so please, for your own safety, stay back!'

Some of them still looked at me, almost pleading. People do that. They want comforting, they want to be told what to do, they want to know what's happened – and what'll happen next. 'We'll do everything we can to get you on your way as soon as possible,' I said. 'Meanwhile, be patient. Be prepared for a considerable delay – and please, stay with your vehicles.'

As the fire engine pulled up I felt the weight on my shoulders ease. These lads were the ones whose job it was to attempt to cut the victims out of the wreckage. I now had the two most important services on scene and dealing with the casualties.

'*Control to 1015.*'

'Go ahead, over.'

'*Mike, I've got Highways on the phone. They want to know where you want the diversions.*'

This was going to prove very tricky, what with the sheer weight of traffic in both directions. Given the location of the accident it was going to be a nightmare trying to re-route them. I needed to give this some thought, but also needed to sort it sharpish.

'If you can stand by,' I said, 'I don't think we have a plan in place for this location. I'll come back to you shortly. Any ETA for the traffic car?'

'Received Mike. Traffic car is aware of the situation and should be with you shortly. The Scarborough car is also making its way.'

'All received.'

My job now was to deal with the queue of cars that stretched back towards the coast, and the other one that was backed up God knows how many miles towards York. Every minute we were there the queues were growing as more and more cars joined the tailbacks.

There was a noise, of metal being cut. Then a smell. Oil on a hot engine block. Or was it the hydraulic cutting gear the firemen were using? Even as I went to ask if everything was OK, they stopped. There was a moment's silence, then one of the paramedics said, 'He's stopped breathing.'

Jayne and Fordy walked past me. They had the lorry-driver between them and were supporting him. He was trembling now, his head hanging low. He was clearly in shock. They put him in the back of their car and spread a blanket over his shoulders. Somebody was jabbering on the fire-engine radio. The ambulance driver was reporting in on his. A paramedic hurried by, panting, with his bag, on his way to check on the lorry-driver. A big guy like that, in shock, he could easily have a cardiac arrest. I'd seen it happen.

'Glad you're here, mate.' Our Ryedale traffic officer had arrived. He was new to our area, but an experienced copper. 'Right Simon, we've got two elderly occupants in the Micra. The female passenger has been killed outright and it looks like the male driver has just proved. The lorry-driver appears uninjured, but is in shock. He's with Fordy and a paramedic in the back of the police car. Don't appear to be any other vehicles involved. AIU are en route, as are a double-crewed Scarborough traffic car. Fordy has got names and addresses of a few witnesses and they're all back with their vehicles. Can I leave this to you now and let me sort out the diversions?'

'Yeah, no problem. I'm going to need a coroner's officer, Mike, to stay with the bodies. Can we have one of your officers?'

'Yep, you can use Jayne, she's done it once before.' I stood with my hands on my hips for a moment, gathering my thoughts. 'God knows how long the tailbacks are.'

He pointed towards York. 'That way it's nearly to Stockton Lane end,' he said. 'The AIU just phoned me as I was arriving.'

'Bloody hell.' I glanced past him, down Golden Hill. All I could see was a solid line, down the hill and out of sight. Thousands of cars and coaches, stretching for several miles.

Fordy was back from the car. 'He all right?' I asked him. 'The driver?'

'Think so, yeah.'

'Right, we've got to do something about this traffic. It ain't gonna get any better by itself. Jayne, I'm sorry but I need you to be coroner's officer. Can you liaise with Simon?'

'Yeah. Will do Mike.'

Jayne was looking at the crushed Nissan. 'What a bleeding mess. How the hell did it happen? Nice sunny day like this . . .'

'That's for the AIU to find out,' I said. 'People lose concentration . . . Ah, here's Thommo.'

'Aye, did my best, Mike.' Thommo was panting, mopping his forehead with a handkerchief. 'Backed up solid, way past Rillington.'

'Right, well, I'm gonna send you straight back along the line, tell them what's happened, ask them to be patient. You know the routine. Meanwhile I'm going to figure out how to get them shifted. They'll be backed up to the coast if we don't get something sorted.'

We had a massive problem here and our options were limited. The Castle Howard route would work for any traffic stuck on the York side of us, but I couldn't see us turning the rest of the queue around, not yet at any rate. Another possibility was to redirect the traffic from the coast through Stamford Bridge and onto the Bridlington road – take them into York that way – but it was narrow lanes all the way across and we'd only end up adding to the queues already forming along the A166.

I must have stood there for a full minute, just thinking. The AIU crew had arrived and were at it with their tape measures, cameras and chalk, marking the road and making notes. Mercifully, the motorists in the queue were now staying well away from the scene. Some were sitting on the grass verge in the sunshine; some were still in their cars, listening to their radios.

I looked back down the hill, towards the bend where the Low Hutton road turned off. Now there's a possibility, I thought. I used to ride that way on my bike when we were kids, fishing at Kirkham weir, and sometimes we'd make a circuit, riding up to the top, above High Hutton, to watch the traffic on the main road before racing back down. That lane came out barely half a mile from where I was standing, on the York side of the blockage. In effect it was a single-track loop that went round the site of the accident. Maybe I could route the traffic in at the bottom, up through the Huttons and out the top, beyond the accident. The problem was that it's a narrow series of lanes, and too long to work on a traffic-light system for both directions. I could only feed the traffic through one way.

'1015 to control, over.'

'Yeah Mike, how's it going up there?'

'The accident scene's under control, traffic and AIU are on scene. Jayne is acting as coroner's officer, but listen . . . I'm trying to work out how to shift this traffic. Can you notify all the local radio stations to tell drivers to avoid the area and expect long delays. The eastbound traffic can be diverted from Whitwell-on-the-Hill round by Castle Howard. I'll send Thommo to start this rolling. Can you get Highways out with the signs to that location?'

'Received, Mike.'

'As for the westbound traffic, can you get Highways to set up diversions off the interchange? Get Fordy and Ed to go down there and start the ball rolling. That'll leave me the queue we've already built up along the dual carriageway, back to the roundabout. I think we might be able to get them round the Huttons Ambo loop. But it'll be tight. I need to go and check it first.'

'Received. I don't think we've ever used that route before, Mike. Will it take the bigger vehicles?'

'I'm about to go and find out.'

'*Do you want an update on the queues, over?*'

'Let's have it.'

'*Ten miles each way.*'

'Right, I'd best get started.'

The trouble with having a bright idea such as I'd had is that other people, locals, in particular, are going to figure it out too. I turned my car round and drove east a few hundred yards, then turned off at the sign that points to Huttons Ambo. I'd only got a couple of hundred yards up the road when I was stopped in my tracks by a convoy of cars pointing the same way as I was, but at a complete standstill.

'1015 to control, over.'

'*Go ahead, Mike.*'

'Yeah, I've got a real problem here. The road's totally blocked. It looks like people have tried to take this route already. Got a line of cars trying to get through from the bottom end – and they've just about stopped the job. I'm going to have to leave my car and go on foot. See if I can sort it out.'

'*Received. We've just taken a call from a local farmer who states that traffic from both directions has met and it is now total gridlock. Tempers are flaring.*'

'Received. I thought that might be the case. I'll cone across the road at this end of the loop, prevent anyone else coming down. Can you get the York traffic car just to shoot to the other end and cone that off as well?'

'*Received, Mike.*'

'I'm going to need some extra staff to get this to work.'

'*1015 from Special Constable Nicholson.*'

'Go ahead, Keith.'

'*Yes Sarge, I've just come on duty. Do you want me to come and assist at the Huttons Ambo junction?*'

'Keith, good timing. If you could make your way and stop anything else coming down here that would be brilliant.'

I got back in the car and went to back it off the road, careful to leave it where it wouldn't cause another blockage.

I was just putting the car into reverse when a stubby finger rapped on the side window. I wound it down to see a bearded, weatherbeaten face peering in at me.

'Now then, Mr Pannett. Are you in trouble, lad?'

It was Bob Ferguson, one of my Country Watch members.

'I bloody well am, mate. We've had a nasty accident on the main road – two fatalities, traffic backed up halfway to Leeds. Now this lot' – I pointed at the line of cars that had stopped in front of me – 'decide they'll take a short cut.'

'Aye.' Bob scratched his head. 'Aye,' he said again, 'I see what you mean.'

I looked at him. 'Any suggestions?'

'Aye, I have.' He looked at the line of cars. 'I reckon I can help you out.'

'What you got in mind?'

'Why, I've a field round the corner yonder. It's right where t'cars from both ends have had a coming together. I left the lot of them shouting at each other to back up. Daft buggers. Anyhow, sometimes I have the Scouts camping in it.'

'Very good Bob, but where are we going with this?'

'It'll take two, three hundred easy. You'll see.'

'Bob, three hundred what? Scouts? What you on about?'
I really wasn't in the mood for Yorkshire riddles.

'No, you daft sod. Cars. Cars, lad!'

'Ah, I get it. You mean stop the job, get one lot in, clear
the road and let them through from the other direction?'

He scratched his head again. 'Aye, sommat like that. It'll
tek a bit of organising, but you can manage that, bright
young lad like you.'

'I'm just worried about them buses on some of these
tight corners. And lorries.'

'Aye, they'll tek a bit of negotiating will them buggers.'

'Will they make it?'

'There's no other way.'

'Right, we'll go for it. Let's get up there.'

It was a good half a mile and I had to field off questions from just about every driver as Bob and I trudged
past. I gave them all a stock answer. 'Just bear with us,
we've had a very serious accident. We'll get things moving
as soon as we can.'

The field was perfect. More or less level, but sloping
gently down towards the river Derwent, and nicely grassed
over. He'd clearly had cattle in it, but not for a week or
two, to judge by the dried-up cow-pats. Bob assured me
that we shouldn't have a problem with vehicles getting
stuck; the ground was dry and firm.

'Right,' I said, 'we'll start with this lot coming from
Malton direction. Can you man the gate, while I bring
'em in?'

It took a good half an hour, maybe longer, to direct the
first line into the field. Then we liaised with Thommo to
get the westbound lot parked up. We got them in lines,

nursing seven or eight buses and a pair of artics through the tight double bend in the road, then sharply round to the field entrance. There must have been a couple of hundred vehicles all told. There was a lot of grunting, swearing and gear-crunching before we were done. I even fielded a complaint from a man in a smart suit about the state of the field. He'd got brown stuff up his trouser legs and wanted to know why I couldn't have found a cleaner place for them all to park.

'D'you know, Bob, I think this is going to work.' We'd got the entire queue of cars parked up and it was time to let the coastbound traffic down the hill, past the farm and away towards the bypass. I held my breath and set them off, keeping my fingers crossed that they'd all get through. Then I shouted up Keith on the radio. 'They're heading your way, should be a steady stream. I'll let you know when the last one passes me.'

'*Received, Sarge.*'

It went more smoothly than I could've hoped for, and once we'd cleared the coastbound we could then open the road as a continuous diversion for the York-bound traffic. I walked with the line of vehicles back down to my car and watched the last of them clear the lane, then shouted over to Keith, 'Just hold them there a minute while I spin my car around, then get them to follow me along.'

'*Will do, Sarge.*'

I got in the car, turned it round and set off back up the lane. Looking in my mirror I could see the convoy winding its way behind. I flicked the blue lights on. This convoy wasn't stopping, and I was a beacon of hope for the stranded motorists who were finally on the move. A few minutes later we joined the main road above the scene of the accident, and there was Thommo waving his arms as he directed the traffic off towards York. 'Aye,' he said, as I pulled over behind him and got out to monitor proceedings, 'reminds me of my young days, standing in Glasgow city centre and watching my old man on point duty.' He squirmed his shoulder round and grimaced. 'Won't do my arthritis any good though.'

As everything fell into place I updated control. Ed and Fordy were now free to organise a flask to take to the scene and take it in turns to relieve Thommo and Keith. I went to see how the Accident Investigation Unit were getting on. Now that we'd got the traffic situation in hand, the next job – and I wasn't looking forward to this one – was contacting the next of kin. The AIU team had been on the radio to tell me they'd managed to identify the victims. They were a married couple, so it would most likely be a case of contacting their children, wherever they were.

It turned out that they came from Leeds, which made it a job for West Yorkshire Police. We passed on the details of what had happened, and got them to organise an officer to attend the address and deliver the dreadful news. It's a horrible business and there's no easy time to do it. You knock on a door and find people putting the kids to bed, or maybe sat around the tea table, or out in the garden enjoying a drink. I once called on a woman to tell her that her daughter had been killed, and found her in the middle of a domestic bust-up with her boyfriend. It's no fun being the bringer of bad news.

The A64 had been closed for well over five hours by the time they brought out a heavy tow-truck to remove the lorry.

The car had been shifted to one side of the road and would be taken away by a breakdown crew from Malton. The undertaker had just left with the deceased couple. There was the eerie silence that usually accompanies this type of scene. The hundreds of cars that would normally be thundering along the road were just a distant rumble on the diversionary routes. Apart from the markings on the road, and a few places where the verge was chewed up, everything would be back to normal shortly; the road would be reopened, and people would be speeding by, ignoring the danger signs. We hadn't established the cause of this particular accident, but most of the ones up there involve people simply driving too fast or losing concentration after a day on the beach.

It was close to nine o'clock, the sun was setting, and I was starting to wind down. My mind was still busy, still alert, but I could feel my energy levels flagging. I was now starting to turn my thoughts to the backlog of calls that would be stacked up since we had all been tied up at the accident. As officers got released we started to pick them up in priority order. Thankfully there was nothing too urgent, but after you've spent several hours dealing with something so serious and demanding you just feel like heading back in for a drink and a debrief. That would simply have to wait, though.

'*Control to 1015.*'

'Go ahead.'

'*Mike, we've got a domestic. Male armed with a knife, threatening a female. Child in the house. The informant is the offender's sister. She sounds pretty hysterical. Are you able to attend?*'

'That's a yes.' They gave me an address not far from the station off Old Maltongate. 'Right, received. Who else have we got going?'

'I'll get Fordy and Ed to attend.'

'All received. Can you flag it up to the ARV unit and make them aware of the situation. I'll give you an update shortly.'

'Received, will do.'

I was in my car, hurrying to the address we'd been given, hoping the urgency of the call would maintain my adrenaline levels, because after all that had happened I really had been hoping for a little respite. But that's the way it goes some days. It's like London buses. You can go for ages without anything major happening, then it's one after another. Particularly on bank holidays. Attending a fatality of any kind drains you emotionally, and now we were going to have to walk into a domestic, with people screaming and shouting; and doubtless we would feel the brunt of it, because nine times out of ten they'll end up thinking it's all our fault. Meanwhile we would be expected to be patient, understanding, calm, rational, perfectly correct in everything we said or did – without offending a living soul.

I took a deep breath and reminded myself that whatever we found we would, in the end, sort it, and that come tomorrow it'd be just another memory. As I put my foot down and contacted Ed and Fordy I could feel another surge of adrenaline kicking in. 'You two got an ETA, over?'

'Just hit the bypass.'

'Received.'

Right, Mike. Time to talk myself into this. You need to think like a supervisor. Depending on how big the job is,

I might need extra staff. I looked at my watch. Too late to call the night duty in early; most of them would be in in half an hour or so anyway. Might need the shields from the station in case we need to go straight in . . .

The good news – if you could call it that – was that we hadn't far to go. Just past the police station to the mini roundabout and off along Highfields Road. I soon found the place.

Here we go, I said to myself. A young woman – she must have been in her twenties – was out into the street trying to flag me down with a shirt or jacket of some kind. Hard to tell in the half-light of the evening.

'Hello. You OK?' I'd stopped the car and got out.

'Oh God,' she gasped. 'You've got to get in there. It's all kicking off. It's me brother.' She was pointing to a mid-terrace, in a cul-de-sac, maybe thirty yards off the main road.

'Right,' I said. 'Tell me exactly what's happening.'

'He's gone totally ape. He's got a knife. He's lost his job, and now his bet's gone down and he's – he's just lost the frigging plot. You've gotta get in there, quick, before he kills someone.'

'OK, now listen, I just need you to take a deep breath and slow down.' I was trying to calm her down, but she wasn't having it.

'They've both been drinking. Just . . . can't you get in there and get him out?'

'Who's they?'

'Him and his wife, and the little lass is in there too.'

'How old is the child?'

'She's six.'

'OK, and what's your name?'

'Janice.' She grabbed my arm. 'You've got to get him out, before he kills her. Or himself.'

'Now listen,' I said. 'Have you seen the knife?'

'Yeah, he grabbed a carving knife out of the kitchen drawer. That's when I legged it and called you. I've never seen him like this. He's really lost it. They had a massive row.' She grabbed at my arm. 'Aren't you going to go in and get him?'

'Listen, Janice, I'm not going to do anything that'll endanger anyone. Not him, nor his missus, nor the child. Now, has your brother actually threatened the child – or his wife?'

'He said he'd kill her – or himself. Oh, for God's sake do something, please!'

'Has he been violent in the past?'

'No. Not him. He's just snapped. It's all got on top of him since he lost his job.'

'What job's that?'

'At the bacon factory.'

I saw Ed and Fordy turning into the street. Janice's phone rang. 'It's my sister-in-law,' she said. 'She's up in the bedroom.'

'Can I speak to her, please?'

She passed me the phone. 'What's she called?' I asked.

'It's Jo.'

'Hello Jo, this is Acting Sergeant Mike Pannett. Are you OK?'

'Oh God,' she gasped, 'I'm up in the bedroom, Rob's downstairs with Rosie.'

'Is anyone hurt?'

'No, no we're all OK. But don't come in. He'll kick off again.'

'What about Rosie?'

'She's downstairs in the living room. I had to run upstairs to get away from him. He had a knife.'

'Are you sure Rosie's OK?'

'Yeah, he'd never hurt Rosie. I can hear her playing. I'm just worried what he might do if you come in.'

'Right, and what about you? Can you lock the door?'

'No, but I've put the bed against it.'

'OK. We're going to have to go steady with this, but don't worry, we're outside if anything happens. I'm putting your Janice back on the phone now. Stay on the line and let us know if anything changes. All right?'

I got on the radio. '1015 to control, over.'

'Go ahead Mike, what's the situation?'

'The situation is this. We've got a male called Rob who is believed to be in possession of a carving knife some- where downstairs. We've got the wife called Jo, who is at this moment in time safe in an upstairs bedroom. She's pushed the bed against the door to make her more secure. I've spoken to her on her mobile phone and the line is still open while she's talking to her sister-in-law Janice. She's here with us. Received so far?'

'All received. Carry on.'

'To make matters worse there's a six-year-old daughter called Rosie who is believed to be safe and well and playing downstairs. This is what I'm going to need. Can you get the ARVs to start making their way and can you let me have an ETA? I'll give you an RV point in a minute. I'm also going to need somebody to bring me a couple of shields from the sergeant's office at Malton down here asap, in case the situation deteriorates and I need to go in. Received so far?'

'*Received, carry on.*'

'Could you inform the late-turn senior officer of the situation and also mention we might need a negotiator. Last thing, could you locate a dog unit?'

'*1015, that is all received. I'll come back to you shortly.*'

I looked over to Janice and mouthed, 'All OK still?'

She put her thumb up and nodded her head. She even gave a sort of smile, but her face was wet with tears.

It was a difficult spot we were in. You learn from experience not to go rushing in unless there's an immediate threat to life. In this case it could in fact inflame the situation, and the fact that the man had a knife could endanger everyone's lives, including ours. I felt that with each minute that passed there was more chance of defusing the situation.

I was just talking through what was best to do with Ed when my own mobile phone rang and made me jump. It took me a while to locate it in my shirt pocket under my body armour.

'Hello Mike, it's Inspector Graham.'

I knew Mark Graham. Based at Scarborough, he was what we called of the old school.

'Hello boss.'

'Now then Mike, baptism of fire for you today, I hear. How's it looking with this domestic?'

I gave him a brief situation report.

'Right, Mike. First things first. I can't get over. It's gone pear-shaped over here at Scarborough. Been a bad day all round, and I've got a couple of serious incidents running as we speak. It's going to be down to you, but the superintendent's aware so you might get a call from him. He's at York at the moment but he's had the sit. rep. and been in contact with the ARV sergeant discussing authorities to arm if need be.'

'OK, sir. Thanks for that. I'll crack on here.'

'Have you got enough officers?'

'We're OK unless we need to do a forced entry. Night duty will be in shortly though.'

'OK, Mike. Good luck.'

Ed was standing beside me. He hitched up his trousers. 'OK then, what's the plan?'

'Number one, we stay out of sight,' I said. 'But as near to the scene as we can.' I pointed out the house to him. 'Just in case we have to get in there sharpish. Number two, we keep obs on the rear of the premises in case he comes out that way. We can do that via a lane at the back. Three, you go with Janice in your car to the school around the corner, that's going to be the RVP. Keep the phone line open with Jo, but get her to describe the house layout in case we have to go in. Where the rooms and stairs are, which way doors open etc, you know the type of thing.'

'Sounds like a plan to me. What do we know about this bloke?'

'I'll find out. You go with Janice.' I was back on the radio. '1015 to control.'

'*Yes, go ahead.*'

'Can you let me know what intelligence we have on the address?'

'*Yes Mike, we've just finished the checks, all negative and no firearms shown listed. Also ETA from ARVs is ten minutes. Have you got an RVP?*'

'All received. RVP is the primary school in Highfield Road.'

'*Received, Mike. Keith Nicholson should be with you any minute with the shields and door-opening equipment.*'

As soon as Keith arrived I threw the equipment across the back seat of Fordy's car and sent Keith to cover the rear of the house. Just so that we could work out which house it was from the back, we counted the chimney pots from the end house. I left Fordy keeping obs on the front from the end of the street before driving round the corner to the school. I felt that we were now a bit better prepared should the situation deteriorate. Everyone had their body armour on and we had a bit of extra protection with the shields. I just had to think. What was the best method to use to make contact with Rob and get the situation sorted? As I arrived in the school grounds and got out of the car, Thommo pulled in behind me.

'Right, I'm free Mike. Where d'ye want me?'

'Thommo, if you could go and join Fordy covering the front, just in case anything happens. The shields are in the back of Fordy's car if you need them on the hurry up.'

'You leave it with me, Mike. I'm used to dealing wi' these type o' situations.' As he headed back to his car he called out over his shoulder, 'Aye, and I've got the war wounds to prove it.'

'But Thommo,' I said, 'we don't want any more, OK? You get down there and look after young Fordy. Keith's round the back out of sight. I can back up either front or back in seconds if needed.'

'OK, Sarge.'

I got into the car next to Janice. 'Now then,' I said. 'Would you say he's a reasonable kind of man, Rob?'

'Yeah, I . . .'

'I mean, would he listen to me?'

'Look, he's never done anything like this.'

I looked at her. She was his sister. She would say that.

It was as if she could see the doubt on my face. 'Never,' she repeated. 'It's not in his character.'

What I'd been wondering was, would it be worth calling the guy and talking to him on the phone. I'd seen it done in the past, in hostage situations. I'd done something like it myself. It can work. It had to be worth a try. I'd just finished writing down the house phone number from Janice when the armed response unit arrived.

'Wait here,' I said to her. 'I need to talk with my colleagues.' I got out of the car and closed the door. 'Now then,' I said. 'Long time no see.'

I knew Derek. He was from Harrogate and we'd been on a number of courses together. I talked him through the situation, and explained what I was thinking of doing.

'Look,' he said, 'if you can talk him into coming out – hell, that'll do me. The Easingwold ARV will be with us shortly. Leave me to sort the containment. I'll use my officers to back up your team.' He thought for a moment, then said, 'Just to let you know, given the present situation, we have not been given authority to arm. But we can self-arm if things deteriorate rapidly. I've spoken to the superintendent on the phone on the way over here, so expect a call from him.'

'OK, Derek. Ed's got a map of the house if you want to brief your lot.'

'Brilliant Mike, good job.'

'1015 to control, I'm going to put a phone call into the house, over. I want to keep it as low-key as possible at this time.'

'All received, Mike. The control-room inspector is monitoring also.'

I pulled out my mobile phone and punched in the number. The phone rang once, twice, and a third time. Then a man's voice said, ''Ello.'

'Hello, is that Rob?'

'Aye. Who are you?'

'My name's Mike Pannett. I'm the duty sergeant at Malton police station. I've had a call from your sister. She said you were having a problem. I just wanted to make sure everything's OK.'

'Nah nah – it's fine, mate. Just had a bit of a falling out with the missus, like.' He paused for a moment, then said, 'All right' and put the phone down.

Bugger, I thought. That's no use to me at all. I'm not having that. I hit redial.

''Ello.'

'Ah, Mike Pannett here again.'

'Now what?'

'Listen, I'm afraid that's not good enough, saying everything's fine. Your sister's worried about you, and your wife, and the little lass. And I'm worried too. I can't leave here until I have physically seen and spoken to all three of you. I need to know that everyone is all right'.

He didn't respond. I could hear him breathing into the receiver. 'Now,' I continued, 'there's been talk of a knife. And that you've made threats against your wife. Come on, let's get this sorted out. I've got a number of officers here and we are not going away until it's resolved.'

'No no no no. No, mate, I wouldn't harm 'em, honest I wouldn't.'

It didn't take a genius to sense a chink in his armour. 'Listen,' I said, 'let's at least get your little lass out of danger, shall we? Can you ask her to come out and see her auntie? I've got her right here with me. Your sister, Auntie Janice.'

'Send the lass out? I dunno about that. She's just off to bed, like.'

I could feel the weight of fatigue pressing on me. The afternoon's dramas, and now this. I was wilting, and I knew it. 'Look,' I said, 'I'm going to tell you something. I've seen two people lose their lives this afternoon, and it makes you realise how precious life is. You've got your life ahead of you, and so's that little lass. Do you want her growing up remembering something like this? Eh? Do you want her to remember something she might blame you for for as long as she lives? Come on, mate. Let her come out.' Beside me the woman Janice was sniffling into a tissue.

There was no reply. I turned around. Derek was stood by his car, not fifty yards away, watching me. I was about to pass the phone to Janice and maybe get her to have a word when Derek came on the radio: '*Got movement at the front door, stand by.*' I held my breath. 'Right, we have a little girl walking alone down the garden path towards the street. Can we have the sister to the outer cordon to meet her.'

I walked from the school to the end of the road with Janice. And there was Rosie walking towards us. She was wearing a red dressing gown and clutching a doll, a little pink plastic thing with its hair tied in a ponytail. She looked about her, then back over her shoulder. That's when Janice ran forward and grabbed her niece with one hand, putting the phone to her ear with the other. 'Jo, I've got Rosie, she's out, she's safe with me.'

Behind me I heard Ed say, 'Let's get her back to the car to keep warm.'

'Thank you,' I said down the phone to Rob, and waited to see how he'd respond. He hadn't hung up on me, but I couldn't be sure that he was still listening. My phone made a beeping noise to indicate someone else was trying to ring me. The main thing from my point of view was that the threat level had been reduced, drastically. Or so I thought. I could hear him breathing, so I repeated 'Thank you' – and the phone went dead. Suddenly I felt exhausted again, and frightened. What was on the guy's mind now? Did he intend to harm his wife? Had he got the lass out of the way so that he could settle with her mother? In situations like these everything can turn in the blink of an eye.

'Rosie!' With no warning whatsoever, the wife was outside the house, looking around for her daughter, then running across to where Janice had hold of her. She grabbed hold of the child and collapsed to her knees, sobbing.

Derek was there beside me, 'So far so good Mike. Just the one to go, lad.'

I shook my head. I had a bad feeling inside me, not for the first time today. Then Derek nudged me. The door was still slightly open. I looked at him, asking the question with my raised eyebrows. At that moment the man Rob appeared at the door, staring at the ground with his hands up in the air.

I could feel all the breath coming out of my chest in one huge sigh. I hadn't even realised I'd been holding it.

Situations like this can go one way or the other and I was thanking my lucky stars it seemed to be going my way. Now it was just a question of securing him and making the arrest.

I looked at Derek and he immediately came back with, 'You keep the rapport going, Mike. Our lads will handcuff him.'

I cupped my hand to my mouth and called across the space between us – maybe thirty yards. 'Now listen, Rob. It's Mike. We just spoke on the phone. Are you listening?'

He was still looking down, but I could see a nod.

'Where's the knife?'

He jerked his head towards the house. 'Back inside.'

'OK, I want you to take five steps forward along the path and then stop outside the gate. Keep your hands where we can see them.'

He stepped forward, silently.

'Now, stop there and put your hands on your head. Then I want you to kneel down.'

For the first time he showed some animation. 'Look, for f***'s sake.' I tensed up. Surely he wasn't going to kick off now?

'No,' I said, loud and firm. 'I need you to do this. You are going to be handcuffed and searched.'

He was thinking about whether or not to comply. Once more I realised I'd been holding my breath. We were so close to a safe result. I hadn't realised that the police dog and handler had arrived behind me. A sudden barking cut through the silence and made both Rob and me jump. That was all it took to finally convince him that it was over.

He dropped to his knees and the ARV crew moved forward to handcuff, arrest and search him.

As he was led to the van I heard control calling me on the radio. I put it to my mouth and realised my tongue was sticking to the roof of my mouth.

'Go ahead, over,' I croaked.

'The superintendent has been trying to ring you on your mobile.'

'Received. Sorry – I was on the phone to the house. I have a final update, over.'

'Go ahead.'

Half an hour later I was back at the station, ready to hand over to the nightshift sergeant. When I tried to sign my name as I was going off duty I saw my hand was shaking.

All of us on the late shift had been relieved, and Jayne had returned from the mortuary, but nobody had gone home yet. It seemed that we all wanted – needed – that little break, fifteen minutes or so, to debrief, unwind, prepare ourselves for re-entry into the mundane world of driving home, greeting our families, putting out the milk bottles, feeding the cat – or in my case the dog – knowing that the next day it would all start again. I got everybody together in the meal room, and over a brew we talked about the day's events. I let everybody have their say about how they'd found things. We'd all had a tough day, no one more so than Jayne. She felt the need to describe in detail what she'd seen when the elderly couple were being cut from the wreckage. We listened in silence. Once everything had been aired, and after a short pause, I thanked the whole team for their efforts and for getting on with things with no fuss. I also passed on a message of 'well done' from the superintendent. He'd finally caught up with me when I got back to the station. 'So, a good day's work, everybody. Let's all go home – and drive carefully.'

'And thank God Chris Cocks is back next week, laddie.' Thommo piped up with a smile.

I grinned back at him. 'I'll second that, Thommo lad.'

As I stepped out of the car at Keeper's Cottage twenty minutes later, an owl was hooting in the trees behind me. Henry was jumping up at the back door, snapping at a couple of moths that had been drawn to the porch light. Ann was up and waiting for me. I'd texted her from the station, telling her that things had kicked off and I'd be late home. Now I was able to give her the whole story over a very welcome beer.

'So,' she said – and she couldn't help laughing – 'welcome to the wonderful world of the supervisor. D'you still want to be a sergeant?'

I kicked off my boots, sat myself down in the recliner and closed my eyes. 'Good question,' I said. 'I think I'll sleep on it. For about fifteen hours.'

Chapter 9

As Sly as a Fox

'There you go, cock-bud. Good as new.' Soapy and I were standing some way back from Keeper's Cottage, over by the gooseberry bushes where we could get a good view of it. My two weeks as acting sergeant were over and I was enjoying a couple of days off before going back to my regular beat. The weather had been kind and I'd managed to get a lot of tidying up done in the garden – in between taking some lengthy tea breaks with Soapy as he put the finishing touches to the roof, replaced a length of guttering and installed a downpipe.

'Not bad,' I said. 'Not bad at all. I have to say you've made a fair job of that. In the end.'

'How d'you mean, in the end?'

'Well, let's face it, you've taken your time.'

'Aye, but you can't be hurrying a craftsman, Mike. No good rushing the job. That's how mistakes get made.'

I let it go. I could've mentioned the elementary mistake he'd made in telling us that the roof was sound, way back in the early summer, but what do they say? All's well that ends well? And, fair play to him, he had made a decent job of it. The new ridge tiles were all cemented in, the chimney was standing tall and straight, freshly pointed up with the TV aerial back in place, and the new lead flashing was glinting dully in the September sunlight. As Soapy said, 'To say your cottage is over two hundred years old, it looks as good as new.' He nodded in the direction of the trailer where he'd just finished stacking the scaffolding, boards and ladders. 'I'll fetch Algy's tractor down tonight and have them away.' He grinned and rubbed his hands together. 'Then it'll be payday, eh?'

'Aye. We all like payday.'

'Specially when there's a decent whack due. Nowt like a big fat envelope in your hand, is there, all crinkly like?' Soapy smacked his lips and grinned at me. I'd last seen that look as he set about one of Walt's sister's cakes.

'Yeah,' I said, 'but I thought Algy was paying you a regular weekly wage these days. Straight into your bank, like.'

'He is, cock-bod, but this here's one of your back-pocket jobs. Our little secret from the taxman.'

'Are you sure I need to know that, Soapy?'

'Well, no, but what I'm saying, like, is . . .' He nudged me and rubbed his thumb and forefinger together. 'Nowt like the old folding stuff.'

'I know what you're saying, Soapy. You've made it plain enough. Cash in hand. The black economy. I did grow up in the country, you know.'

'So, er, when you can you get down the old cashpoint, like?'

'Just run that by me one more time, will you?' I said.

Soapy had me mystified, but that was nothing new. The guy was always talking in riddles.

'Well, you know – the old spondulicks, like. The readies. Friday night coming up, late-night shopping. Me and Becky have a wedding to plan, remember? Seven months and counting, cock-bod. And you know what them lasses are like. Always finding a little sommat to add to t'list.'

'Soapy, I am fully aware of your average female's spending habits. What I don't get is, what's it to do with me?'

'Well, Algy said I'd to settle with you – you and Ann, I mean.'

'He what?'

'He said it were down to you to pay me.'

'Soapy, this is his house, not ours. He's our landlord. Repairs and maintenance – that's his province.'

'That's not what he told me.'

'Well, what did he tell you?'

'He told me you were buying it.'

'Buying it? Soapy,' I said, 'I think I'm going to have a word with Master Algernon. We talked about buying the place all right, but we differed on the price – by a substantial margin, I might add. From which point negotiations, as they say in the football transfer market, were stalled.'

I looked at Soapy. He had a face like a fiddle. 'So I don't stand to get paid while you've sorted out whose house it is?'

'I've sorted it out, matey. This place belongs to Algy. If you want paying, you take it up with him, mate.'

Ann was as perplexed as I was when she came home

that afternoon and I told her what had happened. But after she'd thought about it for a few moments she said, 'You know, he never did come back on that offer we made.'

'Who? Algy?'

'Who else? You know what I'm thinking? Maybe the leak in the roof made up his mind for him. I mean, maybe he suddenly found it all a bit of a faff.'

'Could be – but you'd think he'd come and tell us.'

'I don't know. He's got a lot on his mind.'

'Algy? Nah – he's a gentleman of leisure, isn't he?'

'He's a man of means, Mike, that's what Algy is. And there's a difference. He has plenty of money, but it's all tied up in investments. And people like that, they're always studying the markets, fretting about a percentage point of interest here and there. You'd think if you had all that money you'd rest easy, but they don't.'

'Tell you what, if I had Algy's money it'd be feet on the mantelpiece and break out the cigars.'

'That's what we all think, but do you know, when I was round there for that session on the horse he showed me three separate websites going on his computer. He runs them twenty-four seven. He has the stock exchanges and foreign currencies on one, some kind of investment chatroom going on another, and then he had some sort of fine art auction online.'

'Blimey.'

'Yes, blimey indeed. He has a lot of plates spinning, to coin a phrase. And don't underestimate this latest obsession of his.'

'What, Lord Nelson? I thought you'd written him off.'

'Oh, I have. But I happen to know he's paid for some professional tuition at a stables – over Langton way, I think. This whole hunting thing – he's taking it far more seriously than people realise.'

'Well,' I said, 'that's still no excuse for messing Soapy about – and us, for that matter. I think it's time we gave our friend a bell.'

'I don't think we need to,' Ann said, shaking her head.

'Why's that?'

'Well, don't you think Soapy'll be straight round there demanding to know what's going on? Wouldn't you, if you'd just finished a job and wanted paying?'

'You're probably right there.'

'I'm willing to bet I am. Just you wait, he'll be round here before you can say knife. In fact, if we want our tea in peace we'd better get it now.'

As it happened, Algy didn't come that night, which surprised us. I was all for calling him, but Ann insisted we play a waiting game. 'No. Let him come to us,' she said. 'The last thing we want is for him to think we're desperate to strike a deal.'

'I don't like it,' I said. 'Let's get it sorted. I can't be doing with all this uncertainty.'

But she wasn't budging. 'Trust me,' she said, 'it'll all work out if we play our cards right. And if he thinks Soapy's upset us, or embarrassed us, well, so much the better.'

I knew Ann was probably right, but I'm not good at waiting games. Never have been. As she reminded me, not for the first time, my mum always said I was like a bull at a gate. Anyway, the point is that all this business was very much on my mind, and I didn't sleep well that night. So much so that when the alarm went off at a quarter to six next morning I must have pushed the snooze button, because I suddenly woke up to see that it was six thirty-one, which gave me approximately four minutes to get out of the house.

It's amazing what you can do when you really, really have to. Normally I allow myself a good three-quarters of an hour to get up, wash, dress and have a spot of breakfast, but this day I was into my clothes, out of the house and halfway down the drive in the time it would normally take me to stumble downstairs and get the kettle on. Yes, I admit I ran the electric razor over my face as I drove down towards town – steadily enough, because there were patches of mist at the foot of the wolds – and yes, as I crossed County Bridge I was chewing on one of those cereal bars Ann keeps in the kitchen for when we go hiking, but I made it in time and was feeling pretty pleased with myself when I pulled into the car park just ahead of Fordy, entered through the heavy main door, and galloped up the broad sweeping staircase that led to the first floor.

Even now, after several years at Malton, I still enjoyed climbing that staircase. It's the sort you'd expect to find in a stately home, with a polished hardwood handrail and ornate, carved wood balustrades. Two at a time the first flight, and if I'm feeling on top of my game I'll run up the next two as well, narrower and steeper as they are, all the way up to the locker room, which sits on the third floor. I've always reckoned that the day I can no longer do that it'll be time to think about retiring.

The lockers at Malton are not unlike the ones we had at school, for our games kit and so on: old-style, grey metal things, six feet tall and a couple of feet wide, with just a few slits towards the top to ventilate them – although they seem better at letting the smell of stale sweat out than letting any fresh air in. I always take a deep breath before I enter the room, and try to make it last. There's no handle on the door: you open your locker with a little flat key that has a shamrock-shaped head on it. I always keep it on the same ring as my house keys. I was just reaching for them when I heard Fordy panting up the stairs, one at a time.

'Now then, lad. You should be running up them stairs, young copper like you. I was doing them three at a time when I was your age.'

'No you weren't.'

'Eh?'

'You can't fool me, Mike. They hadn't even built the place when you were my age.'

'Very funny. Listen, matey, when I started out – while you were still chasing girls around the playground in your little short trousers – I learned my craft at the sharp end. Let me tell you there were just as many stairs at Battersea nick as there are here, and I was up them three at a time, several times a day. Why, you came trudging up here like old man Thommo when he's building up to a sickie.'

'Ah, but there's a reason for that, Mike.'

'Yeah, you aren't fit.'

'No, it's an age thing. I mean, you haven't heard what I was up to last night, have you?'

'I'm not sure I want to. I'd rather get down to the

parade room and hear what our sergeant has to say.' I dug my hand deeper into my right-hand trouser pocket. No keys. I tried the other one, then swung my leg at the locker. 'Bugger!'

'Hey, steady on Mike. No need to abuse police property just because you'll never be young, fit and fancy-free again. Out on the town, on the pull . . .'

'I can live with that, me old mucker. It's coming to work without me bloody keys that gets me down.'

'See? The age thing. You're suffering from early-onset memory loss. Any time now you'll wake up sitting in a wicker chair with some lass in an apron feeding you custard on a spoon.'

'Don't you worry, there's life in this old dog yet. Just stand clear while I banjo this door.'

I took three steps back till I was leaning against the locker in the row opposite ours, strode forward and landed a hefty kick smack underneath the lock. The door sprang open, and out fell half the contents, which left me standing ankle-deep in a collection of wellies, fleeces, woolly hats, gloves, welly socks, biscuit wrappers, crushed drinks containers, lunchboxes without lids, lids without lunchboxes, one spare Thermos flask, several handle-less mugs, any number of old notebooks, and the black waterproof coat I'd brought up from the Met and still used when skulking around unseen on night shifts. As I bent down to grab an old fag packet that, by some miracle, had a few cigarettes still in it, Fordy reached into his pocket for his phone.

'This is going on the noticeboard,' he said as the camera flashed. 'In fact, I might send it to the *Police Gazette*.'

'They've seen worse,' I said, 'far worse. Anyway, don't stand there like a pillock, give us a hand. Don't wanna be late for parade.'

'Yeah, but where we gonna put it?' Fordy, his arms full of crumpled rainwear, was staring at the shelf in my locker, where a stack of old *Gazettes* was topped by an empty polystyrene takeaway box, a Metropolitan Police truncheon and a pair of handcuffs.

'Down there.' I pointed to the floor.

'That's supposed to be in the proper store for a start,' he said, pointing at a CS gas canister, 'and that' – he'd dropped the waterproofs and was fishing out my body armour – 'that's supposed to be hung up to protect it. And put on before you go out on patrol.'

'Can't be doing with all this health and safety nonsense,' I said. 'I know when I need body armour and when I don't. Come on, just shove it in.'

'And who the hell are that lot?' He was staring at the faded colour photograph Sellotaped to the inside of the door.

'That lot,' I said, 'is a collection of higher mortals whose shoes you are not fit to clean. You are looking at the York City team – I beg your pardon, the *legendary* York City team – that went to Wembley for the play-off final in 1993 and destroyed Crewe Alexandra after extra time in a penalty shoot-out. And I was there, buddy. Took me a week to get me voice back.'

Fordy said nothing. He was clearly awestruck in the presence of greatness. 'Anyway,' I said, 'while you're feeling free to slag off my locker, let's have a look at yours.'

'Help yourself,' Fordy said, unlocking the door. 'I've nothing to hide.'

'You wanna bet?' I said. Fordy's locker was a picture. It was beyond immaculate. His helmet stood alone on the top shelf, shining proudly. Below it he'd hung one of those things you find in women's wardrobes, a sort of coathanger effort with lots of little clear plastic pockets, and each one filled with some item of grooming equipment: deodorant, hair gel, shower gel, shaving foam, breath fresheners, plus a miniature tube of toothpaste and a pair of nail clippers, and there in a separate hanger was his hairdryer. On the door, below a framed mirror, scrupulously clean, was a collection of cuttings from a glossy magazine – mostly of gorgeous young ladies with no clothes on.

'It's like sommat you'd see in a bloody advert,' I said, pulling out my own phone and clicking away. 'Two guys in a locker room comparing hair products. Because they're worth it.'

'Nothing wrong with keeping your things in order,' Fordy said, making a grab for the phone.

'Nothing at all,' I said, snapping away. 'Except that if this was the Met, you might come to work some night and find it'd been busted open and the contents rearranged. Anyway' – I put my phone back in my pocket – 'it's a level playing field now, isn't it? You put your picture up and I'll put mine next to it. And I tell you what, we'll see who gets the most grief. Anyway, never mind that. It's your turn to mash the morning brew.'

After the briefing I went into the sergeants' office to see Cocksy and have a chat about how things had been during his absence. 'Been hearing good things about you,' he said. 'The feedback from the wendy house – well, I shan't tell you. It'd only cause you embarrassment.'

'Well, that's good to hear,' I said. 'Very gratifying. But I'm ready to get back to my usual beat.'

Acting sergeant had been a change of pace, and something of an education, but it also made me realise how much I enjoyed the independence of my rural round. It got me thinking about the realities of being a sergeant: the extra work on the desk, the added responsibilities, the more pressured atmosphere. For all that I was starting to come around to the idea that it probably was time to go for promotion, there was this other voice inside me saying, yes, some time soon, but maybe not just yet.

There hadn't been a great deal at briefing that morning, but there was one item that I did log away for future reference. We were all aware that over the past fortnight there had been a series of break-ins at golf clubs around our area. Easingwold, Ganton, Kirkbymoorside: they'd all been subjected to smash-and-grab raids on the clubhouses, with clubs, clothing and other merchandise being taken, and it seemed fair to assume that the same individual or gang was involved in each one. Sometimes you get overburdened with information and intelligence. You try to note everything down, but once you're out on patrol, dealing with whatever the day throws at you, you know you're going to struggle to find the time to follow them up. You just hope for a quiet spell so that you can spend a bit of time targeting the various issues. Other than that, you just log them away at the back of your mind.

I had no urgent calls to attend to that morning, so

after I'd gone back up to the third floor and had a bit of a clearout of my locker, then sorted various bits and pieces of admin work, I decided to call in on Walt. It had been a while since I'd seen him.

I drove up through Leavening and climbed the hill that led to Walt's place. It was now a beautiful late summer morning, the sun shining from a pale blue sky. The hedgerows were full of ripe haws and brambles, draped with gossamer and spangled with dewdrops. The fields down in the Vale of York were a patchwork of pale yellow stubble, lush green grass and newly ploughed earth in shades of brown. I paused outside the house, taking a moment to reflect on the events of the last few years, on the time I'd spent living with him in this isolated spot, surrounded by beautiful country and gazing out every day on these breathtaking views. I was so lost in thought that I actually wandered along the hedge a few yards and picked a handful of blackberries. I managed to scratch my hand and get stung on the inside of my arm by a stray nettle, but it was well worth it to taste the warm sweet fruit.

'Don't mind me, lad. You help yerself. I dare say you'll leave a few for an old man struggling to feed himself.' Walt was out in his overalls, carrying a garden fork in one hand and a bulging plastic bag in the other.

'You can spare 'em, mate. I bet you've got your freezer half full of 'em already. I'm just tidying up after you. Besides, you've had all the good 'uns.'

'Aye, I did put one or two away for t'winter, now that you mention it. Come on, out the back wi' you and we'll swap pocket knives, shall we?'

It was a while since I'd heard Walter use that phrase. It suggested that he had something on his mind, and he'd doubtless pitch it to me in his own good time. 'I see your spuds are ready for lifting,' I said, pointing at the rows of yellowing foliage. 'And these.'

'Aye well.' He bent down and caressed a plump onion with his thumb. 'Just want the top growth to wither, then hope we get enough sun to dry 'em off before I hang 'em under me eaves yonder. But come wi' me. There's sommat I want to show you.'

Walt was off through the little gate and into his field. I hurried after him, as ever amazed at how fast he could walk when he had something on his mind.

'Your pond looks well,' I said, grinning to myself as I remembered the fun and games we'd had last year with the unexploded bomb. He'd planted the margins with reeds and had a little patch of waterlilies growing in the middle, but no sign of any wildfowl as far as I could see.

'Aye, she's coming along,' I heard him say as he hurried on across the pasture, pausing to pick up a mushroom the size of a tea-plate and pop into in his jacket pocket. 'But never mind that. This is what I want you to look at.' He'd reached the tall, unkempt hedge that bounded the far side of his land, just to one side of the sycamores we'd disfigured last year in aid of his clay-pigeon shoot.

When I'd caught up with him I looked up at the hedge. It was all of ten feet high, mostly thorn bushes with a few elders growing out of it, and plenty of ivy. Here and there you could see an old oak fence-post, disguised under a layer of grey-green lichen. 'Go on,' I said. 'Tell me the worst. You want a hand trimming it. Am I right?'

Walt shook his head. 'No, I shan't be taking owt off this. Not until I've harvested her.'

'Harvested? Harvested what? Elderberries?'

'I already have some of them,' he said. 'Mix 'em up wi' me brambles to make jam. But tek a closer look, lad.' He was pointing at something up above where we were standing.

I took off my glasses, gave them a rub on my shirt front, and had a closer look. 'What are they?' I said.

'Why, they're sloes, lad. Fruit of t'blackthorn.'

'Oh, right. But you aren't going to eat them, are you?'

'I may do, after they've sat in a jar of mother's ruin for a few months.' Walt's face had the gleeful, slightly guilty look of a schoolboy who's just filled his pockets from someone else's orchard – and who knows he's getting away with it.

'Ah, sloe gin. Yeah, of course.'

'Have you never made it, lad?'

'Never even drunk it, Walt. Is it all right?'

Walt closed his eyes, and took a long slow breath. His face suddenly looked ten years younger. 'All right?' he said. 'Why, you open a bottle of sloe gin by t'fireside on a freezing winter's night wi' the snow piling up on yer windows and a draught whistling under t'doors, and it's like – why, it's as if someone's magically switched t'sun back on and you've a mouth full of ripe fruit, and all that lovely juice trickling down yer throat.' He opened his eyes, looked at me a bit embarrassed, and added, 'Aye, and not forgetting it's got a kick like a bloody donkey.'

'Blimey, Walt. I've never heard you talk like that. Proper poetic, that was.'

'Aye well, never mind that. What I want to know is, can you see them sloes – and more important, can you reach the buggers? 'Cos I reckon they're beyond my grasp, best ones, unless I get me steps out.'

I followed his gaze, up towards the higher branches. 'No,' I said, 'you don't want to be going up a stepladder out here, not on your own at any rate. 'Cos that lot'll take some reaching.' I'd finally spotted the little clumps of fruit, about the size of olives, some of them still green, the bulk of them starting to turn a deep purple. By standing on my tiptoes I was just able to reach out to pluck a handful.

'No! Don't be picking 'em. They want a frost on 'em yet, lad. Wait while it gets a bit colder, then I'll whistle you up.'

'Oh, so you've already got me pencilled in for the job, have you? Before you even asked me?'

'Aye, I reckon you'd do your old landlord a favour.'

'I might do, but what's in it for me, Walt? That's the question. Do I get a bottle of this stuff, or what?'

Walt screwed up his face, as if what he was about to say was causing him physical pain. 'I can't be giving gin away, the price it is. But I tell you what, lad, I'll do a deal with you. If t'crop's as good as I hope it is I'll let you tek some home, then you and that lass of yours can mek your own. How about that?'

'I get it. You mean, I supply me own gin.'

'It'll be worth it, lad. You wait till you're sat in that little house of yours, with young Ann, Christmas time, after you've had your roast turkey. I guarantee you'll be raising a glass to me. You see if you aren't. One of t'great pleasures of winter-time, is a drop of sloe gin.' Walt turned away from the hedge and started to make his way back towards the house. 'Anyway, how you fixed now? Have you time for a cuppa?'

'Aye, go on. If you're twisting me arm.'

We sat in Walt's kitchen, by the stove, and it wasn't long before we got onto the subject that was now on everybody's lips; the proposed hunting ban – and the demonstration that was being planned by supporters of the Countryside Alliance.

'They're all off to London,' Walt said. 'Muriel, Ronny. I believe your pal Algy too. Some's gone on t'train, some on t'bus.'

'What d'you mean, gone? When is this demo?'

'They're having it today. They reckon it'll be on t'news tonight.'

'Oh, blimey. I've been that busy I clean forgot. Of course it is. I'd better make a point of watching that then. But why aren't you with them?' I asked.

'London?' Walt shook his head. 'What do I want to go all that way for?'

'I believe the phrase they use is "to register your disapproval",' I said. 'I presume you do disapprove of the ban.'

'Aye, I do. Not that I've ever been a huntsman, mind. Never appealed to me. But this ban business, it's a lot of nonsense. Blooming townsfolk and politicians meddling in country matters.'

'Well, if you feel that way maybe you should have joined them.'

'No, you won't catch me going all that way just to wave a placard. Besides, what meks you think them politicians'll listen to us? Have they ever? You mark my words, lad; they've made their minds up, long since.'

After I'd left Walt's I drove over the top and down into Birdsall, past the big house and then round the corner towards the yard where they kept the hounds for the Middleton Hunt. I had the window wound down and could hear them yapping in their kennels – but I soon wound it back up. They'd been mucking out that day: there was the usual fire in the yard and the pungent smell of burning straw, singed hair and other matter, all mingled with the smoke, wafted across the road on a strengthening breeze. It got me thinking about the hunt, and the time I'd sat and observed it in action, when I was out on patrol and had Nick the gamekeeper to guide me through the network of farm tracks and green lanes that connect the fields. It's one thing finding your way into some of those enclosures, quite another to find your way back out – and never mind the becks you have to cross. Some of them are barely a yard wide, but they flow through cuttings eight or ten feet deep. As Nick said at the time, 'Aye, there's a lot smarter fellows than us got lost in here.' I would've been one of them had it not been for his intimate knowledge of the landscape and field boundaries. I was impressed, and told him so. 'Why,' he said, 'course I know me way around. I've been walking these fields since I were a nipper – with and without t'landowner's permission. And now,' he laughed, 'I get paid for it. Rum going-on, isn't it?'

I was out with Nick that time because a part of my rural duties included gathering intelligence on the hunt saboteurs who had started to make a nuisance of themselves in our area, especially since the government had proposed the ban on hunting with dogs. We'd soon realised that these people were not to be underestimated, and on a couple of occasions, having searched their vehicles, we'd found offensive weapons. As is so often the case, we came to recognise that you couldn't tar them all with the same brush at all. The majority of protesters were simply advocates of animal rights, passionate in their beliefs, who opposed the sport on the grounds of cruelty – and as such they had a perfect right to demonstrate, peacefully. However, a minority were politically motivated and more inclined to adopt violent measures. They'd start out with letting down the tyres of horseboxes and similar acts – irritating rather than life-threatening – but some of them graduated to pepper-spraying the horses themselves and on occasion getting into fist-fights with the huntsmen and women.

Policing the hunt – policing the saboteurs, and preventing the confrontation from getting out of hand – also gave me a few insights into the nature of the event and the sort of people who are involved in it. Yes, there are the red-coats, and some of them happen to be very wealthy. But it's too easy to label them all toffs. It's downright lazy, in fact. Look around you at a typical meet and you'll see a substantial number of ordinary country people who simply like to ride cross-country and follow the hounds, and quite a few who'll do so on foot or from their cars. As far as I can see, some of the opposition are motivated by the wealth of the hunters, as they see it, just as much as by any concern for animals. And let's not forget that hunting's not exclusively a rural thing.

It's not unusual to find folk from the cities following in their cars. They come for the spectacle.

As for the actual quarry, well, old Rich over at Hovingham had had plenty to say about the fox as a pest – although I think he was more exercised about the domestic cat, to tell the truth. But what I remembered about our conversation was that he spoke of them not so much as hapless victims but as very canny operators. And I agreed with him. I told him how Ann and I had been keeping an eye on the den just across the beck from us, and how we'd watched the dog fox pay regular visits to the rabbit warren in the adjoining field. I already regarded the daddy fox, as we now called him, as something of a character. There was the autumn morning – it must have been in the autumn, because the lane was covered in golden brown needles from the larch trees, but it was still warm enough for me to sit out on my log for a mid-morning cuppa – anyway, what I remember was glancing up the lane and spotting Mr Fox padding his way towards me with a cock pheasant in his mouth, and at the same time, right in front of him out of the long grass popped a rabbit. The rabbit froze, the fox stopped, and I sat absolutely stock-still, my mug halfway to my mouth.

I think we'd all held our positions for about half a minute when the fox dropped the pheasant on the ground and eyeballed the rabbit. It still didn't move. It was quite clear that the fox was weighing up his options. There was no way he could carry a big bird like that, and a plump rabbit, back to the den – even if he managed to catch it – but he was clearly tempted for a few moments. Then he came to the only sensible conclusion. I could've sworn he shrugged his shoulders as he bent down, picked the pheasant back up and plodded on towards me before veering off, crossing the beck and disappearing down his hole – by which time the rabbit had recovered its composure and scooted off into the woods.

So I already had this notion that the fox – the archetypal bad guy of so many stories – was something of a character. And there we were, Nick and I, out in some field on the Wintringham estate, looking down on a little copse, maybe four or five acres. All around us were huntsmen and women, with the pack a hundred yards or so ahead of them, tails erect, scrambling through the undergrowth and cascading over ditches, their barks mingling with the sound of the horn.

'Here.' Nick nudged me and passed me his binoculars, pointing to the right-hand side of the little wood. 'Just down there: d'you see him?'

It took a moment to focus the glasses, but I soon got a fix on a large dog fox running along the side of the trees at what seemed a steady pace, with the hounds maybe a quarter of a mile behind him.

'Now,' Nick said, as first the fox and then the pack disappeared around the back of the trees, 'let's see how he goes on – 'cos he looks a clever old bugger to me.'

Sure enough, a few minutes later, as the field galloped off out of sight, the fox reappeared on the left-hand side of the wood, trotting along as if he hadn't a care in the world. 'Will you look at that?' Nick handed me the binoculars again, and there was the fox, sitting in the long grass and idly licking his privates, before getting back to his feet and sauntering into the woods. They never did catch that one, but, as they say, a good time was had by all – and I was left with the distinct impression that the quarry had run rings around his pursuers.

That night, Ann and I put on the TV news at six o'clock – and got quite a surprise. The demonstration in London was headline news. It seemed funny at first, seeing so many people in checked shirts, waxed jackets and flat caps in the capital. There were filmed reports of what looked like a peaceful demo outside the Houses of Parliament, and shots of a sea of protesters walking down Whitehall with a forest of banners: FIGHT THE BAN, WE WILL HUNT and FOX OFF TONY – a reference, that one, to Tony Banks, the Labour minister whose Department for Culture, Media and Sport was the focal point of the legislation. But later – as the filmed reports showed only too clearly – it had turned ugly, with actual fights breaking out.

'God, I hope Algy and Rich and all that lot steered clear of trouble,' I said. We were watching images of my old outfit, the Territorial Support Group, batons drawn, confronting angry demonstrators. Fists were flying and people were being dragged away to the waiting police vans. It was an odd feeling, seeing my old outfit in conflict with protesters who, in theory, represented my part of the world. I didn't like it. It was confusing. Back in the days when I was on the TSG, it was usually about tackling football hooligans, anarchists, rioters and people who were violently opposed to the establishment. This lot we were watching on the news were people who would normally be law-abiding members of the public. I don't ever accept anyone using violence towards the police, but this just didn't sit right. Folk who would normally work with the police – who could easily have been in my Country Watch scheme – were now head to head with the forces of law and order.

Ann could sense my consternation. 'Probably the usual story,' she said. 'A minority of troublemakers. But you can see how everybody gets sucked into it.'

Later in the report we heard how protesters had actually got onto the floor of the House of Commons, with the result that parliamentary proceedings were suspended for a period.

'It doesn't look good, does it?' Ann said.

'Certainly not for us. I mean, if that sort of trouble kicks off up here we're going to be caught right in the middle, aren't we?'

As soon as the report from London was over we put the telly off. We were both disturbed and upset by what we'd seen. We were sure that the vast majority of the people who'd gone south had done so for no other reason than to make their protest peacefully, but it is so, so easy for order to break down. When people are passionate about their cause – well, it's understandable that things can get edgy.

Next morning I got over to Hovingham as soon as I could. I wanted to hear about what had happened from a reliable source. But Rich was out when I called at the house. I went across to the little shop and post office where Penny worked part-time. 'Now then,' I said. 'You survived.' She was busy tidying up the fruit and veg boxes down in the front corner. 'What time did you get back?'

She stifled a yawn. 'Far too late.'

'Any trouble? Ann and I saw it on telly last night. It didn't look good.'

'Yes well, that's the telly, isn't it? Find the trouble and focus on that. We had a fine time. No real problems at all – apart from trying to find the coach afterwards.'

'So where's your man this morning?'

'He'll be back about lunchtime,' she said, retreating behind the little counter. A couple of customers had come in and wanted serving. 'Why don't you pop in then?'

'Hmm – it may have to wait,' I said. 'I've another call to make. Tell him I came by, will you? And I'll try to call in later in the week.'

'Righto, Mike.'

The other call I had in mind was Algy. I couldn't wait to hear what he had to say about the events in London, and to find out whether he'd managed to stay out of trouble. What always worried me about him was his refusal to bow to authority unless he was utterly convinced it was the right thing to do. It wasn't something he could help. It was the way he was. But I knew from my experience that TSG officers didn't like to get into long-winded discussions. However, I was sure that if something had happened I would have heard, somehow, probably through Soapy. But for now that was all academic; it seemed I was destined not to catch up with Algy for the moment, any more than I was Rich.

I'd come through Leavening and was driving up the hill towards the brow, making my way to Algy's place, when I caught sight of Walt, in his driveway, hopping about from foot to foot with his arms in the air. He had a broom in one hand, a raincoat in the other, and was dancing backwards towards his front gate.

I slammed the brakes on and opened the car door. 'Walt, mate! What you up to?'

As I stepped out he shouted, 'Don't be coming in! Don't be opening that gate!' and carried on dancing around like a demented hippy.

'Why, what on earth's the matter?' I walked towards the hedge and peered over. 'You got a problem in there?'

'If this bugger gets out I will have.'

'Ah.' Now I saw what he meant. Walt was still dancing backwards around the yard, pursued by a large turkey, its dark tailfeathers fanned out and its bright red wattles jiggling this way and that as it pecked at Walt's ankles.

'You don't wanna be going backwards,' I said. 'Get on the front foot, mate. Show him who's boss.'

Walt stopped dancing and turned towards me. 'You get yourself in here and see if you can boss the bugger, you clever young . . .' But he was cut short as the turkey launched itself at his feet.

'Right,' I said. 'Enough of this nonsense. What you trying to do with him anyway?'

Walt thrust his broom at the manic bird, forcing it back, then pointed to a wood-and-wire coop at the side of the garage. He'd got the door open and had a row of logs, like traffic cones, to each side. 'In there,' he gasped, trying to leap backwards and swat the turkey as it came again, gobbling furiously.

'Hang on a bit.' I stepped back and racked out my Asp, then undid the gate. 'Coming in!' I shouted, and slid into the yard – or should I say battle zone?

'Don't you go killing yon bugger yet. His time hasn't come.'

'Well, if he keeps dashing about like this all morning there'll be nowt on him worth eating, Walt.' Then I grinned and said, 'Hey, what if I did, eh? Press would have a field day, wouldn't they? "Police wildlife officer Asps helpless turkey to death"!'

Faced with me on one side and Walt on the other, the unruly bird was clearly confused. He stood still for a moment, flared his tailfeathers some more and then decided he might indeed be better off in the coop where a bowl of grain and a dish of water awaited his pleasure.

'What was that all in aid of then?' I asked Walt as he placed the kettle on the stove and slumped into his chair. 'You aren't going to tell me that landed on your pond, surely?'

Walt tugged out a grubby handkerchief and mopped his face. 'Why, I took it off my pal Gideon,' he said. 'Went and fetched it right after breakfast.'

'Gideon? Him that had the pig that time? And you treated me to some of the bacon?'

'Aye, that's the fellow.'

'I thought he was at death's door. Had a hernia operation or something.'

'Aye, he did. But remember that frozen rabbit we gave him? That did the job. Soon had him back on his feet. Fighting fit, he is. Aye, eighty-nine last birthday and he's strutting about like a little bantam cock. It'll tek more than a surgeon's knife to see yon lad off, I'm telling you.'

'I'm glad to hear it, Walt. By, I still remember that

bacon! Fantastic it was.' The kettle was boiling and Walt was still drying the sweat off his neck. I got up and filled the pot. 'So he raises birds too, does he, your mate Gideon?'

'Aye, he breeds a few gobblers, like; reckons to fatten one or two, Christmas time, only this year he's a bit of a surplus.' Walt rolled up his trousers, exposing a couple of long red scratches on either leg. 'You'd think he were breeding fighting cocks, t'way yon bugger carried on, mind.'

'So' – I jerked my thumb towards the back door – 'that's your Christmas dinner, is it?'

'If he doesn't mind his manners I'll have him next Sunday, lad. Now then.'

'You'll have to be careful how much you feed him.'

'What d'you mean?'

'Trust me, Walter. I know what I'm talking about. My dad had a turkey one year and we kids were always feeding it scraps off the table – especially all that pork fat we were supposed to eat up. God, I hated that stuff. Anyway, in the end he grew so big we couldn't fit him in the oven. Had to dismember him and cook him in bits.'

Walt pointed at his trusty Rayburn. 'Bags of room in that,' he said. 'Anyway, get that tea poured, will you? Before my throat gets too dry for talking.'

Chapter 10

Par for the Course

'I tell you what, Jayne.'

She was sitting opposite me in the parade room, dunking the last Hobnob in her tea. We'd come in from town for a quick brew, it was now getting on for one o'clock, and I'd hardly had two words out of her.

'Yeah? What?'

'Now, don't be all grumpy. Just because you're working with me and not young Fordy.'

'Who says I wanna work with him?'

'Well, you seem very quiet and out of sorts, that's all.'

'Just got a lot on my mind, Mike. Work, exams. You know. Besides . . .' She popped the biscuit in her mouth and closed her eyes.

'Go on. Besides what?'

'I'm seeing someone.'

'Oh. Copper, is he?'

She opened her eyes, stopped chewing and looked at me. 'Who said it's a he?'

'Oh. Well. Sorry, like . . .'

She gave a little laugh. 'Relax, it's a bloke. Lives down south. Teacher.'

'Right, so how are you coping with a long-distance romance and shift work? Can't be easy.'

'You can say that again. It's a sight easier during the school holidays. But other times it's really tough. I·mean, he's off every weekend and I'm working more often than not.'

'Sounds as if it would be easier if you got a place together.'

'Steady on, Mike. I've only known him a few months.' She reached forward, checked the biscuit packet, then tossed it into the wastepaper basket. 'Mind you, I was saying to him the other night, I quite fancy a crack at the Met. What's it like?'

'That's not an easy one. I was only young when I went down – well, like yourself, I suppose – and straight out of Hendon. Let's say it was a shock to my system, young lad straight from rural North Yorkshire and all that; but I tell you what, I loved it. Absolutely loved it.'

'So why did you come back up here?'

'All sorts of reasons. Mostly, though, I'd had enough of living in the big city. But I tell you what, it was great at the time. Really exciting. And fun too. I'm glad I did it. In the end, Jayne, it all comes down to what you want out of life – that and where you want to live.'

'I s'pose so. Anyway' – she looked at the clock – 'what were you going to say just now? When you said "Tell you what"?'

'Oh, that.' I picked up my mug and sipped at the strong, dark brew. 'I was gonna congratulate you, cheer you up.

You looked so miserable. Thought maybe someone had died.'

'No, what's getting me down more than anything right now is all this studying for the sergeant's exam. I hardly ever get out. It's all learn, learn, learn. Couldn't get to sleep yesterday. I'd swear I could hear me brain creaking under the strain. Anyway, about cheering me up . . . I didn't mean to stop you.'

'Ah.' I refilled my mug from the pot of tea and took a little sip. 'I was just going to say, as far as I'm concerned you're halfway there. You, Jayne, have mastered just about the most important skill for a beat bobby – and a duty sergeant, for that matter.'

'Do I wanna hear this?'

'Course you do. This is the ultimate accolade, and it comes from one who knows what he's talking about, a Yorkshireman, born and bred. You have finally learned how to mash a decent pot of tea – and it's only taken you three years. No, don't go pulling a face. I'm telling you, there's fellows in this station – and you know I'm not one to name names – fellows who've got ten and fifteen years' service in, whose tea is not fit to drink.'

'That a fact?'

'It is,' I said. 'But yours – it's coming on.' I took another sip and sighed gratefully. 'Yep, it's definitely coming on.'

'Well, thanks Mike. That's going to be a real comfort to me when I open that exam paper in a few months' time. I mean, it's all right for you, innit? You've got Ann there to spoonfeed you. Any problem, anything you don't understand, you just ask her.'

'When I see her, sure. But we're hardly ever off together.

No' – I drained my mug, stretched my arms and stood up – 'once we get in that exam room, it's a level playing field. You're on your own, and so am I. C'mon, sup up.'

A few minutes later we were on our way through Norton, out towards the bypass. Jayne was driving. She'd got me thinking – and for once she wasn't interrupting my thought processes with her non-stop banter. 'I'll tell you one big, big difference,' I said. 'Between being a copper up here and pounding a beat in London.'

Jayne slowed down at the mini roundabout before accelerating towards the bacon factory. 'Yeah?' she said.

'Well, take your average night shift. It's not like this: steady away, beautiful countryside, rolling hills and driving for miles without seeing anybody. Not like this at all. There's no proper empty spaces, and the thing that started to get me down was, it's a city that never sleeps. There's always something happening somewhere. People are always on the go – especially the criminals and vandals. You've got fights, robberies, domestics, break-ins, riots, suicides – you name it. Morning, noon and night. And complaints? Oh hell, don't talk to me about complaints. You'd always got at least one of them outstanding. It's a different job, really. Shall I tell you the worst part about working nights down there? By the time you finish your shift and you set off for home you're smack bang into the morning rush hour. Up here, if you think about it – well, there is no rush hour really.'

'Same in a lot of cities, I suppose,' Jayne said. 'But I'm not like you, am I? I mean, you're a country boy, aren't you?'

'True. I'll tell you another thing I've really come to

value up here. The one other precious commodity we have. Time. Time to speak to people and investigate things properly. Down there you're running around like a headless chicken. I suppose you could say we're privileged. We have time to' – I was searching for the right phrase – 'time to give to people when they need it. That's the difference. And I hope it continues.'

'We don't always have time.'

'No, not always, I agree. You have your busy shifts, and we've fewer officers, and everything's far more spread out so it takes you ten times longer to get anywhere. But down there – well, if I was you I'd ask to have a look around before I put in for a job. It's manic. You have more cops, for sure, but far more calls. The sheer volume of incidents doesn't give you time to get on the computer and dig into the background, for example. They want you back on the streets as soon as possible. You should see the background staff they have – all so that you can crack on and go to the next job.'

We were out on the bypass now and Jayne had her foot down. She didn't say anything, but she was taking it all in.

'But make no mistake,' I said, 'if I was your age I'd be down there like a shot.'

'Leaving the way clear for old lags like you to grab the first vacancy that comes up. For a sergeant, I mean.'

'Well, that's the other thing Jayne. If you want promotion, there's far more opportunity in a bigger force. From what I can see, to get promoted in North Yorkshire it's not what you know, it's who you know. It's costing me a fortune.'

'What do you mean?'

'Well, the superintendent has a very expensive taste in whisky, let me tell you.'

'Oh my God Mike, really?'

'Don't be daft. Jayne. This isn't the 1980s.' I laughed. 'By heck, you bite every time, don't you?'

She drove in silence for a mile or two, then said, 'Where we going, anyway?'

'Thought we'd just fly the flag around my patch, if that's OK. Tell you what, let's go across the tops to see if we can spot any poachers, then we can drop down Staxton way and call in at the all-night petrol station.'

We took a little detour through Wintringham and over the top to Helperthorpe before cutting back through Butterwick and down to Ganton, but all we saw was a couple of deer, leaping across the road and into the woods. When we got to the petrol station we learned that my mate Jack was on holiday, and the lad who was standing in for him seemed more interested in texting his girlfriend than speaking to us. So we made it a short call, bought a couple of coffees and chocolate bars, and left him to it.

'Gonna be a long old shift,' I said. 'Seems really quiet.'

Jayne was back in the car, which she'd parked to one side of the forecourt, next door to the Little Chef, which was in darkness. I was outside, having a quick smoke and changing my radio to the Scarborough channel. We were right on the border and it meant that between us we could monitor both channels and see what was going on in the neighbouring areas. It was a good place to sit up, right on the crime corridor, as the boss liked to call it, and pretty much out of sight from the road.

'When you gonna give that up?' Jayne didn't approve of smoking.

'After the exam,' I said.

She laughed. 'Right. It was gonna be after Christmas, last I heard.'

'You know what it is,' I said, 'it's boredom as much as owt else. On a busy shift you hardly ever see me light up.'

She yawned. 'Glad I never started.'

'Lucky, you mean.'

I got back into the car and we sat there finishing our coffee and chatting, keeping one eye on the road. There was very little passing traffic and we were just trying to make up our minds where to patrol next when the Scarborough radio came on.

'Can I have a unit to deal. The alarm's just gone off at Filey Golf Club.'

'Eh oop, this could be interesting,' I said. Filey was outside of our patch, of course, but given our location, right at the top of our ground, we weren't a million miles away. A Filey car responded immediately, and a traffic car offered to back them up.

'Didn't we have a briefing about break-ins at golf clubs?' Jayne said.

'We did. Easingwold, Ganton and I think it was Kirkbymoorside. They've all been hit the last few weeks.' I leaned forward and turned up the volume.

'Control, we're just arriving at the golf course now. Stand by . . .' Above the hiss and crackle of the radio we could hear the car door slam as he got out to investigate. A few minutes later he shouted, *'Control, active message,*

we've got forced entry at the rear fire escape. Have we got a dog unit on the way? And ETA for the backup please? There is no sign of any vehicles in the vicinity.'

'Hey Jayne, what's the odds this is the lot we've been hearing about?'

'Yeah, 'cept they'll be away and gone by now.'

'Oh, they'll be away all right, but where to? That's the question. You think about it. I mean, how many routes are there out of Filey?'

'Bit of a long shot to think they'd come our way though. And they could be on foot of course.'

'I dunno. Let's have a look at my maps, I'm sure I've got one that covers Filey area.' I tried to open the Ordnance Survey map, but with Jayne sitting beside me I was struggling for room. I got out and spread the map out on the bonnet, while Jayne shone her torch on it.

'Hmm,' I said, 'looks like there's several ways they could get away.' I started to fold the map up. 'Still, we might as well sit up here for a bit; it's as good a spot as anywhere.'

Before I'd even got the car door open, we heard the high-pitched sound of a car doing almost maximum revs – and it was coming our way.

'They're bloody travelling,' Jayne said.

As we looked at each other across the roof of our car we heard a screeching of tyres at the roundabout, and saw the sweep of headlights across the sky.

In an instant we were both in the car, watching the road. 'Right, Jayne, if it's them we need to be sharp. Doesn't sound like they're hanging about!'

An oldish VW Passat shot past us, heading towards Malton. Inside it we could see three young-looking lads, who seemed to be wearing identical light-coloured woolly hats.

'They look well dodgy. Let's get after 'em!'

Jayne had us out of our spot and onto the road, blue lights on, foot to the floor. I got on to the radio. '1015 to control, active message.'

'*1015, go ahead.*'

'Yes, we've been monitoring Scarborough channel. Are you aware of this break-in at the golf course?'

'*That's a yes, over.*'

'Right, we are behind a VW Passat, three up, travelling at speed A64 westbound towards Staxton. It's come from Filey direction, so a strong chance this could be them.'

'*1015, all received. Any units to back up?*'

I heard the Scarborough traffic car shout up that he was leaving Filey. Then Chris Cocks came on to say he was making his way from Malton along with a Ryedale traffic car.

The lads in the VW knew we were after them OK. As we went over a bump and our lights hit their rear window we could plainly see the youth in the rear seat glancing back over his shoulder, and the puff of burning oil as the driver stepped on the gas.

'They're getting a tune out of that old banger,' Jayne muttered, dropping down a gear to crank the Focus up towards eighty.

'1015 to control, vehicle still westbound, speed approximately seventy-five miles per hour, index mark of VW is . . .'

'*Received.*' We'd barely gone half a mile when control

was back on. '*1015, vehicle reported lost or stolen from the York area earlier today.*'

'All received.'

'I tell you what Jayne,' I continued, 'this has got to be them. Told you I felt lucky tonight.'

'No you didn't.'

'Well I meant to. They stopping or what?' We were at Staxton and they'd slowed right down. Jayne braked hard, then swore as they shot ahead, straight through the red light.

'Not total idiots then, at least they slowed down,' I said. 'Yeah, control from 1015, suspect vehicle just gone through Staxton lights at red.'

'They're pushing that thing to the limit.'

'Don't get sucked in. Just keep your distance a bit. This your first pursuit?'

'Yeah.'

'Well let me tell you I'm a bad passenger – but you're doing OK.'

The Passat was back up to seventy, seventy-five, eighty, clipping the verge on the left-hand bends, cutting across to the oncoming lane for the right-handers. Jayne was leaning forward in her seat, her knuckles white on the wheel.

'You enjoying this?' I said.

'You what? I'm absolutely bloody terrified. But it's one hell of a buzz.'

I wanted to say 'me too', but I held it back. She was having a tough time. 'Watch the adverse camber here,' I said. I knew this road like the back of my hands, so I was able to pitch in to warn her.

'*Control to 1015, over.*'

'Yeah, go ahead over.'

'We've a car ahead of you in Rillington ready to deploy a stinger.'

'Received. That's a good spot for a stinger, Jayne. They'll have to slow down for the bend before the lights, and there's the metal railings to protect the officer deploying.'

In front of us the Passat seemed to be hesitating slightly at every little lane we passed. 'Let's just hope they don't turn up the hill,' I said.

'Why's that?'

'I don't want a repeat of what me and Thommo had that time.'

Jayne laughed. 'Was that when they rolled a caravan down the hill onto you?'

'Never mind you laughing, you just concentrate girl.'

'1015 to control. Just approaching Sherburn crossroads, suspects doing seventy in a thirty zone.' That was another offence racked up and recorded – if we caught them.

'Hello, what they up to now?'

This time the lights were at green, but they braked sharply so that we were within feet of their rear end. I felt my hands tighten on the edge of the seat. I did not like being a passenger, and although Jayne was doing OK so far, she was still an unknown quantity to me. The lad in the back of the car had turned around to face us, and was shouting over his shoulder at the driver. 'Giving a bloody running commentary,' I said as they shot ahead once more.

'Whoa!!' We were speeding towards the crossroads at East Heslerton when they slammed on the anchors once more and veered to the right at the last minute. Or tried to.

'Steady, lads!' I shouted. They overshot the turn and lurched sideways onto the verge, ploughing up two dark, curved furrows and throwing clods of earth into the air. The car spun around one complete turn, then hit the hedge head-on.

'Bloody hell! 1015 to control, it's a crash, crash, crash! East Heslerton crossroads. Stand by.'

Before Jayne had even come to a stop I had the door open, gas in one hand. I was all set for a foot chase, but inside the Passat the three youths sat hunched and still. I ran up to the driver's side and shone my torch inside. As I opened his door the lad at the wheel just blinked at me, shielding his eyes with raised arms. He looked very young, very pale, with a few sparse hairs sprouting from his chin. He was shaking.

'Don't move or I'll gas you.' Jayne had the other side door ajar and was standing with her canister pointed towards the youth in the passenger seat.

I shone my torch into the rear. The lad there had his arms round a bundle of light waterproof jackets, still in their plastic wrappers. The seat beside him, and the footwells, were crammed full of golfing clothes and equipment: Pringle sweaters, boxes of tees, golf balls, an umbrella with a wooden handle, three or four shoeboxes, and a pile of Ping caps, the same as the ones they were wearing.

'Right,' I started. 'Is everybody all right?' I grabbed the car keys out of the ignition.

'I think so,' said the young lad behind the wheel.

'Well, I think you're in a lot of trouble, don't you?'

None of them said anything.

'Right Jayne, do you want to do the honours or shall I?'

'I'll do it, if that's OK. I'll take the driver and passenger and you take the one in the back.'

'Sounds like a deal.'

You do keep a sort of score sheet for your arrests. They count on your record. So when you're involved in a joint job it's the done thing to share the prisoners, so to speak.

'Right you two, you're both under arrest on suspicion of burglary and stealing this car.' Jayne cautioned them both while I arrested and cautioned the lad in the back.

'1015 to control. We have all three suspects detained and a car full of golfing equipment. All occupants held in the vehicle.'

'That's received, you've got the Filey van and traffic car just approaching you. Do you require an ambulance down there? Is everyone OK?'

'Yeah, control, no injuries thank goodness. Ambulance not required.'

'Right, let's get some handcuffs on and then have a look in the boot, shall we?' I said to the lads. 'Well well, well.' Inside were three sets of new golf clubs, a crowbar and a small mound of pound coins in a cardboard box. 'You have been busy, haven't you?' I shielded my eyes as the headlights of the Filey car lit up the night.

We placed all three prisoners in separate vehicles and transported them through to Scarborough, along with all of the stolen property from their car. We left the traffic car to deal with the accident site and arrange recovery of the stolen vehicle.

Because they were suspected of involvement in a series of burglaries that needed to be investigated, the prisoners were booked into custody and would be dealt with the next morning by the CID. This meant that once we'd given our evidence of arrest to the Scarborough custody sergeant, we could make our way back to Malton to complete our paperwork.

As we headed back to our car outside the police station I said, 'Shall I drive, Jayne? You're probably feeling a bit drained, aren't you?'

'Suits me.' Jayne settled back in her seat and fell silent as we cruised along the main road. I waited. The thing with Jayne was, even when she wasn't talking you could generally sense when she had something on her mind. You could almost hear her brain ticking over. She'd frown, or chew a nail or fiddle about with her hair. And sure enough, as we approached the Malton turn-off, she asked the question.

'So,' she began, 'what d'you reckon to this hunting ban then?'

'Strewth. That's a big question. Do you mean am I for it, or are you asking me what I think will happen?'

'Both.'

'Yeah. Thought so.' I took a deep breath, changed down and indicated left. 'First and foremost, as I've said to a lot of people this past year or so, I'm not a fox-hunter. I have bagged the odd gamebird in the past when I've been invited out on shoots, but I much prefer fly-fishing for trout and salmon.' I paused a moment, braking for the thirty zone in Old Malton. You always have to be careful what you say on this subject. It's so contentious. 'It's all part of being a country lad,' I continued. 'It's what you're brought up with. One thing however, I've never shot a deer.'

'Do you eat it though?'

'Eat it? Oh yes. I love it. It's just that I don't fancy shooting one, I like to see them in the wild. As for the ban . . .' I sighed. We were about to pull into the yard now and I was suddenly feeling the effects of what was my third night at work in a row. 'As for the ban, just you mark my words. There will be trouble. Something will kick off. These people out here – and don't forget, Jayne, I know them; they're on my beat, my constituency, you might say – these people will not, I repeat, will not take a ban lying down.' I killed the engine and yanked on the handbrake. 'But what form their resistance takes – well, we will find out in due course. But one thing I do know is that we could well end up right in the middle of it all.'

Inside, we got started on our reports. The station was deadly quiet. Ed and Fordy were in too, both of them hunched over their paperwork. Through the window I could just hear the slightly tinny sound of the church clock striking five, meaning the wind was coming from the south. I was starting to think that we'd got past the time of night when villains are most active, that we were probably on for a sharp getaway and a couple of hours' kip. I was wanting to be out and about mid-morning. I had a few things to see to, then a couple of days off.

'Tell you what Jayne, if you go and put the kettle on, we can celebrate our knock-off over a brew. Give us your statement and I'll go and fax them through to Scarborough custody.'

'Suits me, Mike. I hate that fax machine. It belongs in a museum.'

I wandered through to the front office. It was all quiet,

lit by the sixteen CCTV monitors. The front office is closed at night and the monitors are left on record mode. I began the slow process of loading the fax machine and trying to get a connection to Scarborough by the autodial. I knew it was going to take quite a while, so when the paper started to slowly judder through the machine I pulled up the big comfy office chair and sat down with my feet on the table, grinning to myself. It's the sort of thing you can only get away with in the middle of the night. I'd been sitting there a few minutes when I noticed a couple of shadowy figures walk past the motorcycle shop in Commercial Street. A bit early for people walking to work at the bacon factory, I thought. I logged onto the CCTV system with Phil's password and zoomed the camera in to have a closer look. Both the figures were now nowhere to be seen.

'Now what you up to?' Jayne walked in and plonked my tea down on the front desk.

'Just saw two youths near the motorbike shop, but they've disappeared now.'

Jayne pulled up a chair alongside. 'Do you know Mike, I'm absolutely bleedin' shattered, but I'm really, really pleased with that result earlier.'

'Right place right time Jayne. You need a bit of luck sometimes as I always say . . . eh up, bloody hell. What . . .' I couldn't believe what I was seeing on the CCTV camera.

Papers flew everywhere as I scooted my chair back, whacked the side of the table with my leg, and stumbled towards the door with Jayne right behind me. 'Come on, let's get 'em. Fordy, Ed! Get your stuff, lads. We've a break-in in progress, Commercial Street.'

'1015 to control' I shouted over the radio as I ran to the car in the back yard.

'*Go ahead.*'

'I've just seen on CCTV two youths smashing the front window of the motorbike place in Commercial Street. Looks like they hit it with a sledgehammer. We're all en route, over.'

'*Received.*' Julie's voice was slightly more high-pitched than usual – it sounded as though we'd jolted them into action too.

Jayne and I were in the car and making for the road. Fordy and Ed were right behind us. Over the radio we could hear control putting the call out. *All units. Burglary in progress, Commercial Street.*'

It took no more than four or five minutes for us to arrive at the scene. The place was deserted. The pavement outside was covered with broken glass. Flashing my light inside the shop, I could see where a bike had been knocked over. A couple of helmets and several pairs of leather gloves lay on the floor. A clothing rail had also been toppled over and the alarm was on, full throttle. I glanced around the street to see whether any lights were on or any doors open in the houses nearby. Surely somebody was going to poke their head out to see what was going on. But there was nothing. The intruders must have got in quick, grabbed what they could carry, and left – but where to?

I got on to control: 'Yeah, we're on scene. I can confirm it looks like a smash-and-grab. Looks like the suspects have left. We're going to search the immediate vicinity. Can you put a message out across all channels for the information of all units? We have no further details over.'

'How about we try the bypass?' Ed said. 'They've either gone that way or the Beverley road.'

'Yeah. Sounds good.' Ed was right. They wouldn't have come back through town or we would have seen them, and nothing had passed us on the way down.

Jayne and I set off along the Beverley Road, and travelled flat out for several miles, but it was a forlorn hope. They couldn't have had more than two or three minutes' start on us, but there was nothing to say they hadn't cut across one of the back roads – or that they weren't just lying low in some residential street on one of the housing estates. And of course we had no idea as to what vehicle, if any, they were using.

At North Grimston we gave it up. 'We aren't going to find anyone,' I said, 'unless we get seriously lucky. And I think we've used our quota of luck tonight. Best get back and seal off the scene for the SOCO to deal with it when he comes on.'

'Bugger it.' Jayne was as disconsolate as I was. 'To actually watch 'em at it, and then find they've got away. We couldn't have got there any quicker. It drives you mad at times, this job.'

'I've got an idea. Let's go and have a look around the bacon-factory car park, shall we? Doesn't feel like a local job, this.'

'No, especially this time in the morning.'

It was a long shot, but worth a try. The bacon factory employs hundreds of people, a lot of whom travel from miles away. They also had a shift due to start at six. We left Ed and Fordy at the shop and drove up to the factory where we patrolled the car park. But no, there was nothing suspicious.

Back at the station we reviewed all the CCTV footage we had, but it wasn't a lot of help. The earlier images were fuzzy to the point of being useless. All we could see was two grainy figures wielding what looked like a sledge-hammer, or an iron bar, to put the window in. You could see them leaving within thirty seconds with armfuls of stock. Then they were out of shot on foot more or less straight away. We had nothing – no facial images, and no vehicle.

'Well,' I said to Jayne, as we signed off at seven o'clock, 'could've been worse.'

'You reckon?' Jayne sounded as flat as she had at the beginning of the shift.

'Come on, it wasn't a bad night. I mean, we got one brilliant result at least.'

'Yeah, I suppose you're right, and the bonus being you survived.'

'Survived what, Jayne?'

'My driving.'

I now had two days off to look forward to, and the thing on my mind as I drove up towards home was the future of Keeper's Cottage. We had Soapy wanting his money for the roof repairs, and Algy – well, we hadn't set eyes on him in a while, which was unusual. Was he really assuming we were going to buy the place and pay Soapy's bill? Or was Soapy leaping to conclusions? I was all for popping round with a bottle of wine, sitting down and getting the thing sorted, but Ann – naturally – took a more considered approach.

'Look,' she said, 'we're in the driving seat here. Soapy needs paying, and if we're to believe him Algy wants the whole thing sorted without any hassle. We play our cards right and we could secure Keeper's Cottage for a fair price.'

'So what are you suggesting?'

'That we ask him to meet up with us for a friendly chat. Tell him there's a couple of things we'd like to talk over with him.'

'I s'pose you're right,' I said. 'OK then, how about asking him to meet us down at the Farmers? Tonight. I mean, it's the last time we're off together for a few days.'

We set off to the pub early that evening, thinking we might have a bar meal before Algy arrived. As Ann said, if you're going to negotiate, you need to be on top of your game. And that means starting out with a full stomach.

It was a cold night. We were well into autumn now, and we walked down the lane through drifts of dry, fallen leaves. As a light breeze stirred the tops of the larch trees a shower of needles fell to the ground. Our breath was coming in clouds.

'I love this time of year,' Ann said, clasping my hand in hers. 'I mean, the run-up to the shortest day. Not so keen on January and Feb, mind, but the back-end – I don't know, I find it sort of energising.'

'Aye, me too. If we could have a short sharp winter, a nice lot of snow for Christmas and then go straight into spring, I'd be well happy. Tell you what, though' – I pulled my hat low over my forehead – 'this is cold enough for me. Wouldn't be surprised if we have a frost tonight.'

Ann disagreed. 'Too cloudy,' she said. 'C'mon, let's crack on. Get the old circulation going.'

By the time we got down there we were good and warm – so much so that we had to step away from the fire that was blazing in the hearth. There weren't many in, just one or two regulars sitting in the bar and a couple of lads enjoying a game of pool out the back. We sat and ate our homemade steak-and-ale pie in relative quiet. We were almost done when Walter came in. He didn't say a word, just looked me up and down, peeled off an outsized pair of gardening gloves and held out his hands. 'Now then,' he said. 'Tek a look at them.' He thrust them closer to me. 'Aye, go on, tek a good look.'

'Blimey, Walt, what you been up to?' His fingers were all taped up with sticky plasters, and he had a sort of elasticated bandage round his left wrist.

'Why, it's what you get when folks let you down,' he said, easing himself into the seat beside Ann.

She was staring at his hands. 'What on earth happened to you, Walt? How did you get yourself into a state like that?'

'Why, a certain party said he'd come round and help me. And he didn't. That's the sum and substance of it, lad. It's a good job I still count that certain party as a friend,' he added, pulling a brown paper package out of his pocket and plonking it on the table.

'Is there a connection?' Ann asked, pointing at the package.

'Aye, there is, lass. And if your young man'll fetch me

a drink I'll tell you all about it. I'd get me own, but with these' – he held out his injured hands – 'why, I can't properly get me hands in me trouser pocket.'

'By heck, I've heard some excuses in my time!' I said. 'Can't get your hands in your pocket? I shall have to remember that one.' I got up and fished my wallet out. 'Go on, then. Pint, is it?'

'Aye, that's right good of you, lad.'

I went to the bar, got him his drink. 'And while we're at it,' I said to the landlord, 'I reckon we could do with a couple of desserts. What you got?'

I placed my order and carried Walt's beer back to the table. 'Cheers, lad.' He mumbled the words, his mouth being crammed full.

'I see. Can't get your hands in your pockets, but you're fit enough to nick my grub off my plate,' I said. I put the glass on the table, sat back down and stabbed the last couple of chips with my fork. 'So anyway, have I got this right? You're saying that the state of your hands is all my fault?'

'Very tall, that hedge o' mine,' he said. 'Remember?' He cast an accusing eye at me, then downed half his pint in one go.

'Hedge?' I said. Then I remembered. 'You, Walter, were supposed to ring me to let me know when you wanted me, you daft old bugger.'

'Well I tried, but I couldn't get hold of you.'

'No, that's because I've been at work. Been very busy this last week or so. Why didn't you ring my mobile? It's always on.'

Walter flinched, and lowered his glass to the table. 'You

what, lad? Ring your mobile? D'you think I'm made of money? Anyway, in the end I had to fetch me stepladder to it. And what wi' dodging them thorns . . .' He took another drink, all but draining the glass. 'And remember how all the best fruit was at t'top, out of reach?' He didn't wait for me to answer. 'Aye well, reaching up for them, d'you see, that's how I tippled over.'

'Ouch.' Ann was grimacing.

'Aye, that's what I said as I plummeted to t'ground. And a few other words I wouldn't repeat in front of a lady. Ripped me hands all but to shreds, I should say. And sprained me wrist.' He rubbed it gently and pulled his sleeve back to show us a series of dark scratches that ran the length of his forearm.

'Oh, Walt. I really am sorry, mate. You should have waited for me. I'm off tomorrow, and the next day.'

'Well, it's a good job I'm not a man as bears grudges,' Walt said, downing the remains of his pint and shoving the glass towards me. He was putting me on a guilt trip and loving every minute of it. He reached out and touched the paper parcel. 'Go on, lad, you may as well open her up.'

'Oh, I know what that is,' Ann said as I pulled out a tall jar full of dark berries and pink liquor. 'Sloe gin. Hey, thanks Walter. I've never had it before, but I've heard a lot about it. There's one or two people I know who make it and they've been going on about it recently.'

I picked up the jar and held it to the light. It was a gorgeous warm colour. 'Walt,' I said, 'that's very generous of you. But I thought—'

'I know,' Walt said. 'I told you to buy your own gin.

But that's me, lad. All heart – even though you don't deserve it. I don't know, leaving an old feller like me to go up them steps all on his own.' He took the bottle from my hand and passed it to Ann. 'Here y'are, lass. You tek care of that – and if he behaves himself, mebbe let him have a little taste of it on Boxing Day, eh?'

'He'll be lucky if he gets to sniff the empty bottle, Walter. Don't worry, it's going to a good home is this.' Then she nudged me in the ribs and pointed at Walt's empty glass. 'C'mon,' she said, 'don't neglect him.'

But Walt was on his feet. 'No,' he said, 'I haven't time for another. Got a practice session with that there band of mine.'

'Walt?' Ann was frowning as she put the jar in her handbag. 'How did you know we were down here tonight?'

'I didn't,' he said. 'Not for certain.'

'Well, how come you had our bottle of gin ready for us?'

'Ah well . . .' He adjusted the bandage on his wrist, avoiding eye contact. And at that moment the landlord came over.

'Walter, mate. Thought I heard your dulcet tones. You got that sloe gin you promised us?' He turned to Ann. 'Started up his own distillery, y'know. Not that I should mention it with an officer of the law present,' he laughed. 'We weren't planning to sell it or anything. It was for me and the missus.'

Walt had stationed himself between the landlord and the bottle. 'Aye, tell you the truth, lad, I forgot it. I'll maybe come down tomorrow.'

'Oh, any time.' The landlord took our empty plates

and went back to the bar. Walt put his hat on and slipped away, just as Algy came in.

'Ah, Michael, m'boy! And your good lady.' Algy took off his fore-and-aft hat, adjusted his cravat and gave a little bow in Ann's direction. Then he turned to me. 'Mine's a large one, as they used to say before we got all politically correct.'

'Yeah yeah yeah – the old ones are the best,' I said. 'Is this where I say "Are you ordering or boasting?" and then everyone laughs?'

'Probably so, old chap, probably so. Anyway, we're supposed to be talking turkey, as our American friends would have it, so perhaps just a half measure of the amber nectar for me, for the moment, eh? But it looks as though the good lady's glass needs refreshing too.'

'This is turning into an expensive night,' I muttered to Ann as Algy hung his coat up over a chair and stood there with his back to the fire, raising and lowering himself on his toes.

'Mike, will you stop whingeing about your wallet,' she whispered. 'You'll be wearing a kilt next! Go on, get him his drink.'

As soon as I'd got the drinks in and we were all sat down, Ann laid our cards on the table. 'This is the way we see it,' she said. 'We've enjoyed living at Keeper's Cottage, so much so that we were attracted by the idea of buying it. And we did, as you remember, make you an offer for it.'

'You did indeed. Although, as I believe I said at the time, it fell regrettably short of my expectations.' Algy grinned. 'But a good try, all the same. I admired your spirit, I have to say.' He nudged me, and added, 'She'd make a splendid businesswoman, m'boy.'

Ann ignored this remark and carried on. 'Yes, but circumstances have altered since we made that original offer, haven't they?'

'You mean the dismal performance of the property market in recent months?'

'Well, partly that, but I was thinking of the general state of repair of our humble abode—'

'Ah, you refer to the late troubles with the roof?' Algy winced and sipped at his beer.

'For which you, as our landlord, are solely responsible.'

'Regrettably so. Yes, Soapy's final invoice was enough to make a strong man weep.'

'Oh,' I said, 'so he's billed you for it, has he?'

'Naturally, Mike. I am the owner.'

''Cos last we heard he was round our place huffing and puffing—'

Ann kicked me under the table. 'Yes, he's convinced he left some tools behind. In the roof space. You checked it out yet, Mike?'

'Oh. Not yet, no.'

'Well . . .' Algy was twiddling his empty glass in his hand. 'To tell you the truth, the slump in the market, and certain pressures on the pound sterling – well, let's just say that cashflow has become an issue for yours truly.'

Ann spotted the opening and was in like Flynn. 'And Soapy's invoice has come at a bad time, I suppose.'

I knew Ann wanted me to play it cool, but I couldn't help myself, I've always been the same. I like a bit of haggling – it's a Yorkshire thing, just comes naturally.

'Well, look, I've got an idea,' I said, making it sound as though it had just popped into my mind. 'How about if you agreed to our original offer—'

Algy almost yelped. You could feel his pain. 'But that was a long way short of my original valuation,' he said.

'Yes.' Ann leaned forward and stared him straight in the eye. She spoke slowly, as if explaining a simple calculation to a seven-year-old. 'Yes,' she repeated, 'but that valuation was based on the property being sound. Then the roof caved in. Not only is there the cost of repairing it, but there's the material damage we suffered.'

'And the setback to my studies,' I added. 'Not to mention the emotional wear and tear. I mean, how would you feel if you were sitting there after a hard day's work and a shower of rubble came down the chimney, followed by a builder?'

Ann was nudging me under the table. I didn't need to go any further. We both sat there waiting for Algy to respond. There was just the ticking of the clock above the fireplace and the faint clack of cue against ball from the pool room.

'I see,' Algy said. He sounded tired, and resigned. 'So you're offering to accept the costs of the repair, and pay Soapy his due – if I agree to that earlier offer?'

'In a nutshell, yes. It's like meeting halfway, don't you think?'

Algy shook his head. 'Well, you two, it's a difficult one this.'

'It is Algy, but it would suit all of us right now, don't you think?'

Algy clutched his head. 'I think I need another drink,' he said.

And that was that. We could've gone home there and then, but we couldn't resist a celebratory drink or two. So it was late by the time we made our way up the hill, having secured a verbal agreement that would be followed within a few weeks, according to Algy, by the legal documents.

'Only one question,' I said, as we walked the last hundred yards up the lane to Keeper's Cottage.

'Which is?'

'Soapy's bill.'

'What about it?'

'Well, if it brought a tear to old Algy's eye . . .'

'Don't worry about that,' Ann said.

'But—'

'Just don't worry about it.'

'You can't just tell me not to worry, Ann. Come on, what's the deal?'

'Mike, I have an idea and all will be revealed, OK?'

'In due course, am I right?'

'Right.'

Chapter 11

A Strange Encounter

Several days passed, and we heard nothing. I really didn't know how to feel. Ann and I knew we were on the brink of a major change in our lives, but had been left on tenterhooks. From worrying that we might have to move on if we wanted a home of our own, suddenly it seemed that our future at Keeper's Cottage could be secured. We had the verbal agreement with Algy, and we knew we could trust him as a man of his word. There was just this matter of Soapy's bill to sort out. It felt so close, and yet so far away. But Ann said she had a good feeling and I shouldn't worry, so I tried not to.

I did my best to put such thoughts out of my head, to try to keep work life and home life separate. As I drove into the station car park to start a night shift I wondered whether there might be some good news waiting for me there. Maybe something would be resolved. Had there been a breakthrough on the smash-and-grab raid we'd caught on CCTV a week or so earlier? Had the offenders been caught – or the stolen goods recovered?

No, no and no, was the answer I got off Chris Cocks as soon as I walked in the door. So what had they got away with?

'Eight leather jackets,' was his answer. 'Value three or four hundred apiece. Plus a couple of very expensive crash helmets. The main thing is, the jackets: we've got the maker's name – brand name, whatever – and it's been fed into the intelligence system, as have the helmets. It's upmarket gear.'

'Did SOCO manage to get anything?'

'Not really, but they took samples of the broken glass just in case. You never know.'

'Damn. We were so close to having them. What about the CCTV? Has that come up with a getaway vehicle or anything?'

Chris shook his head. 'Nothing. Nothing to say there even was a car. They could have been on foot for all we know. Opportunists.'

'Hmm . . . I don't know. I'd say it was a pretty well-thought out operation. I mean, they disappeared sharp enough, didn't they? You think about it. We were down there before you could say knife – and we never caught sight of them. If they'd been lugging a pile of jackets—'

'Eight jackets? Four apiece? Wouldn't weigh a huge amount.'

'Maybe . . .'

My opinion was that we might have been dealing with a fairly smart pair of operators – always assuming there were only the two of them. There could well have been a look-out, and there could well have been a driver. Maybe even both.

'They'll come again,' I said, as Ed and I drove through town later on.

'You reckon?' he said.

'They always do, buddy. If these lads have got a taste of it, if they think they've got away scot-free – which they have, for now – they'll be feeling good. They'll be wanting more. Another throw of the dice.' I switched on the wiper blades and gave the windscreen a wash. It wasn't raining as such, but there was a heavy dampness in the air. It had been one of those dull, grey days when it never actually rains but everything's wet and grimy. It was now a thoroughly gloomy night, with every streetlight surrounded by a halo of mist, the black trees dripping onto greasy pavements. 'I mean, when you look at what's on offer, you wonder why there isn't more of the smash-and-grab sort of crime.'

'How d'you mean?'

We were coming down Wheelgate and all the shops were lit up with attractive window displays, getting into their stride for the festive season. 'Well, it's only a sheet of glass separating the burglar from all sorts of goodies, isn't it?'

'Yeah, you can see how people get tempted. Still quite unusual round here though, smash-and-grabs.'

We crossed the lights and headed into Castlegate. 'Look at that,' I said. 'Just what I'm talking about.' In Yates's window was a brand-new, gleaming quad-bike, draped in tinsel.

Ed laughed. 'Yeah, but not exactly at the top of everybody's shopping list, is it?'

'May not look very exciting to you or me, buddy, but

there'd be plenty of takers out there if it was on offer cheap.'

'Fair point.'

'Must be worth three four grand, easy. I think that's the first time they've put one of those right in the shop window. Look at it, sitting there like a little jewel. Might as well have a label on it. Come and get me. I could quite fancy one of them to ride around on, couldn't you?'

'Steady on, Mike. You're on our side, remember?'

'Ed, I've said it before. It pays to think like a criminal. Get inside their heads.'

'Yeah but . . .'

'You think about it, coppers and crooks – we're in the same business, in a way. Our minds run along similar lines.'

'To a point.'

'Take me, when I was a kid. Seven, eight years old. I used to quite fancy being an outlaw.'

'You what?'

'No, don't get me wrong. I didn't want to be a criminal as such. But that was the dilemma. I was brought up to respect the law, of course I was. But I was a young lad with a taste for adventure. Do you know what I'm talking about?'

'Course I do. I was the same. I wanted to be a pirate. Swinging through the rigging with a sword between my teeth. Boxes full of gold coins.' Ed laughed. 'Pieces of eight, and a black patch over my eye. Yeah, that was the dream all right.'

'There you go. Adventure, action, danger. It's what little boys fantasise about. I used to sit there watching the TV, and night after night what was it? Cops and robbers. And who had the most fun? The bad guys. Blowing things up, smashing through fences in getaway cars. The cops – well, the way I saw it they were spoilsports.'

'Yep, the poor old baddies never quite got away with the loot, did they?'

'Just like in real life, Ed.'

We were passing the motorbike shop now, a new steel grid covering its front window. 'Yeah,' I said, 'I was always looking for excitement. A challenge. That's why I joined the T.A., in the end.'

'I didn't know you were in the Territorials.'

'Yeah you did. Must've told you about it.'

'Can't say I remember.'

'I did seven years. Then I decided to go for the police and I had to give it up. Yeah, really enjoyed my time in the Terriers. And Lumley barracks? Right slap bang next to York City football ground? Just the job, lad.'

'How d'you mean?'

'If you sat on top of the barracks roof you could see right into the ground. Watch the match for nowt!'

Ed yawned. We'd driven up the Beverley road as far as the last row of houses and were now making our way slowly back through the deserted streets of Norton. It seemed as though everybody was treading water, knowing that the Christmas rush would soon be upon us but hoping it wouldn't hit just yet. From a policing point of view, there was that feeling that most of the burglars and break-in merchants would be lying low, hoping for richer pickings in the not too distant future.

'Makes you wish you could hibernate,' I said, giving the windscreen another wash.

'Wake up about April time, eh?'

'Yep. Either that or give us some action. Something to liven things up. Where's an enterprising criminal when you want one?'

'Hey, careful what you wish for, Mike. I thought we were aiming for a crime-free society.'

'Yeah, OK – the voice of reason. But I get bored, that's all.'

Nobody wants to see a surge in criminal activity. It's simply that you like to do the job you're paid for and trained for. If the criminals aren't at it, so to speak, you've precious little chance of catching them.

We had an early break back at the station, taking advantage of the lull to catch up with a bit of paperwork, and set off again around two o'clock. 'Oh well,' I said, as we left town along the York road, 'at least the weather looks as though it's changing.' The wind had got up, the mist had dispersed, and a few stars were peeking through the ragged clouds. We drove out onto the A64. At the bottom of Golden Hill, where the road leads off to Huttons Ambo, I pulled up. 'Let's stay here for a bit and see who's out and about, shall we?'

'Clutching at straws, aren't you? We haven't seen a vehicle since we passed the showrooms.'

'Hey, you never know,' I said. 'Let's just wait and see.'

We sat up, as we call it, for fifteen, maybe twenty minutes. A paper van passed us, heading towards town. I got out and lit a cigarette. A fox darted out from the hedge bottom, spotted me, and slipped quietly away out of sight. That was about as exciting as it got. Back in the car Ed was yawning extravagantly.

'Yeah,' I said, 'point taken. We'll head back to town, shall we?' I put the car in gear and was about to move away when a bright light caught my eye. 'See that?' I said. It was about four hundred yards away above the hedge, near an old stone barn of some sort. My first thought was that something had set a security light off.

Ed was peering through the windscreen. 'I see it, but . . . what the hell is it?'

'Search me.' I could see something – something that looked like a kind of vehicle about the size and shape of a double-decker bus – but I was dazzled by the light that surrounded it.

'Weird. Is it on the road, or in the field?'

'No idea. It's got to be on the road, surely. Or . . . is it above it?'

'Looks like a bloody combine. Except it's airborne. Isn't it?'

'I think you're right, Ed.'

'No, it can't be. Couldn't be lampers, could it?'

'Way too big and bright.'

We'd probably been looking at it for no more than ten or fifteen seconds. Then, as suddenly as the light had appeared, it was gone. Vanished.

'Come on, we'd better check this out,' I said, putting the car into gear.

We drove slowly up the lane to where we thought the mystery object had been and got out. I can't deny that I felt nervous now. My mouth was dry and my hands were sweaty. I walked in through a gatehole towards the old stone barn. It was more or less a ruin. No door, hardly any roof, and inside just a pile of rotting boards with the roots of last summer's nettles poking through the cracks. And there was no sign whatsoever of any security lights.

'See anything?' I asked Ed, making his way along the other side of the hedge.

'No,' he replied, almost whispering. 'You?'

'Not yet.' I was looking at the ground under my feet now. It was ploughed earth, and where I'd expected at least to see wheel-marks or a set of footprints, there was nothing, no sign of anything having been there.

Just then a car came along the main road from Malton, its headlights making a long, slow sweep to illuminate the entire field. It was completely empty. Nothing but the neat furrows curving away towards the woods on the far side.

'Well, my friend, whatever it was, it's gone.'

Ed had finished checking along the hedge and joined me beside the barn entrance. 'Looks like it.'

I shone my torch over the ploughed earth around us. 'But why no tracks?'

'You know – you know what I'm thinking?' Ed's voice was unsteady. He sounded well and truly rattled.

'Don't even go there,' I said, flashing my torch into the barn and over the rafters.

'Well, why not?' he said. 'Why couldn't it be a UFO?'

'Could be,' I said. 'I s'pose it could be, but – you're surely not suggesting we log it, are you?'

'Why not?'

I sighed. 'Because we don't want to look like a pair of prize prats,' I said. 'Come on, let's get back to the car. We need to think this through for a minute.'

'No, I want to have another look around.'

'Aye, go on then. But we aren't going to find anything, trust me.'

We searched all around the outside of the barn, along both sides of the hedge and into the road itself. Apart from our own footprints we found nothing. Whatever we'd seen – or thought we'd seen – had departed without leaving a trace. Neither of us could come up with any reasonable explanation of what we had seen. I didn't like this one little bit.

We trudged back to the car, casting an occasional glance over our shoulders, half hoping that the mystery object, or its light, would reappear. We even scanned the sky, now clear and star-spangled.

'What's that?' Ed had spotted a winking light, away to the north and moving towards the horizon.

'Aircraft.'

'You sure?'

'Positive.'

'So, we gonna call in or what?' Ed had his radio in his hand. 'I mean, it's a sighting, isn't it? We're supposed to report them.'

I didn't answer. I was still coming to grips with the fact that I knew – absolutely knew – I'd seen something, something of which there was not a shred of evidence. If I'd been on my own I would've tried to shrug it off as an illusion, the result of being tired. Eye strain. The perils of shift work. Anything. But I was left with the uncomfortable realisation that we'd both seen exactly the same thing. Or had we?

'Hang about, Ed.'

'What is it?'

'Just before we go any further, tell me what you saw. I mean, describe it to me.'

'What you on about? You saw it, same as I did.'

'No, we both think we saw – something. Just tell me what it looked like to you. You're going to have to write it up in your report, if you do one.'

Ed exhaled through half-closed lips. 'Well, it was big. That's for sure.'

'OK. And what else?'

'You writing this down?'

'I am.'

'Right. It was big, it was sort of rectangular . . .'

'How big?'

'I'd say like a bus, maybe bigger. And it looked metallic. And it was glowing. Or there was bright light, around the whole thing. Very bright.' He turned to look at me. 'Sound familiar?'

'Exactly as I remember it, my friend. So I don't think you're going round the twist.' I closed my notebook. 'No, the only thing I'd add is the little green figure with huge brown eyes that walked down the ladder and beckoned to us.'

'Yeah yeah yeah. In a silver jumpsuit. Listen, this ain't funny.'

'Sorry. You're right.' I got in the car. 'So, next question. What we gonna do?'

'Call it in.'

'You realise everyone's going to be listening?'

'All right, say we don't report it. What then? I mean, what if it turns out there was something?'

'Ed, there's an old saying. I think it's some Chinese

philosopher. If a tree falls in the forest and nobody sees it . . .'

'Yeah, I know. Has it really fallen?' Ed sat there for a moment, then banged his fist on the dashboard. 'Look, I'm going to report it, OK? And if you don't want your best buddy to look like a total plonker you're gonna back me up.'

'Can't we just say it was sommat to do with the base? Out at Fylingdales?' I was referring to the early-warning station out on the moors. UFO spotters are always prowling about in that neck of the woods, hoping to see something weird and wonderful.

'How would we know they had anything to do with this?'

'Fair enough.' I groaned. 'Go on, then, but you do realise that they'll take the proverbial out of us for the rest of our service,' I went on. 'You and I could end up getting referred to welfare.'

'Listen, Mike.' He spoke very slowly and very deliberately. 'I know what I saw, OK? Now, if you're not up to a bit of mickey-taking, then all I can say is it's a poor do.'

'Go on then.' He was right, and I knew it. 'No, give me the radio . . .' I took a deep breath. Here goes, I thought. '1015 to control, over.'

'*Go ahead Mike.*' Damn. It was Brian in the control room, our most experienced hand. I wished it could've been Julie.

'Yeah, we're at the bottom of Golden Hill. We've had a sighting of a large, unidentified object in a field. Showing bright lights . . . very bright.' It was hard to know how much else to give him. Sometimes you hear yourself speaking and you just know the listener's going to think you've lost the plot. Brian was saying nothing – yet. I decided I'd better keep it short. 'We've investigated. We're satisfied there's nothing there now.'

'Was it moving or stationary?'

'Stationary. Well, no, it was sort of . . . hovering, a few feet off the ground I'd say.'

'Hovering?'

'That's correct, over.'

'So where is it now? Where'd this thing go to?'

'It didn't go. Look, I know this sounds far-fetched, but it just . . . vanished.'

'Vanished, as in "disappeared"?'

'That's a yes. Listen, there was definitely something out there. We both saw it. We've searched the area thoroughly. All I can tell you is there's nothing there now.'

'Some kind of helicopter, Mike?'

'That's a negative, Brian. More like a double-decker bus job.'

'That's received.' There was a short, but pregnant, pause. Then Brian said, *'Mike, you do realise I am about to create an incident. Once I've done that it can't be deleted. Do you understand, over?'*

I looked at Ed and he nodded, then closed his eyes. 'Yes, Brian I understand, but Ed and I confirm the sighting, over.'

'Er, received Mike.' I was sure I could hear the tittering of the control-room staff in the background. I turned to Ed.

'You see, Ed. It's bloody started already. We could end up getting sectioned before hometime at this rate.'

It was no surprise when Chris Cocks rang me on my mobile phone. 'Mike, what the hell's going on out there?'

'Sarge, I'm simply telling you what we saw. And what we did, and what happened.'

'This had better not be a wind-up, Mike. You're not in the Met now, you know.'

'Chris, when an ex-Met officer wants to wind everybody up, trust me, he doesn't start a UFO rumour. We were a bit more sophisticated than that.'

There was a long silence. Maybe he was wondering whether this was a double bluff. Then he said, 'So you'll be writing it up fully on the computer then?'

'Yes. Both of us.'

'OK. On your own head be it, mate. You do realise the bosses will see it, if you're after promotion, you know . . .'

Christ, I thought. I turned to Ed. 'Now look what you've made me do. Dropped me right in the . . . mire.'

Ed shook his head. 'We know what we saw, Mike. They weren't here to see it.'

We knew what to expect when we got back to the station at the end of the shift – and we weren't disappointed.

'Mike! You made it.'

'Yes, Jayne, I made it.'

'That's such a relief. There's all sorts of rumours flying about. I heard you'd been abducted by aliens.'

'Well, here I am, Jayne. The living proof that you heard wrong.'

'Oh, they took Ed instead, did they?'

'No, Jayne, they did not take Ed.'

'So there were aliens, that what you're saying?'

'Jayne, we are police officers. We go out at all hours, and we report what we see. We are not responsible for what we see. Sometimes, as you well know, you see strange and mysterious things. Or unlikely things. And we report them, OK?'

I knew we hadn't heard the last of it. Despite my misgivings, Ed logged it on the computer in big bold letters for all to see: 'UFO sighting.' And we both put our names to it. Did I regret it? Not entirely. Not yet, at any rate.

I was disappointed not to see Ann when I got in that morning. I was anxious to run the thing by her, get her take on the subject. But she was on an early turn and had already left the house. Maybe we'd talk it through later, over a glass of wine.

But word had spread around the North Yorkshire police quicker than even I expected. As I took Henry for his walk, my phone beeped, and there was a text from Ann. 'Now what u gone and done?!' I fired one back immediately. 'Not as bad as it seems. Ed was w me.' Ann's reply was brief and to the point. 'York nick buzzing w it. Story is two country cops have lost the plot.'

I didn't reply. I took Henry home, put him in his kennel and took myself off to bed. By the time I pulled the duvet over my head it was gone half past eight.

Somehow I managed to sleep right through. I awoke to the smell of smoked bacon which, mingled with the aroma of freshly ground coffee, drew me straight down to the kitchen in my dressing gown.

'What time is it?' I yawned.

'Three thirty. Thought you'd appreciate a calorie-fuelled start to the day. Before we have a little chat.'

'Too right,' I said. 'I'm starving.' Then I told her what had happened with Ed, out on the York road. She didn't say anything at first. Just pushed the plunger on the cafetière and fetched a couple of mugs out of the cupboard.

'So d'you think me and Ed did the right thing?' I asked. 'You know, logging it. Or should we have kept schtum?'

'Course you did,' she said. 'I mean, who knows what's out there? It could be anything. Keep an open mind, I say.' She poured a cup of the fresh brew and handed it to me.

'So, as a sergeant, if someone rang in to say they'd seen a UFO, what would you think?'

'Doesn't matter what I'd think. But if an officer started seeing them regularly, well, then I might start to wonder. Here, pass me those eggs. I mean, we've all seen weird stuff before. Haven't you?'

I handed her the box. 'Weird things? Oh hell yes. One night coming through the woods near Sand Hutton. Middle of winter, it was. There was this red glow, right across the sky, sort of a veil. Remember those big long curtains they used to have in the flicks before the film started, with lights behind them? Like those, it was. Very eerie.'

'And what did you do?'

'I called it in, of course. Far as I was concerned it could've been anything. A fire, an illegal rave; God knows what. Turned out it was the northern lights – which had crossed my mind, to be honest. Got back to the station and they'd had dozens of calls. People thought we were being invaded. I mean, that's why you log things, isn't it? Give you a reference point when the calls come in. And reassure the public.'

Ann laughed. 'I saw something once. I was on duty in the middle of Wandsworth Common, and this bright light shot across the sky. Too fast for a plane, way too bright for a firework. Turned out to be an asteroid. Want them flipped?'

'Eh?'

'Your eggs. Shall I flip them?'

'Aye, go on. So how could you tell it was an asteroid?'

'It's all to do with the trajectory, the speed, the luminosity, that sort of thing.'

'You what?'

Ann laughed. 'No, I saw it in the papers next day. Turned out the scientists had been tracking it. Even managed to locate the spot it landed, in a field out by the coast.'

She served the food out of the frying pan and onto our plates, grabbed a pile of sliced bread, then shoo'd me through to the sitting room. 'Anyway,' she said, as I stuck my fork into a rasher of bacon, 'while you were sleeping . . .'

'What? Something from Algy?' I said.

'Better than that,' she answered. 'Something from Soapy. He's coming round later in the week to talk about his bill.'

'What's there to talk about?'

'The size of it, mostly.'

'What are you saying, that he's willing to negotiate?'

'I don't know about willing, but he knows he's going to have to argue his corner. By the time we're done with him, he'll be begging for mercy. Ready to agree to a reasonable and honest settlement.'

'Strewth.'

'Indeed. Listen, have you any idea what he actually spent on materials for that roof?'

'Must have been a fair bit.'

'No, not at all. Think about it. He re-used the old tiles, replaced three or four timbers – which I'm willing to bet he half-inched from Algy's outbuildings – and bought a few bags of sand and cement to reassemble the chimney.'

'Plus a few bits of guttering,' I mumbled, my mouth full of egg.

'Right, and some lead flashing. A roll or two of felt. And what's the betting he ran them up to Algy's account?'

'Hmm – but they'd still be ours to pay for.'

'True. But even so, most of his costs would be for his time. Large chunks of which were spent supping tea and sitting on that log in the sunshine.'

'What about his hired hand? That youth with the tea-cosy on his head?'

'Hired hand? Don't make me laugh. That was his nephew. One of his nephews. There's dozens of them. They work for the price of a pint. If you call it work. What did he do? Run up and down the ladder with a bucket of cement every now and then?'

'So come on, Ann, give us the final reckoning.'

'I'm hoping he'll settle for about half his original bill. In fact, if you offer to pay him cash he'll bite your hand off. Mike, the man's desperate.'

'Because of the wedding?'

'Precisely.'

'So long as we aren't shafting him. I mean, don't forget I look on Soapy as a mate. We've been fishing together and that.'

'True, we need to be fair about it. But there's fair and then there's paying way over the odds. He's slippery as an eel, mate or no mate.' She refilled our coffee cups. 'Yes, slape as a fox, as my old uncle from Lincolnshire used to say.'

'Right then. When d'you say he's calling by?'

'This week. That's as far as he'd commit himself. You know what he's like. A man of impulse.'

'OK, then. I reckon we'll be ready for him.' I grabbed a slice of bread and mopped up the last of the bacon grease and squashed tomato from my plate. 'Cheers, love, that was excellent. Now then,' I said.

'Yes?'

'I've been thinking. It's been a while since we managed a night out together.'

'Too right it is. Must be about six weeks, I'd say. Have you got something in mind?'

'I have, as a matter of fact. I was thinking about a night out in York. Maybe pick you up from work, take a tour round town, do a bit of Christmas shopping, then go for a meal.'

'Are you offering to treat me?'

'I am.'

Ann looked at me, a shadow of suspicion on her face. 'This doesn't end up with us going to watch that shower at Bootham Crescent, does it?'

'If you mean my favourite football team that I've

supported man and boy for I don't know how many years – no. We're going shopping, having a meal, and I'll drive you home so you can have a glass of wine with your dinner. How's that for an offer?'

'You're on. And no changing your mind.' She got up from the table and started gathering the plates together. 'Just wait till they hear this at work. A man, offering to take me shopping.'

All that talk about the possible house purchase put the work situation out of mind for a while, but as I drove in that night I started to think about what I might be in for. As a copper, when you do something that your colleagues think is out of order – something odd or weird – you can expect what they politely call 'a bit of banter'. Or, if you want it put more bluntly, you can expect to have the piss taken, mercilessly.

The first thing I saw when I walked into the locker room was a giant inflatable alien, all in grey plastic except for its eyes, which were a nice shade of green. Its head was huge, its arms and legs long and thin, and it was dangling from the ceiling, right above my locker, spinning slowly around as the draught caught it.

'Good, innit?' Jayne had followed me into the men's locker room. She was reaching up and prodding it. 'And look, if you wiggle it the eyes move.' She grabbed one of its spindly legs and tugged at it, then scowled. 'Oh. Well, it's s'posed to, anyway.'

'That's the problem with cheap imported toys, Jayne. They don't always do what it says on the packet. Did you put this up?'

'Me? No, we just came into work and there it was.

Complete mystery. They're all over town. Haven't you seen 'em? Sarge reckons they must've come in on that spaceship you and Ed saw.'

'Nice try,' I said, 'but it wasn't a spaceship. If you look at the log it says "UFO". Unidentified Flying Object. Notice the word "unidentified".' I went to my locker, brushing the inflatable alien out of the way. 'Tell you what,' I added, 'why don't you fetch in some tinsel, and we can incorporate it into our Christmas decorations.'

It didn't stop there. Of course it didn't. When I got downstairs, there on the table in the parade room was a flashing blue globe, inside of which stood a little green man with the same eyes. Thommo was standing beside it, grinning from ear to ear. 'We could only afford the one,' he said. 'You and Ed'll have to scrap over it.'

'How d'you mean?'

'Tae see who gets to put it on top of the car, of course.' He reached over and pressed down on the thing, setting off a tinny alarm sound. 'Got it from the Alien Investigation Unit, Scotland Yard,' he said. 'If this doesn't put the fear of God into the criminal fraternity . . .'

'That's really thoughtful of you, Thommo.

'Aye. Thought you'd appreciate it.'

I went to check my tray for any new corries – or correspondence, to use the correct word – and found a copy of *UFO Magazine UK*. I peeled the bright pink Post-it note off the front cover and read, 'Mike and Ed – for reference. See article on how to identify UFOs'.

'Can't wait for briefing,' I said. 'I suppose they'll be sending out mock alerts, circulars, all sorts.'

Thommo looked at the note and laughed. 'Very probably, son. But it's all good clean fun, isn't it?'

'No worries, Jock. I can take it. Big broad shoulders, me.'

We went in to briefing and took our seats. Nobody said anything, but Jayne and Fordy had their hands over their faces. Neither of them looked at me.

'Right.' Chris Cocks had walked in and was ready to start. 'You've all had a bit of fun, but it ends here. OK? I think there's been enough banter about the UFO stuff. At the end of the day Mike and Ed saw what they saw. End of.' There was an uncomfortable silence. Everyone was looking at each other, trying to work out if Chris really meant what he was saying, but nobody dared push it. I noticed Thommo with his eyebrows raised questioningly and Jayne stifling a giggle behind her notebook. Ed had been sitting there stony-faced and silent. He leaned forward and said, 'Thanks very much, Sarge. It was no laughing matter, let me assure you.'

Chris then read out our postings for the shift. Ed was on his own, Jayne was out with Fordy, 'and finally, if Thommo and Mike could cover the rural UFO patrol . . .'

As we went out I grabbed Ed. 'Hey, we got off lightly, mate. They could have crucified us.' I couldn't tell whether he welcomed my comments, and I decided to let it go.

Out on the road, Thommo and I got off to a quiet start. Not much happening and very few people out and about. We steered clear of Golden Hill, concentrating on the area around Castle Howard. We'd had reports of lampers at work, but after half an hour or so driving around the edges of the woods and fields out there we'd found nothing.

'Ah well, we may as well enjoy the lull before the storm,' Thommo said. 'Another couple of weeks and your season of goodwill kicks off. Christmas parties – and the inevitable fights and domestics. Christmas shopping – and the shoplifters out in force. Christmas presents all stacked up under the tree – and the annual spate of burglaries.'

'What put you into such a positive, upbeat mood?'

'I am not a devotee of the festive period. We Scots prefer to save our energies for Hogmanay. Christmas – you can have it.'

'I look on the bright side, mate. If Christmas brings a little cheer into our drab lives, and draws out the best in people, I'm in favour of it.'

'You reckon it does that?'

We were dawdling, heading back towards town with no particular purpose in mind.

'Course it does. Take me,' I said. 'In a moment of festive madness I promised to take Ann Christmas shopping.'

'Och, you sure those little green men didnae brainwash you the other night?'

'Thommo, you are talking to an old-fashioned romantic, a man who knows how to put a smile on a woman's face. And it ain't what you're thinking. It's quite simple, really. Just treat 'em to a night out now and again.'

'But shopping, mon? In York? At Christmas time?' He shuddered. 'That is a bridge too far.'

'Yeah well, you may have a point there. Tell you the truth, I made the offer without thinking it through.'

'There you go, see! And now the seeds of doubt are

starting to grow. Still, we've all done things on a tidal wave of passion . . . And there's no going back, I suppose?'

'Nope. My word is my bond, matey.'

'Ah see. Mind, the good thing about York is, there's always something going on. Music, street theatre, the floodlit walls . . .'

'Designed to keep the Scots out, Thommo. Along with other marauders and savages.'

'And a lamentable failure, I might add, if the average Saturday night is anything to go by.'

'Aye, the place is crawling with your fellow countrymen. They ought to check the statute books if you ask me. They had a law once where it was perfectly legal to kill a Scotsman within the city walls. In fact I'm not sure it's ever been repealed.'

'I believe it's still extant, laddie – so long as it's with a bow and arrow, am I right?'

Before I could answer Phil was on the radio. '*Malton CCTV to control and all units. The alarm's just gone off at Yates's in Castlegate. I've got what looks like two youths – pushing a quad-bike onto a flat-bed trailer. All on CCTV. Stand by for description and direction of travel.*'

'I don't believe this,' I said as I put my foot down and headed towards town. 'Right under the cameras and they have the gall to . . .' We were already speeding over the bypass. '1015 to control, show me and Thommo en route. Just approaching town on the Castle Howard road.'

'OK, Mike. *We have Chris leaving the station now in the van. Malton CCTV to units. The quad-bike's on the trailer, pulled by – looks like a Cavalier, making its way down towards County Bridge. Both youths wearing dark-coloured hooded tops and dark trousers. Unable to get a vehicle index on either the car or trailer.'*

As we raced down the hill towards the red light we had to brake sharply to let Jayne and Fordy out from Wheelgate. We approached Yates's right on their tail. The window had completely gone and the pavement was covered with broken glass.

'Malton CCTV to all units. Cavalier and trailer now heading into Commercial Street, towards the motorbike shop. Stand by . . . camera that covers Commercial Street is not responding . . . vehicle is now out of vision.'

'Typical, just when you need the camera.' I turned onto County Bridge. 'D'you know, I told Ed just the other night.'

'Told him what?'

'That that quad-bike was a sitting duck.'

We bumped over the railway crossing hard on Fordy's tail, and swung left past the petrol station.

'Shit.' We were arriving at the mini roundabout outside the shuttered-up motorbike shop – and, just as we had been for that earlier job, we were left to guess which direction our friends had taken.

Fordy took the right turn and shouted over the radio. 'We're heading down the Beverley road; will you take the A64, over?'

'All received, Fordy.'

Within a minute or two we'd passed the bacon factory and were on the A64, speeding towards Scarborough looking for any tail-lights in the distance. Nothing. We carried on through Rillington, and sped towards the Heslertons. By now I was calculating the time over distance equation. 'If they went this way, Jock, we'd have caught them by now.' I pulled over at West Heslerton crossroads and banged on the steering wheel. 'Sod it,' I said.

'What you doing, laddie?'

'Thommo,' I said, 'times like this I could weep, I really could. I mean, that's twice this week CCTV's picked up smash-and-grabs, and twice we've lost them. The chances of that happening! It's not as if we get this sort of thing on a weekly basis, is it? Once a year, if that. And we blow it.'

'D'you think it's the same youths?'

'Don't know, but two smash-and-grabs in the same week? You'd think so.'

'So what's your plan?'

I didn't answer for a moment or two. I was thinking. Something at the back of my mind was nagging away at me. 'Thommo,' I said, 'have you been following the briefings that Amanda puts out?'

'I've flicked through them. Cannae say I remember anything special.'

'I can. And I'm remembering something that just might help us out here.' I put the car in gear and set off on the road towards the wold tops.

'Well? Don't keep me guessing.'

'OK, last week, or maybe the week before, she reported a very active criminal from Leeds; does burglaries, vehicle theft, that sort of thing. Apparently he's travelling across quite regularly to see his ex-wife in Duggleby. Information has it that she doesn't want owt to do with him, but she still lets him stay over now and then to see his kids.'

'Go on.'

'It's a bit of a shot in the dark. But you think. Those lads – they've set off this way after both jobs.'

'Possibly.'

'Probably. Anyway, they could've gone anywhere: this way, or to York, or Humberside, but they chose this way – we think. So why not Duggleby? I mean, if it is this fellow from Amanda's report, it'd be the perfect place for him to hide out.'

Thommo exhaled loudly. 'It's a hell of a long shot. But worth a look. There can't be more than a couple of dozen houses at Duggleby.'

'You exaggerate. But in any case, shouldn't take long to check them out.'

'Aye – but for what?'

'For a Cavalier, my friend, for a Cavalier.'

Thommo got on the radio and established that Fordy and Jayne had drawn a blank. Then he let them and control know we were heading out towards Duggleby and the Luttons area. Fordy and Jayne would back us up.

I've said it before, and I'll say it again. You need to be lucky in this game, and I was born lucky. I cut across the wold tops towards West Lutton. The road is narrow and there are a couple of right-angle bends, but at that time of night it was deserted, and I was making good speed when Thommo turned around and shouted, 'Whoa! What was that? Back up, laddie, back up.'

I stood on the brakes.

'Something in the field back there.'

'What was it?' I was reversing at speed. Thommo had

the window down and was sweeping the beam of his Dragon Light across a field of winter barley.

'How did we miss those?' The planting was scarred by two dark, parallel gouges.

'Look! Right there. See the reflector?'

We were out of the car now. The hedge along the road-side was sparse and low and we were able to step right into the field.

'Well, well, well.'

There was a trailer and, several yards away, on its side, the shiny new quad-bike.

'1015 to control, we've found the trailer and quad-bike overturned in a field. It's on the back road about a mile and a half out of West Lutton. No sign of any vehicle. Looks like they've lost it on the bend.' Thommo was training the Dragon Light on the trailer so that I could read out the registration number.

'They can't be too far ahead,' I said. We'd left the trailer and quad and were speeding towards the Luttons. We'd gone less than a mile when Brian in control came on. *The trailer was reported as stolen from just outside Leeds two weeks ago. I've got the double-crewed Eastfield car in the area just approaching Foxholes on the back roads. No sightings past them.*

'Thanks,' I said. 'Can you send them towards us via Butterwick and get them to hold there and keep obs?'

All received.

It took us no more than three or four minutes to get to Duggleby and start checking in driveways, looking for any sign of life – or of an old Cavalier. But the village was dead, just the odd security light coming on as we cruised by. And no sign of the car. Once we'd located the ex-wife's place I parked out of sight and we crept around the back to see if there were any lights on or any signs of life. But there was nothing, and the garage was empty. We returned to the car, pretty dejected. Should we wake up the occupants? It seemed pointless. There were no obvious signs that the youth from Leeds was about, and it was still a long shot that it was him we were looking for anyway.

'Right,' I said. 'Sod this. Let's try West Lutton.'

'Why West Lutton, laddie? Am I missing something here?'

'Well Thommo, this is my beat, we're in the middle of nowhere and there's only one other person that I know near here who might be involved. He's a young lad, not the sort to go out and do it on his own, but he's easily led. If he's got involved with this lad from Leeds then he's daft enough to go along with this sort of job.'

'Bloody hell Pannett, ye don't half like going out on a limb.'

'Thommo, what do you think I do all day? When I'm out and about supping tea, matey, I'm absorbing intelligence. All day, every day. Taking it in, drip-feeding the memory-bank.'

We came into West Lutton nice and slowly, lights dipped, and made our way towards a row of cottages. The one I wanted was one of a pair, ex-council.

'Here we go.' At the side of the house was a Cavalier, eight or nine years old, parked nose first to reveal a towbar. I glanced up at the house. There was one light on, bathroom or landing by the look of it. We drove on twenty or thirty yards before pulling up. I got on the radio to control and explained the situation to them, then we got out and walked up the short drive. I squeezed my way along the side of the car to place my hand on the bonnet.

'Re-sult!' I whispered. It was warm. Hot, in fact.

'Are ye wanting to go in?' Thommo was there beside me, looking at the house.

'Let's wait for backup, shall we?'

'Looks like they're here already.'

It wasn't the Eastfield unit, but Jayne and Fordy. 'Right,' I said, keeping my voice low, 'you two watch the rear and side of the house in case me-laddo decides to make a run for it. We're going to knock on the door and find out what's what.'

While Thommo updated control I walked up to the door, lifted the metal knocker and gave it a sharp rat-a-tat. Nothing. I banged on it with my fist, really hammered it. A light went on in an upstairs window. I saw the curtain being tugged to one side, and a head appeared. A woman, maybe fifty, opened the window. 'What's going on? What do you want?'

'North Yorkshire police, madam. I'd like you to come down and have a word. Is Sam in?'

'He's asleep. What you want him for?'

'Who are you, his mother?'

'Aye, what you want him for? What's he been up to?'

'Just want to clear something up, that's all.'

'Hang about. I'll go and wake him.'

A moment or two later she appeared at the door with the lad, red-faced and stretching as he forced a yawn.

'Got you out of bed, did we?' I said.

'Aye, been asleep for hours, like. What's the problem?'

I glanced down at his legs. 'You always sleep in your jeans?'

'Nah – I just fell asleep, like.'

'Been out, have you?'

'No,' he mumbled. 'No.'

''Cos this car's been used. The engine's still hot, lad.'

Before he could answer his mother turned on him. 'You been tekkin' our car again? 'Cos if you have, you tell 'em, right now.'

As I waited for an answer the lad's father appeared from upstairs. 'What's all this, then? Why're we being woken up this time of night?'

'We're wanting to know who took your car out, and brought it back not many minutes ago.'

'Well, it ain't me and ain't her . . . we bin in bed since eleven.' He turned to look at the lad, who shuffled awkwardly on his bare feet.

'Well, aye, I did tek it out for a ride, like, but—'

His Dad cut in. 'Officers, can you tell us exactly what's going on?'

'I can, sir. A vehicle matching the one on your drive has been involved in the theft of a quad-bike in Malton. We've found the bike and trailer just down the road.'

'Bloody hell.' He moved to one side to make room and said, 'I think you'd better come in.' Then he turned to the lad Sam and said, 'What the bloody hell have you been doing now?'

'Nowt Dad, honest.'

His mother erupted. 'Haven't I been telling him and telling him?' she said. 'And tried to keep him in? It's that' – she raised her hand to point in the general direction of Duggleby – 'that other lad – him from over yonder. He'll be behind this. They've been meddling with each other for long enough.' She turned to her son. 'You daft . . .' and then dried up as suddenly as she'd started, her hand over her eyes.

Thommo had been back to the car for some evidence bags. 'Right,' I said, addressing the father and mother, 'I'd like to search your son's room. Is that all right?'

'Yes, go on, go right up.' The mother was fighting back tears. 'We try our best, you know. But he's just so stupid at times.'

'Right Sam, lead the way,' I said.

I followed Thommo and Sam up the stairs, almost tripping over the family cat in the process. 'This it?' I asked, as the lad's father followed us onto the landing.

'Aye, on yer left there.'

On the bedroom floor was a dark hooded fleece lying in a heap, and a jacket. I held the fleece up and nudged Thommo. 'See that?' I whispered. Little bits of broken glass were sparkling in the light. I put some into one of the evidence bags. There was no point beating about the bush. 'Right Sam, you're under arrest on suspicion of burglary.'

As I cautioned him his mother began to sob. His father was shouting at him. 'Bloody burglary? That's the final straw, Sam. What the hell are you trying to do to us, eh?'

There was nothing else of any significance in the bedroom, but before we went back downstairs we seized the rest of the clothing that he'd been wearing, including his trainers. It could all be helpful for forensics.

Downstairs we explained to the lad's parents that we were taking him to Malton Police Station. Fordy had come in and was looking around the living room. 'And I'm afraid we'll be taking the car too,' I said. 'It's been used in the commission of a crime. We need to have it examined by our scene of crime officer.'

'Well, what we – what we gonna do for transport? I've a hospital appointment tomorrow.' The mother was trembling. Her husband put his arm round her.

'I'm sorry,' I said, 'but we've no choice. Can you get a lift off a friend, or a taxi?'

'Don't worry,' her husband said. He seemed resigned to it all. 'We'll sort something out.'

'Whose name is it in?' I asked him. 'Who's the registered owner?'

'That's me,' he said.

'We'll let you know when we're done and you can come and get it back. I'm sorry,' I added. You do sympathise with people like that, innocent people whose kids have gone off the rails and landed them in trouble – not to say shamed them. People tend to think that the only victim of a burglary, for example, is the property owner – end of story. But it extends further than that. This lad had traumatised his parents. In their own way, they were victims of his crime as well.

Thommo had taken the lad out to the car and was on the radio to control to arrange for the removal unit to collect the Cavalier. Just as I was about to follow, Fordy produced another find. 'Behind the settee,' he said, holding up a nice new leather motorcycle jacket.

'Whose is this?' I asked.

'That's Sam's,' the mother said.

'Oh, is it? When did he get it? Do you know?'

'Just a couple of weeks back, as far as I remember. He hasn't stolen it, has he?'

'I'm afraid to say I think he has.' I said. 'We're going to have to seize it as well, as possible evidence.'

We took Sam back to Malton. At the station he didn't ask for a solicitor, and even though there was only an hour or so of the shift to run we were able to get his interview completed. He didn't have a lot to say for himself.

'Can you tell us about this jacket?' He made no comment.

'So where have you been tonight?' No comment.

Thommo then produced the exhibit bag. 'See this hoodie?'

'Aye.'

'It's yours, is it?'

'Yeah. What of it?'

'I wondered if you could explain what those fragments are. They look like glass to me. Any idea where they came from?'

No comment.

'Tell you what,' I said, 'let's get it matched up with some other fragments we have, from that window that was smashed in tonight.'

I was taken aback by what happened next. The lad slumped back in his chair and said, 'Fair enough, like. It's down to me, down to me.'

He then confessed to the Yates's break-in. But no way was he going to give us the names of his accomplice or accomplices. No way at all. And as for the stolen biker jacket, he refused to give any explanation for that. We were unable to prove that he'd actually stolen it from the shop, so he was charged with handling stolen goods. He could have helped his cause at court by naming the others involved, and he was aware of that fact, but he refused to co-operate any further. Honour among thieves, I suppose you'd call it.

So we hadn't managed to locate the youth from Leeds, let alone pin anything on him. After we'd arrested Sam, Fordy and Jayne had gone round and searched the house, but the ex-wife was adamant that he hadn't been there that night and the search had proved fruitless. He was later located in Leeds a few days later, brought to Malton and questioned. But he said nothing, and with no forensics or other evidence to tie him in, that was that.

We only recovered one of the stolen biker jackets, so in that sense we'd failed. Still, the stolen quad-bike and trailer had been recovered. As far as I was concerned it was a draw. Sometimes that's how it is. I'll never know if young Sam did the job at the bike shop – he might have, or he may after all have just been given the jacket, to get him to do the quad-bike job. Policing is like that. Things aren't always nicely wrapped up like they are on the telly. But then that, as we say, is just the job.

Chapter 12

Penny

'It's a big 'un, isn't it?'

Walt didn't answer me. He just stood there with his old dog Tess by his side and gazed admiringly at the turkey. I hardly recognised it from the thing we'd chased back inside earlier in the autumn. It was a fair size then, but it had been piling on the pounds, and now, with its brindled feathers all puffed out, it looked absolutely huge. Plump, sleek and almost as proud as its owner. And then, as I approached the wire fence, it flared out its magnificent tail.

'By heck!' I said. 'He is a handsome beast, isn't he? Looks like one of them Indian chiefs with all those feathers. Wouldn't mind a few of those myself, cold day like this.' I pulled my scarf out of my pocket and wrapped it round my neck. Winter had really kicked in the last week or two.

'Aye, he hasn't done badly.' Walter beamed with pride. He looked like a man who'd lost a pound and found a tenner. Cold as it was – and with the sun going down you could feel another sharp frost coming on – he was a picture of health. He stood there with his hands in his trouser pockets, cheeks all rosy, a broad smile on his face, and I could've sworn I saw the slightest hint of a paunch under his donkey-jacket. 'Aye,' he said, 'he's been a good old bod. Eats everything I put out for him. A proper little gobbler,' he added, then looked at me to see whether I appreciated the joke.

'I can see he likes his grub. What you feeding it on?'

Walter pushed his hat back and scratched his forehead. 'Bits and bats, like,' he said, kicking the ice off a frozen puddle with the toe of his wellington boot. 'Pellets . . . scraps . . . the usual going-on.'

There was no point pushing it. If he didn't have a secret recipe he wasn't going to admit it. And if he did he wouldn't be parting with it.

'All I can say is, when the time comes I just hope he fits in that oven of yours.'

'Don't you worry, lad. If I have to shave a few sharp edges off him there'll be no shortage of takers. Will there, old girl?' He leant down and tousled Tess's head, then turned to make his way back towards the house. 'You coming in for a minute?'

Through the skeleton outlines of the trees I could see the sun sinking into the murky horizon, painting the streaks of cloud and jet trails a pale red. I rubbed my hands together and shivered. 'Course I am.' I wasn't going to stop out there any longer than necessary. I followed him into the kitchen and warmed myself on the stove. The old kettle was simmering away on the hotplate, the brown china pot beside it. As Walter spooned out the tea he turned and looked me up and down. 'Not in uniform, eh. I suppose you're working under cover, are you?'

'Don't be daft,' I said. 'This is my day off.'

'Oh, and you've nowt to do, eh?'

'I've plenty on, Walt. Just thought it was a while since I'd been round. Old bugger like you, you need checking on. No, I've been busy with the chainsaw most of the day, cutting logs.'

'Best thing to burn, wood,' he said. 'My old dad always said the best thing about logs is you get warm twice over.'

'I know,' I answered. 'Once when you're cutting 'em and then again when you burn 'em.' I watched as he emptied the kettle into the pot. 'By the way, I've been meaning to ask you, how did Muriel and them get on when they went to London?'

'You mean for that there march on Whitehall?'

'Yeah. You did say she was going, didn't you?'

Walt sniffed and handed me the pot. 'Here – put this on t'table. And help yourself to them biscuits.'

'Cheers, mate. So what did she have to say about it?'

'She said it was a good turnout, and it showed them townies what us country folk think of their daft ideas.'

'I saw there was a good turnout. What about the bother we saw on the telly?'

'She said it were a lot of fuss about not very much.'

'What, the trouble with my old lot? The TSG? I didn't like the look of it. It didn't sit well with me.'

'She reckoned it were no more than a spot of bother. Then when you read the papers you'd think it was World War Three.'

'So she steered clear of the troublemakers, did she?'

'If you want my opinion, I reckon they steered clear of her. She isn't a lass to tangle with.'

'I can well believe it,' I said. Walt got up to check on something he had simmering in his oven. He pulled out a big brown earthenware pot and lifted the lid.

'What's that?' I asked.

'Braised haunch of venison, lad. Shot in them woods up on t'Brow, barely a mile from here.' He took a long-handled spoon and sipped delicately at the gravy, closing his eyes as he savoured it.

'You got company tonight then?'

'I may have.' It was a typical Walter answer. He leaves you in no doubt when he isn't taking questions. As if to underline the point, he shoved the pot back and slammed the oven door on it.

I let the matter drop and glanced around the kitchen. I went over to the dresser where he had a pile of Christmas cards. 'Hell,' I said, 'you're keen. I haven't even bought mine yet. Creeps up on you, doesn't it, this festive-season malarkey.'

'Lot of blooming fuss,' he said. 'And expense if you're not careful.' He picked up the pile and sat down at the table across from me with a pair of scissors, a roll of Sellotape and a sheet of white card.

'What you doing?'

'Saving money, lad.' He started snipping pieces out of the Christmas cards. 'These are last year's,' he said. 'What people sent me.'

'You surely don't send them back out, do you?'

'Aye, just cut out where they've signed 'em, like, or stick a blank bit over it.'

'Well!' I said. 'It's no wonder people think Yorkshiremen have deep pockets.'

'Good housekeeping,' he replied. 'Like fattening your own turkey. Besides, I'm trying to reduce me environmental footprint, d'you see?'

'And damping down the economy at the same time, matey. If everyone were like you, why, half the shops would be out of business. Just make sure you shuffle them around though.'

'How d'you mean?'

'Don't send people the same card they sent you, is what I mean. Anyway, when you going to – you know, deal with Mr Gobbler out there?'

'Won't be long now,' Walt said. Then he leaned back in his seat and shoved his cap to the back of his head. 'Although, d'you know, I reckon shall miss him. I've tekken a lot of pride in that bird.'

'Aye, but that won't stop you eating him, will it?'

'Course not.' He carried on snipping. 'It has to be done, lad. We don't feed our livestock for the love of 'em, do we now?'

I glanced at Tess, plump as a little porker and curled up next to the stove. 'Not in every case,' I said.

We chatted on until we'd drained the pot and cleaned out the biscuit tin. I was just thinking I ought to be getting back home when my mobile rang.

'Hello?'

'Mike, it's Fordy here – Gary. Sorry to catch you off duty, like, but . . .'

'What is it, mate? Something on your mind?'

'There's been an armed robbery over at Hovingham. At the post office. And I think the people are friends of yours.'

'Anybody hurt?'

'No, thank God. But one of the women, she works in the shop—'

'Not Penny? The gamekeeper's wife?'

'That's her. Lives in a little cottage just off the main street?'

'What's happened, mate? She all right?'

'She's at home now. But the intruders tied her up. She's pretty badly shaken.'

I was on my feet, putting the phone down for a moment while I squirmed into my coat. 'Walt, mate, I've got to go. Bit of a crisis. There's been a robbery at the post office over at Hovingham. Yeah, carry on, Fordy. Where you calling from, anyway? Are you dealing?'

'Yeah. It was me and Jayne got the call. And Cocksy's come out as backup. We're waiting for the SOCO, and the CID.'

'I suppose the robbing bastards have got away, have they?'

'Yeah, we never got the call till a customer came in. She untied them – the women in the shop, I mean.'

'Right,' I said. 'I'll be over soon as I can. Don't worry, I shan't interfere, but I want to see how Penny is – and we'll need to speak with Rich. He there yet?'

'That's the point, Mike. He hasn't shown. She said he was on a shoot, out of mobile range, somewhere up on the moors.'

'Well, listen, if he comes back before I get there just be careful how you handle the lad. He will not be impressed when he hears that his wife's been hurt. Not impressed at all.' I gave Walt a wave and was out the door, making my way across the darkened yard to the car.

It took me the best part of half an hour to get through town. First I had to clear the frost off my windscreen, then once I got on the road I didn't dare push it. The thermometer on my dashboard was showing minus three degrees and there was every chance of black ice on the roads. In town I ran into the early-evening traffic, and of course Sod's Law said the railway crossing barriers had to come down right in front of me. After that, though, it was pretty much plain sailing.

I saw the blue flashing lights before I'd even turned the corner into the main street at Hovingham. Fordy was outside the shop, with two or three villagers standing talking to him. I pulled up beside him, got out and took him to one side.

'Go on, then. Tell us the tale.'

'Nasty business. There were three of them, they reckon, in balaclavas. Just came bursting in. Threw the staff to the floor, then tied them up and threatened 'em. One of them had a sodding great rock to break the safety glass. It's still in there. And one of them was brandishing a meat cleaver.'

'Hell-fire. What did they get away with?'

'Quite a bit, they reckon. They do a lot of business on pension day.'

'Got anything to go on?'

'Not really. We've got brief descriptions of the suspects circulated. We're going to be doing house to house, see if we can get anything else – like a description of their vehicle.'

I nodded towards the shop. 'So is everything in hand?' I said.

'Yeah. The CID and SOCO's in there now.'

'What about Rich? He shown up yet?'

'You mean the woman's husband, the gamekeeper?'

'Yes.'

'Not that I'm aware of. Don't even know what he looks like'

'You'd spot him OK. Drives a Land Rover? Fore-and-aft cap? Green wellies?'

Fordy shook his head. 'No. Unless he's at home. Jayne's there, with Penny, she's really shaken up.'

'Right, I'll go and have a word.' I turned the car round and splashed through the little beck, skidding slightly on the icy ramp as I got to the other side, then turned up the darkened lane to the house.

'You home?' I shouted, opening the side door and walking in through the utility room.

'Mike? Come in.' Penny's voice sounded subdued, distant. I found her in the sitting room, sitting in the easy chair with a duvet wrapped round her shoulders, her hands clasping a steaming mug. Jayne was beside her, squatting on a little stool with her notebook in her hand. The fire in the grate looked more dead than alive.

'Now then,' I said, 'what happened to you?'

Jayne looked up at me as Penny dabbed at her eyes with a tissue. Her nose was all red and her hand was shaking.

'Sorry,' I said, 'I dare say you've told Jayne here all about it.' I reached out and felt her hand. 'You're freezing half to death, girl. Here.' I went to the fire and gave it a good poking, then put some fresh coal on and opened the damper. 'That should help. You got any spot heaters about the place?'

She pointed to the door. 'Under the stairs. Oh, thanks for coming by, Mike.'

I fetched an electric heater through. Just as I was plugging it in I heard a vehicle draw up outside.

'Here he is at last,' Penny said. 'I was starting to worry.'

I hurried outside and met Rich at the front gate.

'Mike,' he said. 'Wasn't expecting you, mate.' He grinned and held up a brace of pheasants. 'You should've said. Could've got you some birds. They killed about fifty-odd.' In his other hand he had his shotgun.

'So you haven't seen the police cars out on the main road?'

'Police cars? No, I've just come down through t'woods.' He frowned, and swung the door of the Land Rover shut. 'What's been happening?'

'Look, the first thing to tell you is, Penny's all right. She's in the house. Really shaken up, but . . .'

'Penny?' He was already brushing past me, in through the gate and up the path to the door. 'What the bloody hell's happened to her?'

I hurried after him. 'There's been a robbery at the shop. But look, it's all right. Nobody's been seriously hurt. It's all under control now.'

He was in the house, not even bothering to kick his muddy boots off. 'Pen, love. What happened? What they done to you?'

She got as far as, 'Oh Rich,' before she started sobbing into her hands.

Rich dropped the pheasants, propped the gun against the mantelpiece and fell to his knees, comforting her. Then he turned to me, his eyes narrowed.

'C'mon, Mike. What they done?'

'You need to ask Jayne here. I've only got the barest details. I got a call off duty and came straight over.'

He stood up, and turned to Jayne. 'Well, what's happened?'

'Briefly,' she said, 'it seems that three armed robbers entered the shop and threatened the staff including your wife. Then they—'

'Armed? Why, the . . . bastards.'

Penny cut in, her eyes full of tears, her lips trembling. 'They just came bursting in. They had masks on. Sort of bags over their heads. I thought they had a gun at first but it was a meat cleaver. Then they rammed this rock through the glass. It all happened so quick. They made us lie down, then they tied us up.' She paused and rubbed her wrists. 'They – they gagged us. I could hardly get my breath. I thought they meant to kill us.' She winced as she spoke and put her hand to her side.

'What is it, love?' Rich's face was creased with worry.

'I don't know. My side really hurts where he held me down. Hurts every time I breathe.'

Rich turned to Jayne. 'You hear that? We need to go and find these bastards, before they kill someone. Where are they? And why aren't we out there chasing after 'em?'

'Rich,' I said, 'just hang on a minute. Penny, have you been checked over? Shall we get an ambulance?'

'No, no Mike. Like I said to Jayne, I don't want any fuss.'

'Well, I think it's best if you get checked over just in case. Now listen, Rich, every man and his dog are on the case. There's plenty of officers out there and it's been circulated across borders.'

Rich turned to me. 'What about you and me, Mike? We know our way around. We could join in the search.'

'Rich, I think we should leave it to the officers searching.'

'I've gone after poachers before now and I don't see why I shouldn't get after this bloody lot. I'm not afraid, cleaver or no bloody cleaver.' He grabbed the gun and went through into the hallway. I followed him. He pulled a key from his trouser pocket and opened the cabinet, grabbing a box of cartridges.

'No.' I looked him right in the eye as I reached forward, grabbed the ammunition with one hand, and closed the door with the other. 'No, Rich. I know exactly how you feel, but this isn't the way. I want to catch 'em just as much as you do, trust me. But you're going to stay here and sort that lass of yours out. She needs to get to hospital and she needs you with her. You can see how badly shaken she is. Seeing you like this – it'll only make her worse.'

For a moment I thought he was going to carry on arguing. It's not something you relish, having to restrain a friend. We both had our hands on the door, me pushing, him pulling. Then he sighed and let go.

'OK,' he said. 'But I'm telling you, if those buggers show their faces round here again . . .'

'Rich, I know how you feel.'

'No you don't, Mike. They've just threatened my missus with a bloody cleaver and probably busted her rib. You telling me you know what that feels like?'

'OK, Rich. But just be thankful Penny hasn't been badly hurt, OK? Just try to stay calm. None of the cops round here will like this. Trust me, they'll be doing their damnedest to catch whoever's responsible.'

He was still reluctant. 'All right then, but I'm telling

you, the minute they set foot round 'ere again I'll give 'em both bloody barrels.'

'Yeah, and go to prison for the rest of your life! Come on.' I lowered my voice. I didn't want Jayne hearing any of this. 'Listen, there's no reason why they'd come anywhere near you, or your home. So let's not have any of that talk, OK?'

'Oh hell, Mike.' I could see the tears welling up in his eyes. 'I just feel so bloody useless. When she needed me – I mean, where the hell was I?'

'Look, this isn't the sort of thing that happens round here, is it? Eh? How were you to know? We need to concentrate on getting your Penny to hospital. Get her ribs checked.'

'Right, well, I've got all I need for now.' Jayne had come through into the hallway. 'I've got the best descriptions I can. CID said they'll be round to take her statement later. If we can just get Penny checked over then I think I'll be more use out there with the others.'

'Aye, go on, me and Rich'll sort her out. If she won't have an ambulance, one of us'll run her to Malton hospital,' I said. 'I'll see you out. Back in a minute, Rich.' I followed Jayne outside and down the front path.

She paused at the gate and glanced back at the house. 'He won't do anything stupid, will he?' she said.

'Don't worry. He'll calm down. But listen, keep us posted, OK? You've got my mobile number, haven't you?'

'Yeah.'

'See you later, Jayne.'

Back inside Rich was looking a little bit calmer, but he still had his coat on. He was standing there, itching to get out and do something. 'Come on,' he said, 'I tell you what,

I'll tek Pen to hospital, you can tek me Landy and have a scout around the estate – they could just be lying low, Mike. And listen, tek that shotgun with you just in case.'

'As much as I would like to Rich, I can't do that. Apart from anything else the place is crawling with armed response officers. Just leave it to our lot. You get Penny off to Malton.'

'Aye, I suppose you know best.'

'Rich, trust me. They'll be well away by now. I very much doubt they'll be from around here, so I can't see them hiding out in this neck of the woods. They'll be scuttling back to – to whatever rock they crawled out from under.'

He paused, took out a cigarette and lit it. 'I suppose you're right. But why do they need to attack defenceless women like that? Bloody cowards, the lot of 'em – by God, if I ever lay hands on them . . .' He threw the match into the fire, which was now blazing nicely.

'I know, I know. I'd probably be the same if I was in your shoes. Look, is there anything you want me to do? Do you want me to drive you through to Malton?'

'No, no, Mike. We can manage.'

'In that case I'll be off.'

'Aye, you get on your way – but listen, whatever you hear, you let me know, will you?'

'Course I will, mate.'

Outside I lit up a cigarette and stood in the lane for a few moments. After the heat of the sitting room the icy-cold air was welcome and refreshing. There was no moon, but the sky was clear and studded with a million stars. A man was making his way towards me with a dog on a lead. 'Nasty business at the shop,' he said, without looking up.

'Aye. You wouldn't expect it in a place like this, would you?'

'It can happen anywhere these days,' he said, as he walked on by. 'They've got the upper hand, these crooks. We need more policemen on the beat. Stiffer sentences.'

I didn't answer, and he turned the corner and disappeared.

Back outside the shop Fordy was talking with the scene of crime officer. Stuart had just about finished and was packing his evidence bags and equipment into his car. As he prepared to leave I got a few more details from Fordy. It seemed the gang had struck just as it was getting dark, a little after four. They'd used the rock to smash through into the post-office kiosk.

'So where was the cash?' I asked.

'In the till.'

'No safe?'

He shook his head. 'They said they'd talked about getting one, but the guy who owns the place wasn't sure it was worth it.'

'This is the trouble in these village shops. You have to wonder, though. I mean, will they try it again if it's that easy?'

Fordy shrugged. 'Who knows?'

'Who knows indeed. But I tell you what, I'm going to make sure all the shopkeepers on my beat are well aware of what's happened, and get them to sort themselves out, sharpish. Anyway,' I said, 'I'm away home.'

The frustrating part of police work is that you can get

deeply involved in a case like that, then have to go home with things still unresolved. It's like if you leave a book on a train when you're halfway through it, or have to walk out in the middle of a film – you can't wait to find out what happened. Except that half the time, for us, there is no outcome, no real conclusion. In this case, of course, I wasn't actually involved in any official capacity, but Rich and Penny were people I'd come to regard as friends. Ann and I had been for a pint and a meal at the Malt Shovel with them more than once. So of course I wanted to know how the investigations were proceeding – and how Penny was recovering. The next day then, back at work, I made a point of getting across to Hovingham as soon as I could find time.

I was able to take one piece of news, which I'd got from Fordy. He came bounding up to me as I was signing in to tell me they'd found a bundle of ten-pound notes, right under the wheels of the SOCO's car after he drove off. Four hundred quid's worth. That brought a wry smile to Penny's face when I told her. 'Aye,' I said, 'just sitting there in the gutter. Squashed into a puddle and frozen solid. They had to use a garden trowel to dig it out. The useless sods must have dropped it as they made off.'

It was only a moment of levity. Rich was still fuming about the whole business. The fact that Penny had been found to have a cracked rib didn't help. I tried to steer away from the subject. 'By the way,' I said, 'I never did hear – how did you go on in London, on the demo?'

'Oh, that.' Rich lit a cigarette and settled back in his chair.

'We really enjoyed it, didn't we?' Penny said. 'It had a

real sense of community. You felt you were part of something.'

'Aye, it was a strange sensation.' Rich actually allowed himself a shadow of a smile as he remembered. 'There we were in t'middle of London and all you could hear was hunting horns. It was like – like a Mexican wave coming closer and closer to us, louder and louder.'

'And then it went past and sort of faded,' Penny added.

'Aye, all down Horse Guards Parade. It was like a train coming towards you and rattling off into t'distance. And all the soldiers were at their windows waving at us. It was bloody marvellous – and do you know, they reckoned afterwards they never had a single scrap of litter to pick up.'

'At least we showed them how country folk are,' Penny said. 'That we know how to conduct ourselves. We never caused a spot of bother.'

I glanced at Penny. She'd said she was already feeling a little better, physically – and she certainly looked perkier – but there was no way she would be ready to return to work for a while yet. As it happened, the post-office side of the shop had been closed down anyway while a safe was installed. But in any case, she said, the idea of going back filled her with dread. When someone's been manhandled by an armed robber – tied up, assaulted, shouted at, threatened – well, your personal space has been violated. More than that, your familiar surroundings, ones in which you've been comfortable, be it the home or the workplace, suddenly feel unsafe; tainted, you might say. As for Rich, he was still fuming, but he was about to go off on a prearranged visit to an estate in the Midlands. Penny's sister would come over to help out and keep her company at night because, not surprisingly, she didn't want to be around the place on her own.

I had little to do with the enquiries that followed. As with any armed robbery, the CID took over the investigation, so our involvement as beat officers was limited, and we would only hear indirectly or at briefings about the later developments. Among them was the discovery of the vehicle believed to have been used in the robbery. It had been found abandoned and burned out. I found myself speculating as to who might have been involved. I was convinced it wouldn't be locals, so where had they come from? York? Leeds? Or maybe the north. Of one thing I was pretty sure: this was not the work of your run-of-the-mill rural villain. Maybe, I suggested to Des the CID man, they were from Middlesbrough way. 'And what makes you think that?' he asked.

'Well, there's quite a few travel down from there to work at the bacon factory. They travel via Stokesley on that B road, down Bilsdale. And you ask at the shop there – they often call in for cigarettes or a paper on their way to and fro. And at the bakery. They stop there for their pack-up, quite a few of them.'

Des agreed it was a strong possibility, that they were looking at all options along with other similar crimes in neighbouring forces that might be linked. But in the end, it grieves me to admit, we never got to the bottom of this one. I kept hoping something would break, but there was nothing. What did happen was that the post-office facility in the Hovingham shop closed down a few months later. Somebody had decided that the measures required to make it secure were going to be too expensive, and that it just wasn't worth the hassle any more. They say crime doesn't pay – but it certainly costs a lot.

Still, there was, as ever, plenty to keep me on my toes, at work and at home. Because that's another thing about police work – the way you can find yourself one minute dealing with serious and complex crimes, the next helping some little old lady across the road. It was just the luck of the draw that had taken me from that double fatal on Golden Hill to a hostage situation on the same day that August Bank Holiday weekend. It could just as easily have been a couple of kids scrumping apples, or some equally lightweight case; or, indeed, another accident. It all depends where the wheel of fortune stops spinning, as Thommo liked to say. That's where you can get a real emotional battering – when you break off from an emergency, or some sort of violent confrontation, and go straight to the next call without having had time to unscramble your mind, to rid your memory of the gruesome sights that are part and parcel of our job. This is when your laid-down procedures help, of course. If there's a prescribed way of going about things, a checklist you can tick off, you're halfway to coping, no matter how shaky you're feeling. If you remember those, you can operate to some degree on autopilot and spare yourself another emotional storm.

We were now only a few days from Christmas, coming up to the shortest day. It was well past midnight and I'd just come from sorting out a dispute between neighbours, way out above Rosedale, the sort of spot where you'd imagine life would be all peace and tranquillity. It was late at night, and there I was standing between opposing neighbours who were arguing over whose kids had kicked a football that had then knocked over the illuminated reindeer in the garden. It was an argument that had started earlier in the evening and escalated as the stresses of Christmas, combined with alcohol, set in. Both sets of parents had been drinking, and both of them were mad as hell. But once we'd established that the reindeer was not in fact beyond repair and could still take pride of place on the front lawn, things calmed down. I saw the parents back into their respective homes and left with a glow of satisfaction, and the warm red reflection of Rudolph in my rear-view mirror.

I'd taken a circuitous route, largely so that I could bring myself back down to earth and normality. I skirted the forest plantation above Cropton and took a back road into Pickering. I was just passing through a patch of woodland when I spotted some sort of creature lying on the road in front of me.

At first I thought it was a young rabbit, the way it seemed to be crouching there. You often get them at night, grazing on the verges and oblivious to the traffic. But as I approached it I realised it was in fact some kind of bird. I stopped the car a few yards short of it, dimmed the lights, and got out.

It looked just like an owl, except for one thing: it seemed far too small. I'd seen plenty of barn owls and tawnies over the years and they're a fair size, a foot and more in height. This little fellow – well, let's say it wasn't much bigger than a thrush. But as I got up close to it I could see that it was, unmistakably, an owl. And it was injured.

It sat there quivering, sort of hunched up but with one wing hanging loosely by its side.

I went back to the car and opened the boot. I put on my leather gloves, picked up one of the blankets I always have with me and went back to where the bird sat staring at me. Small it may have been, but on each of its feet it had three long curved talons. I reached out with one hand, dropped a corner of the blanket over it with the other and quickly scooped it up, wrapping the cloth tight enough to stop it from lashing out. 'Right,' I said, 'you're coming with me, lad.'

I soon had the injured owl securely wrapped in the blanket in the boot of the vehicle. I glanced at my watch. Two forty-five a.m. Now what was I going to do? There was no way any vet would come out at this hour, and anyway I wouldn't be able to justify the expense. This is the problem when you come across injured wild animals. During the day it's not such a problem because either of the two vets that I knew would have known what to do. But I couldn't go dragging them out of bed at this hour. Then I thought about what Jean Thorpe, the badger lady, had said. She'd told me that if I had an injured animal I should call her any time, night or day – and I'd kept her number on my mobile.

'Jean Thorpe?' I was taken aback at how quickly she picked up her phone. It had only rung twice.

'Yes?'

'PC Mike Pannett here. Sorry to get you up at this time of night but I've found an injured bird at the side of the road – looks like some sort of owl. Right little thing, it is.'

'Oh? How little?'

'I'd say a quarter of the size of a normal one, maybe a third.'

'I see. And where are you now?'

'About three miles above Pickering. I can be across in twenty minutes, if it's not disturbing you.'

'No problem. I was up anyway. Been bottle-feeding a litter of pups.'

I got back in the car and made tracks. Thank goodness for people like her, I was thinking. I wouldn't have had the faintest idea what to do on my own. I suppose I could've just ignored the bird, left it to its fate, but that would have gone against the grain.

Jean was at her gate waiting for me. She came to the rear of the car and carried the bird into the house. In the kitchen she unwrapped the blanket. 'Ah,' she said, 'a little owl. There aren't many of them around these days. There used to be plenty, years ago before the war. So they tell me,' she added.

'So what's happened to them?'

She grimaced. 'Pesticides, habitat loss. People taking pot-shots at them.'

'Well, you live and learn. I have to say I never knew there was such a creature.'

Jean was examining the bird's feet and wings, gently manipulating the joints. 'Well, they're very localised. The difference with them is, they'll be out and about in the daytime.'

'What, hunting?'

'Yes – insects, small mammals.' She had the bird's right wing spread out in her hand. 'Here, I think it may have broken a bone, can you see?' I bent forward to get a closer look, but wasn't sure I could see anything. 'Hard to tell,' she added. 'I'll maybe get it x-rayed in the morning. Then we'll let it rest and hopefully it'll be fit for release in a week or two. Where exactly did you find it?'

'Above Pickering, out towards Cawthorne.'

'I'll need to know exactly. You can't just release these any old place. They have to go back to their home territory.'

I got the map out to show Jean the exact location, and described it to her as carefully as I could. 'Tell you what,' I said, 'soon as it's fit, give us a buzz and we'll ride out together. How's that? Be nice to see it set free.'

By the time I made by way back to town it was getting on for the end of my shift. The temperature was down to minus seven. Whoever was in early would doubtless have the usual crop of accidents to deal with as people grappled with the black ice and, in many cases, ended up off the road and into hedge bottoms. They're caught out, year after year, by the first bit of icy weather. The trouble is they think they can drive at the same speed as normal. I had a little skid myself on the way out of town past the gallops, and took it very steadily indeed the rest of the way home.

Back at Keeper's Cottage I sprayed some de-icer on Ann's windscreen and spread a plastic sack over it before turning in. I hadn't been asleep long when the phone rang. At least, it didn't feel like long. Normally I turn the ringer off but I'd managed to forget it this morning, what with trying to save Ann a job. I let it ring three times, then a fourth, hoping that the caller would give it up. As if.

'Hell-o!' I didn't try to disguise my grumpiness. If it was somebody trying to sell me a new internet deal he was going to get both barrels.

'Now then, lad.'

'Bloody hell, Walt. What you wake me up for?'

'Well, you want to be up and about, grand morning like this.'

I pulled at the curtain and screwed up my eyes against the low, dazzling sunlight.

I looked at the alarm clock. Eleven forty-five. Later than I thought. I already knew I wouldn't be going back to bed.

'Aye, I wouldn't mind being out and about, if it wasn't for having been at work all night, protecting people like you from marauding criminals and only having had four hours' shut eye. But go on, what's on your mind, mate?'

'You need to be round here with that chainsaw, lad. Right away.'

'Walt, I am not climbing trees in this weather. Not till I've had breakfast at least.'

''Tisn't a tree job, lad. It's me turkey.'

'Hell-fire, Walter. There's rules about slaughtering live-stock, you know. And in case you forgot, let me remind you that you are talking to a police officer. And a wildlife officer at that.'

'We shan't be killing him.'

'I'm pleased to hear that, old chum. So – don't tell me . . . you're gonna trim his tailfeathers, right? Teach him a lesson.'

'He's well past learning now, lad. I dealt wi' him night before last.'

'You killed him? That's a bit previous, isn't it? You won't be cooking him for a few days yet. Won't he go off?'

I could hear Walt's exasperation mounting. 'Course he won't go off, you daft bugger. I've hung him in t'shed. He's frozen. Frozzen solid. That's what I'm calling you about.'

'Sorry, Walt, it's a bit early for me. I still don't get the connection. Turkey? Chainsaw? You've got me beat.'

'Just get yourself over here, right smartish. I've got some of that home-cured bacon on the go if you're interested.'

I didn't hang about. I was up that hill like Jensen Button – and when I got there Walt was just clearing his plate.

'Oh, that's great, that is,' I said. 'There's me galloping up that bloody hill, and you've cleaned up.'

He didn't say a word, just reached into the oven, pulled out an oval dish full of crispy bacon, sausage, fried bread and tomatoes, and set it in front of me.

'Eat up, lad, then we'll get cracking.'

Ten minutes later I found myself in the sort of situation that was all too familiar these days. Part of my ongoing association with Walter seemed to involve one hare-brained enterprise after another – some might say downright bizarre. Unexploded bombs, clay-pigeon shoots, and now this. I found myself standing astride a plucked, frozen turkey, tugging away at the string as I tried to fire up my trusty chainsaw.

'Aye, it'll fit in me oven. No problem, lad.' I glared at Walter, my voice heavy with sarcasm, but if that man has one standout quality it's a thick skin. Elephant hide, at a guess.

'Why, it would've fitted nicely if I'd topped him a few days sooner,' he said. 'But he kept on eating till the bitter end. And don't you be complaining. I've said you can tek half of it.'

'Yeah, OK,' I said, giving the string another tug. 'But which half?' I shouted, as it roared into life. 'Or is it a case of "I cut, you choose"?'

'No, we'll toss a coin,' he said, rubbing his hands and fastening the top button of his coat. 'It's t'fairest way.'

'Go on, then.' I let the saw idle. 'Get your purse out, you tight old . . .'

'Eh, I weren't born yesterday,' he said. 'What if you win?'

'That'll be my good fortune,' I said.

'Aye, and then you go and slice the bugger all on the slant so's you get three parts of t'bird, and leave me t'rest. No, we'll toss after you've cut it, then weigh the two bits.'

'However you do it, Walt, it's going to be a tough decision. You're dealing with a master of his craft here, so prepare yourself for a photo-finish.' I lowered my Perspex goggles, brandished the chainsaw with a flourish, and cranked it up to maximum revs.

'By heck, it takes some cutting! It's like a piece of oak,' I shouted, as the whine of the two-stroke engine dropped a couple of octaves and the motor started to cough. Slowly, though, it sliced into the frozen flesh. 'I say, it's taking some cutting!' I repeated, but there was no answer.

I eased off on the trigger for a moment and looked around. Walt was crouched down at the side of his woodshed, trying to smother a grin. Looking down, I saw the front of my dark-green jacket splattered with a gruesome mixture of shredded turkey meat, bone and ice.

'Aye, it has to be me in the firing line,' I said. 'All right for you, hiding away there. This is a decent jacket, y'know.'

'Used to be,' Walt said.

'Aye well,' I shrugged, 'you can't make an omelette without breaking eggs.' I revved the saw up again and sliced through the rest of the bird, then stood back and cut the motor.

'Bloody hell Walt, that was a job and a half. What do we do about the oil on it?'

'Don't you be worrying about that, we'll wash it off while it's still frozen. I'm more concerned about how much turkey we've lost out the back of your chainsaw. Must be half a pound stuck to your clothes, lad.'

'There's plenty left.' I eyed up the two halves. 'You'll have a job on, splitting these,' I said.

Walter edged his way forward, stooping to inspect them.

'Aye, I can see that. I shall have to fetch me scales.'

'No, first we toss the coin.'

Walt fished out a fifty-pence piece and prepared to flip. 'Your call, lad.'

'Heads,' I said, and watched as he tossed it right up in the air, only just catching it at the second attempt with his outstretched right hand. Then he whacked it over onto his left.

'Aye, heads it is,' he said, and set off for the house.

'Go on,' I said. 'Don't you worry about me. I'll manage.' I staggered after him, clutching the two halves of the butchered bird, aching with pain as the cold penetrated my fingers.

Back in the kitchen I found him dusting off a set of bathroom scales. 'Never remember you having them,' I said. 'Getting figure-conscious in your old age, are you?'

He screwed up his face, placed a metal tray on the scales and reset the needle to zero. 'It's Muriel. Says I've to watch me weight. Anyway, never mind her, let's see what we have.' He took the first half from me, placed it on the tray, then got down on all fours to read the weight. 'It's just over t'stone mark. Sixteen pounds and – why, it's betwixt and between. Call it fifteen and a half pounds. Now give us t'other one.'

I passed it to him and watched as he placed it carefully on the scales. 'Ee, look at this,' he said. ' Sixteen pounds . . .'

'See, what did I tell you? Close call.'

'Aye, it is. D'you know, lad, it's near enough level pegging.' He stood up and handed me the second half of the bird. 'There you go, lad, and a happy Christmas to you.'

'Cheers now, Walt. I really appreciate it. Saves us a trip to the auction market. Got well and truly ripped off there the last time I went. Anyway, happy Christmas to you too. Ann and I'll drop in and see you some time over the holiday.'

'Aye, and don't forget to raise a glass of sloe gin, will you? After you've eaten all that free turkey.'

'We will, Walt. Don't you worry.'

Chapter 13

Ghost Busters

It was a proper wintry night when I met up with Ann in York. The city was shrouded in fog and despite the sunshine we'd had earlier in the day, patches of frost still lingered in the shadows of the ancient shops and houses. Along Petergate the old stone pavements, liberally sprinkled with salt, glistened under the streetlights. Barely fifty feet behind us the west face of the Minster rose like an ornate, illuminated cliff. We joined the small crowd – perhaps a dozen or fifteen people, mostly couples – huddled under the gaslamp, shoulders hunched, hands deep in pockets, feet stamping. It was that kind of night.

We'd done our shopping. Well, to be perfectly truthful, Ann had done the shopping and I'd tagged along with her as we worked our way down Stonegate, along Davygate, into Parliament Street and then squeezed our way through the shoppers jostling the narrow pavements of the Shambles, where the upper storeys of the medieval houses almost meet above your head. I had to chunter long and loud about the crowds, the heated shops – and the prices of some of the goods – before Ann finally cracked. 'Listen,' she said, 'if you don't stop complaining about the cost of stuff, we're going to have a falling-out. It's not 1973, you know. Stop being such a Scrooge, comparing prices with what you paid when you were fifteen. Now go on, get yourself off to HMV and check out those computer games. Hey, and see if you can find a couple of CDs or something for the nieces and nephews,' she called after me as I scuttled off towards Coney Street grinning to myself. This was my kind of shopping.

'Ah well,' I said to her after we'd met up again and were hurrying back down Marygate to drop our purchases in the car, 'all good things come to an end. That's the shopping. Now for the entertainment.'

'A ghost walk, eh?' I couldn't tell from Ann's tone whether she liked the idea or not. It had certainly taken her aback when I sprang it on her. It was a spur-of-the-moment thing. Only an hour or two earlier, while she was sifting through the calendars, tea towels and jars of local produce in the National Trust shop, I'd picked up a leaflet.

'This looks like value,' I said. 'A guided tour of the city's most haunted sites? For four quid? Has to be worth a try.'

'Just so long as none of my colleagues spot me. I'd never hear the last of it.' Ann pulled her fur hat low over her forehead. 'If we so much as smell a patrol car you are personally responsible for making sure I'm invisible, OK?'

So there we were, hidden away in the crowd, collars turned up, scarves up round our chins, stamping our feet, when a tall figure emerged silently from the darkness. He wore a black top hat and a frock coat, and carried a silver-topped cane. Around his neck was a white silk scarf, and on his hands a pair of those fingerless gloves that street-corner newspaper vendors and bus conductors used to wear. When he spoke it was with the voice of an old-school actor: slow, deliberate, with every syllable – every letter in fact – perfectly enunciated.

'Good evening, ladies and gentlemen.'

'Strewth. Sounds like Alfred Hitchcock,' I whispered.

Ann nudged me sharply in the ribs as our guide continued. 'It is my pleasure on this dismal winter night, the longest of the year, to lead you brave people – some might say you reckless, foolish people – along the forgotten byways of this great city and introduce you to some of the lost, forlorn, tormented souls whose spirits still infest its darkest corners. It is on a night such as this that we might see the tragic face of the little girl imprisoned behind the stone walls of a plague house over three hundred years ago, still beseeching the unhearing passersby to set her free, her cheeks hollowed by hunger, her parents dead and decaying in the rooms below her.' The guide closed his eyes and took a deep breath. 'Should you hear a piteous wailing as we repair to the narrow alleyways behind this magnificent cathedral, let me suggest to the more sensitive of you that – who knows? – you may have heard nothing more sinister than a cat calling to its mate. But, on the other hand . . .' He swung round, twirling his coat, and marched off, swinging his cane, savouring the tension in the cold night air, then turned and said, 'Kindly follow me into York's murky past.'

'I tell you what Ann, he's good is this bloke.'

She smiled. 'He can certainly talk,' she said. 'Like some-body else I know.'

I took her hand. 'I wonder who that could be.'

We'd followed him no more than a hundred yards when he stopped outside the south door, just beside the statue of the Roman emperor Constantine, and looked up at the south side of the Minster. 'They say Rome wasn't built in a day,' he began, 'and neither was northern Europe's largest Gothic cathedral. It wasn't completed on schedule,' he said, with a trace of a smile flickering along his lips. 'In fact, it took well over two hundred years, spanning the lives of several generations of artisans and craftsmen. And during that time,' he continued, 'there was a certain stonemason who liked to bring his little dog to work with him. Now, this dog annoyed the mason's workmates so much with his constant barking that they decided to silence him once and for all. They waited until his master was otherwise engaged and bricked him up in the wall – this wall, not fifteen feet from where we stand.' He paused while a murmur of sympathy rippled through the crowd. 'And to this day,' he said, tapping the pale stonework with his cane, 'it is regularly reported that the sounds of his piteous yelping and whimpering may be heard at certain still moments.' He paused, and cocked his ear theatrically. As if on cue, somewhere across the city, a dog barked. A lady standing close by me let out a little shriek. 'But I'm not sure I believe that,' the guide said, and moved swiftly on.

'Goodness,' said Ann. 'Proper showman, isn't he? It's a bit gloomy though.'

It certainly was. This fellow knew his history all right. He told us about the miseries of the plague year, and he expanded on the story of Guy Fawkes, born not a stone's throw from our point of departure in what was once Young's Hotel; and then outside the Treasurer's House he gathered us round, got up on a stone pediment, and told us about the Roman soldiers of the lost legion. The legendary Ninth, he told us, vanished without trace in Scotland almost two thousand years ago but still appear from time to time in the lower reaches of this very building, bearing their eagle standard. 'With the changes in floor level over the centuries, and each new city being built upon the last,' he added, 'they are visible – I am reliably informed – from the knees up.' He moved on and we trailed after him, moving into the narrow streets behind the cathedral, where he told us the gruesome story of a man who used to run an orphanage. This delightful character starved his charges to death, buried them under cover of darkness and continued to collect the money to support them. 'And upon occasion,' our guide intoned, pausing beside a stone wall and rapping his cane against a low, wooden doorway, 'people have reported a ghostly apparition in this very spot – although speaking personally, I have never had the pleasure and therefore must remain a sceptic.' And with that he glided away once more into the fog.

Ann and I had just passed the doorway when there was a loud gasp, followed by a scream – and then a peal of maniacal laughter. Turning round, I saw, framed in the arch, a crouched figure in a black hooded cloak. He stepped onto the pavement, waving his arms at the stragglers of our party, and cackled again. Then, just as he turned to go back inside, a camera flashlight popped, illuminating a gaunt but familiar face.

'Well!' I couldn't stop myself. 'Well,' I said, 'if it isn't Ronnie Leach!'

Turning to look at me, he dropped all pretence and said, 'Mike Pannett. What the hell you doing here?'

'I might ask the same of you,' I said.

As the remainder of the party put away their cameras and hurried on, Ronnie shoved the dark cowl off his head, pulled out a cigarette and lit up.

I looked him up and down. 'Still got your sights on a career as an actor, eh?'

'Nah, that was a load of – why, it was a con. But this – 'tisn't a bad number. Thirty seconds' work and' – he patted his hip – 'a tenner in the old back pocket.'

'Yeah, but what about your expenses? Travelling in from Norton every night? You'll hardly be breaking even, will you?'

Ronnie shook his head and grinned. 'I get a ride in, and a spot of supper.'

'Who off? Him in the frock coat?'

'No, her in the frock.' I couldn't recall having seen Ronnie look sheepish before – except maybe when I arrested him in Bulmer cemetery that time – but that's the only way I can describe the look on his face as he said, 'Works in a hotel restaurant just down the road there. Brings me in whenever matey needs me. Then about nine, when they finish serving, she meets me at the kitchen door and slips me a plate of grub. She fetches me steaks, chops, all sorts.'

'You always were a slippery customer, Ronnie. Anyway' – Ann had grabbed hold of my arm – 'I'd better be off. And by the way . . .'

'Yeah?'

'Keep out of trouble, won't you?'

Ronnie grinned and touched the side of his nose before slipping away down the alleyway.

Despite our guide's stories about mysterious apparitions in unlikely places, there were no more ghoulish figures leaping out from dark corners. By the time the Minster clock struck half-past eight we were on our way back to where we'd started, and just a few minutes' walk from the place I'd booked for our supper – during which I found myself eyeing the waitress and wondering whether she might be Ronnie's lady friend. We had a super meal, and, true to my promise, I let Ann have the wine while I stuck to Coke.

'Well,' I said, as we got in the car and headed out towards the Malton road, 'I reckon that just about wraps it up.'

'Wraps what up?' Ann sounded every so slightly tetchy.

'Why, the Christmas shopping. Nicely timed, too. No major panic. We go in, we get the gear, and we get out. Job done.'

'Mike, we are three days away from the Christmas holiday – such as it is.'

'That's what I'm saying. We timed it to perfection.'

'You may have timed it to perfection, having a quick rummage round HMV, but some of us have wider responsibilities, a slightly longer list of presents, and are running out of time.'

'You mean there's more to be done?'

'More to be done? It's a good job you're in that driving seat, Michael Pannett. Otherwise you might be feeling my hands around your neck right now, applying a little pressure to your windpipe.'

'What have I said?'

'You men really are hopeless, aren't you. All the Christmas arrangements – they don't just happen, you know.'

'Oh, so we've still got a few more bits to get then?'

'Just the odd one or two,' she said, through clenched teeth.

'I tell you what, it's late-night shopping every night at Monks Cross. Shall we stop off?'

'Mike, it's gone ten o'clock. It says "late night", not "all night". You just concentrate on getting us home. I need my bed. On an early tomorrow. And I've plenty on at work.'

We'd begun the run-up to Christmas now. From here on, from a policing point of view, things were likely to get really busy. Kids were out of school, workplaces were preparing for lengthy shutdowns, and everywhere you looked on a night-time there were works parties in progress. The pubs were busy too, and the landlords were rubbing their hands. Maybe it's peculiar to our area, but there's a sort of tradition in the building trade that everything shuts down for at least a couple of weeks around the turn of the year. What that means is that you'll often have a bunch of lads with large pay packets in their pockets and not a lot to do apart from descending on the town looking for a good time. And for one or two of them a good time isn't really complete unless the night ends up with a bit of a rumble. We had one particular character who ran a scaffolding business, staffed mainly by members of his extended family. They were like a clan, really – and they were all built like brick outhouses. The main man they called Jacko, and he was a seriously hard case. I suppose it's in the nature of things that if you spend your working days running up and down triple-extension ladders and clambering over roofs you have to be tough. He certainly was, as were his lads. And they were proud of it. I'd only come across them in town once or twice, but I'd heard plenty about them. They actually came from over Kirkbymoorside way, and they had quite a reputation. People were scared of them, in awe of them.

It was on Christmas Eve itself that the trouble kicked off. I came in for my night shift to be told by the lads on the late turn that this lot were in town and threatening to stir something up, and the warning was underlined at our briefing. Cocksy told us they'd already been upsetting the customers in the Spotted Cow and were now working their way through town towards the Blue Ball in Yorkersgate. Still, we were well up to strength that night, which, as you can imagine, you want to be. We had four officers off the late shift, then me, Jayne, Fordy and Ed, plus a couple of Specials: Will MacDonald – the lumberjack, as I called him – and Keith Nicholson. And not forgetting Thommo. The sort of crew, in other words, that you want with you if trouble's going to break out.

The late-turn lads had actually made a couple of arrests – although none of them were Jacko's men – but

I found myself wondering whether it was enough. That shift, in my opinion, tended to let things go a bit too easily. They'd soft-pedal it. There are various ways of dealing with situations such as you get on a busy weekend, or at times like this when everybody's out on the streets drinking. Call them differing styles of policing. I believe in staying good-humoured, but not getting too pally with the public. These are mostly younger people you're dealing with, and they're easily influenced. Wherever you decide to draw the line, you have to make it quite clear that you're there to keep the peace, that you're not going to stand any nonsense, and that if anyone crosses that line you will come down on them, hard. They'll try it on – they're bound to – and if you get a shift on whose mentality is to let people get away with a bit here and a bit there, well, you're likely to have problems. It stands to reason. So we as a shift prided ourselves on generally being able to maintain order better than most – providing the previous lot hadn't let things get out of hand.

Ed and I had barely been out an hour. There were plenty of people in town: lots of girls with tinsel in their hair being chased by lads in Santa hats, and, it being after eleven, they were a bit boisterous; even so, it was all pretty light-hearted, as you'd expect on a Christmas Eve. As good-humoured as it was, however, we were very aware that a lot of people were pretty drunk, and with Jacko's crew in town it wouldn't take a lot for things to kick off. Our job was to keep a lid on it, and to do what we needed to be out and about, and highly visible. We wanted to be seen around town and make it clear to people that we were there, in numbers. We even had two of the late-shift

officers out on foot, one with each of the Specials. We'd
visited the pubs and chatted with the doormen, getting
a feel for how things were developing. Our hope was for
people to have a good time, celebrate Christmas Eve and
trot off home having had a fun night out.

I was over in Norton with Ed. We'd parked outside the
Derwent Arms and were having a quiet word with a group
of lads who were getting a bit rowdy. We tried to reason
with them. 'Come on,' I said, 'spare a thought for the resi-
dents around here. Think of them kids with their Christmas
stockings hung up. They'll be trying to get to sleep.'

'Will they f***?' someone said. 'They'll be trying to
stay awake and see Santa flying by.'

'Look,' I said above the laughter, 'we're all for everyone
having a good time. Just tone it down a bit – and watch
your language. Better still, stay inside the pub, eh?'

Ed and I were just persuading them inside when the call
came over the radio. *'Urgent assistance, urgent assistance!'*

Those are two words that guarantee an instant
response. You're trained never to use them unless you or
your colleague is in big trouble, when a situation is
life-threatening and you need the cavalry, fast. It's not a
call you send out lightly, because you're asking for your
fellow officers to abandon whatever they're engaged in,
make you their number-one priority and get to you as
quickly as they possibly can. If it's a road traffic accident, for example, and the road is blocked – even if a
death is involved – you'll send out a call for additional
units. You wouldn't ask for urgent assistance because it's
a done deed, a *fait accompli*. You ask for urgent assistance when you go to a domestic incident and someone

pulls a knife on you, or when you stop a car and four people pile out and come for you; or when, as in Fordy's case, you've gone to a pub in answer to a call from a bouncer and found the place in uproar.

We'd barely got in the car when Fordy was back on. *'I'm at the Blue Ball . . .'*

As loud as he was shouting, I had all on to hear what he was telling me. I could make out *'all kicking off . . .'*, then there was a moment's pause in the signal, then the sound of breaking glass, followed by a shout. *'Need some help down here . . . quick as you can. There's a ri—'*

When a radio goes silent, that's when you really start to worry. It could mean anything.

Control were straight onto the call and everyone on duty was jostling to find the radio space to answer. The good news was, we had Brian on duty. He had vast experience of this kind of thing, both as a former officer and as an old hand in the control room at Northallerton.

'Control to all units, I have all units assigned to the Blue Ball. Can we have radio silence until we get a sit rep from the pub.' Brian wanted to make sure that Fordy could pass on any further information as the situation unfolded without being cut out by other radio traffic. In a situation like this you might only get one chance to say something critical.

There's nothing quite like the feeling you get when you've called for urgent assistance and you hear everyone shouting up to come and help you. You know that they've heard you and they'll all be doing their utmost to get to you as fast as they can. It can give you that extra bit of strength to hang on in there.

We were speeding away from the Derwent Arms, blue lights on and two-tones blaring. As well as warning people we were coming it would, hopefully, let Fordy know when we were approaching him. That's a sound you long to hear when you're in trouble – the cavalry coming over the rise. We raced over the railway, swerving out into the middle of County Bridge to avoid a girl who'd stumbled on her high heels, grabbed a friend's arms and dragged her off the edge of the pavement with her.

'We've one officer down and injured.' Fordy sounded out of breath, indistinct. *'Can't see the other.'*

'Do you need an ambulance, over?'

There was no reply, just the sound of shouting, and a kind of grunt.

'1015 to control, there in about one minute. Confirm ambulance en route and CCTV monitoring outside?' At least if we got some record on camera, it'd be a help if it came to prosecuting any troublemakers.

'Confirmed Mike.'

We arrived at the Blue Ball to find a scrum of bodies outside the door, mostly males trying to force their way back in, but impeded by others – mostly female – trying to get out. In the melee were a couple of doormen trying to hold back two or three handy-looking lads. As I opened the car door a bottle smashed on the pavement beside me.

'Bloody hell! You're here.' One of the doormen stumbled his way out of the crowd. He had a smear of blood across his cheek, his tie had come adrift of his collar and his shirt was all untucked and open to his stomach.

'Where are the cops?' I asked.

'Inside. It's all kicking off.'

I turned to Ed. 'You ready?'

He was speaking into his radio. 'Control, 1015 and myself on scene. We've got quite a crowd outside the pub and according to the doorman there is large-scale disorder inside. We're about to go in to try and find Fordy.' He glanced at me, and at the doorway as a chair-seat flew over the scrimmaging bodies and clattered against a lamp-post. I've been in many a situation like that back in my TSG days, but always in full riot gear, with shields and helmets, and plenty of officers. When you're fully kitted up and surrounded by as many as thirty trained riot police – yes, I'll admit it – you can almost get a buzz out of going in to do battle. You have that extra confidence. Sure, you have the fear, but you also have a feeling that you can take on the world. You're good at what you do, better organised than the opposition, better prepared, and you know that the guy to your left, and the guy to your right, have been through it all dozens of times with you before. But a situation such as we faced here, with fewer officers, scantily protected, and some of your colleagues lacking experience, I have to say I wasn't approaching it with total confidence.

Ed extended his Asp and gave his CS canister a reassuring shake. 'Right,' he said, 'let's get in there,' then he jumped as a pint glass shattered on the pavement just a few feet from where we were standing.

We launched ourselves at the mass of bodies around the entrance and started pulling them out one by one. There was a bit of effing and blinding, but they didn't resist once they saw the uniform and realised we meant business. Most of them were more interested in getting a ringside seat than joining in.

Inside the pub it was a different matter altogether. Fists were flying, guys on the floor were being kicked; women were screaming, tearing each other's hair; glasses were being smashed, chairs and tables tipped over. It looked as though it had degenerated into a free-for-all, with people hitting out at random. How the hell anybody could tell whose side they were on was beyond me. With the low ceilings and cramped rooms it was going to be a nightmare getting it sorted. There was another melee at the rear exit, where a doorway led into a sort of garden. I was scanning the room trying to locate my colleagues, but I couldn't see anybody in uniform. I was suddenly barged into by a drunken knot of youths tussling over a chair. I shoved them backwards as hard as I could with both hands. 'Get back,' I yelled. 'Go on'! F*** off or you'll get nicked.' I stood as tall as I could and gave them the hard stare. They needed to know I meant business. I was deliberately trying to frighten them. They needed it. Who they hell did these people think they were?

In a far corner I spotted someone on the floor curled up in a ball, and a solidly built youth kicking him. I pushed my way through the crowd, took a swing and kicked the lad on his thigh as hard as I could. The shock of what I'd done made him stop long enough for me to grab him by the shoulders and drag him away from the lad on the floor. 'Get back!' I shouted. 'Outside, now!' Ideally I would have arrested him, not to mention any one of several others, but right now I needed to find Fordy and the other officers. Once we got a decent number of us on scene and had the situation under control, maybe then we could start making arrests. I recognised quite a few of the people involved in the fighting, so if we didn't get them tonight we could round them up later.

'You all right, Mike?' Ed was beside me, getting his breath and straightening his coat.

'Yeah, you found Fordy yet?'

'I think he's outside. The rest of the shift have shown up.' He jerked his thumb towards the door. 'It's kicked off out there now.'

Ed and I made our way through the bar, pushing people apart and making it quite clear they would be arrested and locked up over Christmas if they didn't calm down. The landlord had finally turned off the music and switched the lights on, which had an immediate sobering effect, on some of them at least; a reality check. Behind the bar two of the staff, both of them young women, were pressed back against the wall, clearly shocked at what they were seeing.

'All right, girls,' I called across. 'Don't worry. We're winning.' The tide inside was starting to turn in our favour, but the radio traffic told me the situation outside was bad. As fast as we dragged the fighters off each other, others were heading for the doors, responding to the shouts we could hear from the street.

With the room cleared we finally found Derek, one of the late-turn PCs, on the floor, propped against the bar, clutching his shoulder. He was a young lad and still in his probationary period. 'Sorry, lads. Reckon I've broken it,' he said.

'You sure?'

He tried to move his right arm and winced. 'Feels like it. Bloody well hurts, anyway.'

'Right, gimme your good arm. You don't wanna be sitting there, mate; you're a sitting target.' Between us Ed and I got him to his feet.

'1015 to control.'

'Go ahead.'

'I've located Derek. Looks like he's got a dislocated shoulder or broken collarbone. The pub's starting to clear. I think it's a safer option to leave him with the bar staff inside.'

'All received. I'll get a message to the ambulance crew to make them aware. Are you aware that officers are asking for further assistance outside?'

'Yes, yes, just making our way now.'

Ed was struggling through to the door, doing his best to clear a way for us, shoving people aside, removing a glass from one youth's hand all in one swift movement. I followed him through.

Outside it was mayhem. There were groups of youths all over the main road hurling abuse and gesticulating, and small fights were breaking out. A paramedic was hurrying towards the pub doorway. 'Got an injured PC?' she asked. 'In there,' I said.

Jayne and Thommo had handcuffed a young lad and were shoving him into the back of the van, pausing to let him throw up on the road. Then he was locked away. Thommo closed the door on the prisoner, paused to flick something off his jacket and headed back towards me. That was when I heard the shout. Well, it was more of a growl. It was coming from some way away, about fifty yards down Wheelgate. I stepped out into the road just in time to see Fordy being dragged across the road by one of Jacko's gang. I knew the lad; Fatty Wilks, they called him. There was a squealing of brakes as he stepped right out into the traffic, dragging Fordy with him. He had his head in an armlock. I ran towards them. He'd crossed the road onto the pavement, grabbed Fordy by the body armour and was pounding him against Thomas the Baker's window. I was sure it was going to break, but instead it seemed to bend as Fordy's body thumped against it. Christ, how long would it hold out?

A small group of youths, maybe four or five, had followed me down the road. I knew most of them by sight and I'd had dealings with one or two of them in the past. I could tell they were thinking about wading in, and I was now on my own. I needed to sort this Wilks character out, make them think twice, give myself a chance to get some backup. They were hard on my heels, shouting abuse at me and encouragement to their mate Wilks.

If ever there was a time to make a pre-emptive strike, this was it. In our neck of the woods, you can generally count on people hesitating before actually assaulting a copper. I ran at Wilks, steadied myself, then kicked his legs with all the strength I could muster. I caught him just right, round the back of his knees. Down he went like a felled tree. I jumped on him, grabbing an arm. Fordy wriggled out from his grasp and grabbed the other. Bingo. The cuffs were in place and matey was spluttering his venom into the icy pavement.

'You bastards.'

'You take one of us on, buddy' – I was gasping from the effort of the run and bringing him down – 'and you take us all on. You know that.'

He was torn between giving me more verbals and struggling to free himself, but it was all he could do right now to catch his breath, writhing about on the ground on his stomach like a beached whale.

'Fordy.' I stood up, straightening my jacket. 'You OK, mate?'

'F***ing hell Mike, it was touch and go. I thought I was going through that window.' He rubbed his head and tried to smile.

I turned on the group who had followed me down the road. They'd backed off and were across the other side of the road. 'Right, you lot,' I shouted. 'Disappear now or you will be arrested.' They stood there for a moment, clearly looking for a lead from someone. Then one of them said, 'C'mon lads, let's get the f*** out of here.'

'Right Fordy, you keep him there.' I pointed at Wilks, who'd fallen silent. 'If anybody else comes near you, gas 'em. I'm going to help the others.'

I ran back up the road. One or two cars were edging slowly past, the occupants winding down the windows to see what was going on, then speeding away up the hill. Will the Special and one of the late-turn lads had got another youth on the floor and were struggling to get the cuffs on him while a crowd of his mates shouted and jeered. Jacko was there, muscles bulging under his short-sleeved shirt, geeing everybody up. As I approached I saw him draw himself back and kick Will as hard as he could from behind, catching him in the middle of his back and hurling him forward. Then he was in, raining punches down on him. Tough as Will was, I could see he was getting hurt, but he still didn't let go of the lad on the ground. I was within twenty yards of them, running flat out, shouting at Jacko: 'You! Get off him! Now!' I reached them just as Jacko started pulling Will's body armour to one side to try and get his punches into his ribs. Just as I was about to hurl myself on him he turned to face me, his hands on Will's body armour. The look of pure malice and aggression almost stopped me in my tracks. I was trembling with anger and fear. It was like being in a boxing ring when the bell's just gone, that moment when you know the fight's about to start.

'Get back! Get back!' I saw Jayne, leaning forward and emptying her CS gas canister into Jacko's face, then turning to spray it on the lads who were swarming round.

It's amazing what you're capable of when you're really, seriously, up against it – not to mention scared. One moment the guy was staggering, coughing, the next he was coming at us, lashing out with his fists. I ducked under a huge swing, reached forward, grabbed hold of his shirt with both hands, and lifted him clean off the ground. He must have weighed fourteen stone, minimum. God knows how I did it, and God knows what his shirt was made of, but it held, and there I was throwing him back down. Before he could get himself upright I jumped on him, turned him over so that he was face down, and pinned him to the ground. Jayne followed, piling on top of him, knocking the remainder of his breath out of him. The thing that struck me then was the smell of his aftershave combined with the CS gas. It was sickly sweet and made my eyes water.

As I fumbled for my cuffs, Ed came running up and snapped his own set on the prisoner. Next thing I heard

Jayne gasping out, 'You're under arrest . . . for assaulting a police officer . . . and affray.'

As I stood up the big fellow's mates were crowding in on us, jostling us. I shoved them back, cracked my Asp open, and stood there with Jacko at my feet. 'One step nearer, any of you, and you'll get this. I'm warning you.' Jayne was by my side with her canister in her hand, ready to give them another dose. She shook it, just to make her intentions clear, then looked at me. 'Mike, I'm out of gas, mate.'

'Here,' I said. 'Take mine.'

Jacko may have been on the ground handcuffed, but he was still trying to get his mates to have a go. 'I know who you are,' he snarled. 'All of you. Just wait until I see you off duty. You might think you're tough now . . .' But somehow he didn't convince. I could see that he was shocked; we'd come at him hard and fast, and he hadn't expected that. As far as I was concerned we'd done absolutely the right thing. The situation was still in the balance. If Jacko's cronies and the eight or ten other youths who'd gathered around had decided to go for us, we might well have been in trouble.

You don't always realise how tense you are, how frightened, until the danger passes. The stand-off with the youths had lasted barely thirty seconds when the faces of our potential assailants were lit up by the blue lights as more backup appeared from all directions. In an instant I felt my shoulders drop as I let out a huge sigh of relief. The 'cavalry' consisted of a York traffic car, a York dog unit and a double-crewed unit from Eastfield, available for the simple reason that this was still relatively early, and the clubs in York and Scarborough had yet to turn out.

'Right.' I moved a couple of steps closer to the group. 'Back off – now – or you *will* be arrested.' They took a quick look at the back-up officers – and the dog – and started to disperse.

Our arrests that night numbered eight, and another two would be picked up later. We had room for four at Malton and the rest had to be taken through to Scarborough. It meant that all our available officers, bar two, were off the streets.

We could've lost it that night, but we'd scraped through. As it was we had one officer spending his Christmas morning at the hospital with a dislocated shoulder, Will MacDonald nursing a stiff back and bruised ribs, and Fordy with bad bruising, or shaken but not stirred, as he put it. It could, of course, have been much, much worse. If further disorder had broken out while we were all involved in transporting prisoners, God knows how we'd have managed. But I preferred to look on the positive side. For me, whatever else it was, it had been a useful bit of team-building and the younger officers would be all the better for the experience.

Back at the nick everyone was upbeat, on a high. The place was buzzing, a bit like a dressing room after you've won an important football match. 'I hope the late shift take note of this,' Jayne said as she took off her body armour. 'That's how you deal with aggravation. No messing, eh? Get into 'em.'

I found Fordy slumped in a chair opening his sandwich box. 'Look,' I said, 'I know you've got a thing about that lass who works in Thomas the Baker, but come on – trying to get in through the front window using Fatty Wilks as a battering ram? If you have to try that hard to impress a girl, well . . .'

'Yeah,' he said, 'but who got the cuffs on him and made the arrest, eh?'

While I was taking the mick out of Fordy, Thommo couldn't resist having a go at me. As he banged his helmet and Asp on the mess-room table he said, 'Just how many prisoners did ye bring in, laddie? I mean, fair shares and all that – young Jayne here's made two arrests and we've all got one. Where were you?'

'What you're forgetting, Thommo' – I gave him my best choirboy smile – 'what you're overlooking is, I was far too busy bailing you lot out so you could make those arrests in the first place.'

'Yeah, right,' Jayne said.

'No no,' I said. 'It's the season of goodwill, isn't it?'

'What you on about?'

'Jayne, you've missed the point. You lot need the figures. I don't. I just thought I'd help you out, that's all. Can't have you giving our shift a bad name, can I? So, you know, how's about a bit of gratitude?'

I could see her getting ready to give me a mouthful when Cocksy came in. 'Here, don't you know what time it is?' He was carrying a tin of mince pies and a tray of teas. 'It's well gone three o'clock, lads and lasses.' He placed his tray on the table. 'Christmas starts here. So go on, get stuck into 'em.'

The rest of the night was a good deal easier. It needed to be. Maybe, as Jayne suggested, word had got around town that the A team was on duty. That was one way of looking at it. I preferred to think that the majority of those who

were out and about were there for a good time, to celebrate the holiday. We see so many pictures, and hear so
many stories, of people behaving badly when they've had
a drink. It's easy to forget that most people who go out
to the pub are perfectly well-behaved and willing to go
home quietly – well, reasonably quietly – when the night
is over.

It's a traditional goodwill gesture for the early shift to
come to work a bit ahead of time on Christmas morning,
so that the night duty can get away sharpish, so I was
home in good time. Ann, of course, was already on her
way to work and had left me a note propped up by the
kettle to say that Henry had been out for his morning
walk. I gave him a biscuit out of his bag of Christmas
treats and headed off to bed.

Ann had hung mistletoe above the bed and strung tinsel
round the bedpost. On the pillow was a chocolate reindeer. I carefully placed it on the bedside cabinet and
slipped under the duvet, which was still nice and warm.
I put my head on the pillow and tried to relax, but of
course I immediately started thinking about what I needed
to do to prepare our Christmas dinner. Turkey, I thought.
How big was that bird? Was it thoroughly defrosted? How
long does it need to be in the oven? Is it twenty minutes
a pound, plus the extra twenty? Or is it twenty-five? That
got me worrying about how long I could sleep before I
needed to put it in. Sod it, I thought. It needs to go in
now or we won't be eating till ten o'clock tonight.

I jumped out of bed, threw on my icy-cold shorts and
T-shirt, grabbed the reindeer and headed downstairs. I
needed an energy boost; one bite and the reindeer's head

was gone. I put the rest on the table, turned the oven on and started to prepare our half of Walter's gobbler. It was only when I'd got the chestnut stuffing ready that I noticed there was nowhere to put it, the usual orifice having been sliced in half by the chainsaw. I shoved the stuffing back in the fridge, then crossed my fingers as I prepared to slide the big bird into the oven. In it went – just. Nice and snug. I was now wide awake, of course. I made a brew and nibbled the hind legs off the reindeer. Then I wandered into the living room, where Ann had put our gifts under the tree. I remembered how excited I used to get as a boy on Christmas morning, and couldn't resist picking up one or two of the nicely wrapped boxes, giving them a shake and a sniff and wondering what they might be. Then, for the first time in my life, I found myself wondering what it would be like if I had a little Pannett beside me by the tree. Strewth, I thought, where did that come from? Still pondering, I double-checked the oven setting and went back to bed.

I got up just after two, had a peep in the oven and lit the fire. Then I cracked on with the vegetables.

Everything was just about ready when Ann came home. The house was warm as toast, the whole downstairs smelled of roast meat, and I'd got a bottle of sparkling wine in the fridge. We sat by the fire and opened our presents, helped by a highly excited Henry, before tucking into a very tasty Christmas dinner.

It was early evening. I'd just been outside to get a breath of fresh air and check that Henry did what dogs need to do. It was a crisp, starlit night, with a rime of frost over the grass, and not a breath of wind. I looked up at the chimney that Soapy had rebuilt all those months ago and watched a plume of smoke drift straight up into the sky. Back inside Ann and I cuddled up by the log fire.

'Just one thing you've forgotten,' she said. 'Something we've been looking forward to for weeks. Months.'

'No,' I said, 'you've got me there. Not something else to eat is it, because I'm ready to burst.'

'That's a point. The chocolate reindeer. Where's that?'

Quick as a flash I pointed at Henry, and to my great relief Ann laughed.

'That blooming dog. Ah, never mind,' she said. 'No, I was thinking of something to drink.' She stared at me. I hadn't the faintest idea what she was on about. 'Oh dear, Mike. You and your memory. What do they say, you'd forget your own head if it wasn't screwed on?'

'What, have I put the hairbrush in the fridge again?'

She got up and went to the kitchen, returning with a couple of sherry glasses in one hand and Walter's sloe gin in the other.

'Oh, that,' I said. 'Yeah, get it open. I just hope it lives up to expectations. The way Walt built it up I'm expecting a life-changing experience.'

She poured us a glass apiece, smelled hers, then closed her eyes and raised the plum-red liquor to her lips.

'Hang about,' I said. 'Toast first.'

'Oh, right.' She clinked her glass against mine.

'Here's to us, and whatever the future may bring.'

Chapter 14

Full-steam Ahead

Our Christmas break lasted all of twenty-four hours. After having Boxing Day off together it was straight back to work for the pair of us. It was well into January before we got so much as a day off together and were able to drive out to the coast, to Staintondale, where I used to spend my holidays as a lad. The December cold spell had given way to much milder weather and we managed a few hours' hiking along the clifftops before heading for the eighteenth-century coaching inn at Hayburn Wyke where we had dinner. It was good to be able to relax for a few hours, enjoy each other's company, and look back over the past twelve months.

Ann felt she'd had a decent year, settling into her new job in York. The travelling had been easier than she'd expected, and she was getting on well with her new colleagues. On the home front, after all those problems with the roof during the summer, things had started to come right. Algy had shaken hands on our offer on the house, leaving us to settle up with Soapy. Ann and I had calculated what we were willing to pay, and I'd gone to the bank to withdraw it in cash. Soapy's eyes were out on stalks when I flashed the bundle at him. 'Job's a good 'un,' he said, holding out his hand. Then he counted it out and his face fell. 'Yeah, cheers Mike. It's a lot of cash, and it's a big help,' he said, 'but I sometimes wonder if we'll ever save enough money for the wedding Becky wants. We'll just have to put it back again.'

'How much longer have we to wait?' I said. 'You've been threatening to name a day since this time last year.'

Soapy weighed the cash in his hand. 'This is all very well, but it'll still leave us scratching around,' he said. 'It ain't cheap, I'm telling you. We're aiming for April, but there's still the car, the cakes, the flowers.' He re-counted the pile of notes.

'Soapy, my old mate,' I said. 'Cards on the table. Me and Ann had a feeling you were struggling. But here's what we reckon. Algy owes you a favour or two, so you can tap him up for the loan of a car. There's that little sports job – or the Frazer Nash. Yes?'

He nodded, but I could see he wasn't convinced.

'Look, it won't cost you a penny. Maybe a drop of juice in the tank. Then, as for a cake, here's the deal. We've arranged for Walt's sister to knock one up at cost, and we'll see her right. She used to make them professionally and she can decorate it any way Becky wants.'

'Aw, that's brilliant Mike.'

'And as for flowers, I know just the person to speak to.'

'Who's that then?'

'Ann's aunty. She's a dab hand. No, she's more than that. She's a bloody marvel. She's done loads of weddings.

We'll pick up the cost for that as well, which means you've got a fair rate for your building work – and we can spread the costs over the next few months, yeah? That way everyone's a winner.'

'Mike, you've done me proud, cock-bod. Becky'll be over the moon. Hey, make sure you say thanks to Ann for me.'

'Too right I will. It was her daft idea in the first place. You don't think that I'd be quite that generous, do you? Anyway, just remember: if anything goes wrong with that roof, you owe us a free repair job.'

Soapy went home grinning from ear to ear. Paying him off had nearly cleaned us out, but we knew we'd got a good deal that suited everyone. Next day we were able to instruct our solicitors to make our offer to Algy formal, and early in January we received confirmation from the bank that we could get a mortgage on the place. Once the solicitors had done their work we could look forward to calling Keeper's Cottage our own.

Somehow, in between work and all the commotion at home, I'd managed to cram in the bookwork for my sergeant's Part One written exam, which I'd be sitting in just a few weeks' time. I'll never actually enjoy that kind of studying. I'm just no good at sitting still. But I did find – to my surprise – that putting in a few hours each week at odd times depending on what shift I was working, I was able to retain the information. I suppose I'm quite lucky in that I seem to have a really good short-term memory. All I had to do was peak at the right time. Of course, I also had Ann around, and that was a massive help. She was always ready to answer my questions, explain some of the more difficult aspects of legislation – and reassure me that I would, eventually, get the hang of it all. She said it was all a bit like driving. You don't so much learn to drive, she said, as learn how to pass the test. When the exam's behind you, that's when you start acquiring the skills and confidence that make you really competent. With Ann being a sergeant herself, she was able to back up all the theoretical stuff I was reading with day-to-day examples of what the job actually entails. If there was one thing that was still worrying me, however, it was that I'd only had the one brief spell standing in as acting sergeant at Malton – albeit one that had ended up with the manic activity and high drama of that bank holiday afternoon back in August. You need to grab all the experience you can get, because the Part One written exam is followed several months later by the Part Two, and that's where the fun really starts. You're confronted with live scenarios, with actors playing out the roles of suspects, fellow officers, solicitors and members of the public, to test your skills to the absolute limit. If you pass that, then it's a matter of waiting for a vacancy to come up. In London or one of the other big-city forces, that's not much of a worry; in a small force like North Yorkshire, though, you're more or less waiting to step into a dead man's shoes, as the saying goes. But all that was a long way off. Right now, I knew I needed more experience as a sergeant. And I wasn't getting it.

'Maybe you should put in a request,' was Ann's suggestion. 'How about asking Birdie if you can do a bit more acting up?'

She had a point, but I wasn't sure I wanted to approach

Birdie. Not yet, anyway. I prefer people to come to me and I didn't want to appear desperate, which of course I wasn't. Besides, we were about to have a short break. It was Valentine's Day, always a dangerous time for me. I was walking past a travel agent in town, saw a bargain and – well, I was simply overcome with a romantic impulse I couldn't resist. Without bothering to consult Ann, I lashed out on a week's all-inclusive midwinter break in Fuerteventura. It probably wasn't what our bank manager would have advised – we were supposed to be saving for the inevitable expenses when we completed the house purchase – and I worried on the way home that Ann might want my guts for garters. But I'm a canny operator. I paved the way with a big bunch of flowers, then fessed up. To my huge relief she was over the moon when I broke the news. She's not a lover of winter weather; this year she'd had one cold after another since Christmas and was feeling properly run-down. This break, she said, would be the perfect tonic for both of us. So she packed a collection of her favourite chick-lit books, I agreed – under duress – to take my Blackstone's manuals so that I could carry on preparing for the exam, and we booked Henry in for a refresher course in discipline at Walter's boot camp, in return for some duty-free goods to be delivered upon our return.

After our week in the sun, we flew home feeling properly rested for the first time in months. We were both relaxed, tanned, and ready to face whatever came our way. We arrived back at Keeper's Cottage to find the sun shining, the crocuses in full bloom and a pair of blackbirds gathering bits of twig from under the hedge. It's a good job I didn't know what was about to hit me.

Out on my patch opposition to the government's policy on hunting with dogs was growing stronger by the week. Or perhaps I should say that those who opposed it were getting progressively more organised, and making their feelings felt. Spray-painted pro-hunt slogans in huge lettering began appearing along North Yorkshire's roads. 'Fight the Ban' posters were popping up just about everywhere. People had always been against the legislation, but now they had decided it was time to raise their game and take action, which put me in a difficult situation.

All sorts of people had been telling me how fed up they were about the whole business. Rich and his wife, Algy, even Walter had a bit of a chunter when I called on him to collect Henry after we came back from our holiday. 'Look,' I said to him, 'this ban's nothing to do with me. It wasn't my idea.'

'I know that, lad, but you're goin' to be in t'firing line, aren't you? How you goin' to feel when they tek to t'streets and you're sent out to keep the peace? Answer me that.'

I played a straight bat. 'Our job,' I told him, 'is to uphold the law.'

He gave me a funny, sideways look. 'Even if it is a stupid daft law?' he asked.

'Look, Walt, it's nothing new. Anything controversial that the government does, who's in the firing line? Us. And I can promise you this: whatever the outcome, rest assured, it'll be the police's fault. I can guarantee it. It goes with the territory, mate.'

But Walt wasn't really listening. 'Us country folk, we can't win, lad. First it's hunting, next time it'll be shooting, then fishing. They keep on chipping away. Next thing you know there'll be nowt left. Them townie politicians know nowt about countryside ways.'

'Hell-fire, Walt, you're starting to talk like a paid-up member of the Countryside Alliance.'

'I am. I joined 'em six months since. I tell you, I've had it up to here wi' bloody politicians, southerners, whatever they are. They come up here for a fortnight's holiday and rattle on about how beautiful it is. Well, how do they think it got that way? Who do they think keeps the countryside looking the way it does? It dun't maintain itsen, y'know. When it comes to countryside matters, it should be left to them as knows what they're on with. Them other lot should – why, they should just keep their neb out.'

'Well, this is where you're in a privileged position, Walt.'

'What's that supposed to mean?'

'At least you're entitled to an opinion. I'm not. Not in my job. We have to be impartial, regardless of what we think. All I hope is that I don't find myself in the middle of it, having to confront people I regard as friends. That's my biggest dread. And if they do decide to protest, let's hope they do it peaceably.'

That conversation with Walter was the first time I'd fully expressed my fears about the hunting ban business. And, typically of the way things unfold, it wasn't long before I was forced to confront them. Just a couple of weeks later, on a Thursday afternoon in March, Birdie called me at home to say that Chris Cocks had put his back out and rung in sick. I would be acting sergeant for a week or so until he was fit for duty again. Although it wasn't great for Chris, it was good news for me, another opportunity to gain experience in the role and, hopefully, show what I was made of. And I had every confidence. There was no way, surely, that I'd be tested the way I had been the first time I'd stepped into the sergeant's role?

The Friday was quiet, I would almost say dull. Everything went like clockwork and I felt quite comfortable with what I was doing. I had very little to tell Ann when I got home that night. I arrived back at work nice and early on the Saturday and went through the normal briefing with the team. Things were so quiet that we met up at Malton Hospital for a team breakfast in their canteen. It's quite rare these days to have the time to get a cooked breakfast, so that was a bit of treat. The rest of the morning was steady away, as we say, with just the odd minor job and a few statements to take for cases that had been handed over from the night shift. With so little going on, I was able to go out on patrol for an hour or so.

After I'd had a bit of a look round I landed back at the station for a brew and checked through the jobs on the computer. The church clock was just striking twelve noon when Jayne and Thommo poked their heads around the door.

'Now then, what you two doing here?' I was surprised to see them. As far as I was aware they weren't due on till two.

Thommo grinned. 'Ye see the advantages of being a mere PC, sarge? I've been called in on overtime tae cover the match at that so-called football club of yours. Apparently you were supposed to be going – until you got promoted in the field.'

'Bloody hell, so I was. I forgot I was down for the York match.'

'Well, with any luck we'll be outside the ground and won't have to watch that poor excuse for a team.'

'Thommo, let me tell you, that so-called poor excuse of a team is on a roll.'

'Is that a fact?'

'Aye, unbeaten in two. They're on the march, lad.'

Jayne groaned. 'Come on Thommo, we need to get a move on. We're due at York for the one o'clock briefing. We'll be here all day if you get Mike onto his favourite subject.'

I turned back to the computer. 'Typical,' I muttered – but I consoled myself with the thought that I probably wouldn't have got to see the match anyway. It's very rare that you actually get to police the inside of the ground these days. That side of thing is mostly left to the stewards; they come a lot cheaper.

'*Control to 1015.*' Brian's voice sounded a little more urgent than normal.

'Go ahead, over.'

'*Yeah, are you free for a phone call?*'

'Yes, yes. Sergeant's office Malton.'

'*Received, standby.*'

I didn't like the sound of this. As a rule, control give out messages over the radio. They only pass it to the sergeant when it's not straightforward and the response needs to be given some thought. It might be something sensitive such as a sudden death, a complaint against police or an allegation of a very serious crime. As I drummed my fingers on the table and waited for the call to come through, I thought, who knows, maybe it's just a call to ask how I'm getting on.

'*Right Mike, are you ready for this one?*'

'Go on, Brian.'

'*Hmm, not every day you get a job like this. We've just had reports from North Yorkshire Moors Railway that they have a number of pro-hunt protesters gathering at Pickering station.*'

'Oh hell.'

'*Apparently you've got the MP for Scarborough and Whitby, Lawrie Quinn, on the steam train travelling down from Grosmont. He's a supporter of the hunting ban. Looks like the pro-hunters have got wind of him coming and they're planning an impromptu reception committee.*'

'Have we got any numbers, Brian?'

'*The station manager reckons about thirty to forty at present. All quite vocal, banners and placards, but not aggressive at present.*'

'Right, show me en route. Get Fordy to meet me there. Is Ed still dealing out at Kirby Grindalythe?'

'*Yeah, afraid so Mike. I'll get him to break off and start making his way, but he could be some time. You've got Brenda the new PCSO on foot in Pickering, don't forget.*'

'Yeah, I'm aware but we just need to be a bit careful if there's any disorder. She's not kitted out for that. I tell you what, ask her to make her way, but wait for my arrival. Can you scope around for some extra staff in case things escalate?'

'*Will do Mike, but we've got two football matches on today.*'

'Typical. All right, then. Let me know how you get on.'

I jumped in the car, hit the two-tones and blue lights and headed out on the A169. As I sped along I was trying to think of the best way to handle the situation. There are thousands of protests every year, but ordinarily they're pre-planned, so you have the opportunity to liaise with the organisers and put your staffing in place as best you can. But in this case we'd been totally caught out, with no prior intelligence whatsoever.

Quinn, as a supporter of the hunting ban, had spoken in its favour in the House of Commons on a number of occasions. None of that mattered, however, as far as I was concerned. What mattered was his safety and that of the general public. It was our duty to protect him while ensuring that any demonstration was conducted peacefully and within the law.

I got on the radio. 'Fordy, how long till you get to Pickering?'

'Ten minutes, with luck.'

'Ed, how you doing over there?'

'Just about squared up, bud. About thirty minutes, I'm afraid.'

This wasn't looking good. Experience told me we'd probably want to maintain a low profile, but we needed bodies on the ground – now. My guess was that the protesters would be mainly locals, the sort of people you would count on, ordinarily, to be co-operative towards police, certainly not aggressive. But lately feelings in the countryside had been running high. And wherever there's a crowd, whatever their intentions, there can be safety issues. Especially where you have trains involved.

'Control to 1015.'

I turned the radio volume up to counter the sound of the two-tones. 'Go ahead.'

'Mike, the good news is the Scarborough inspector has released the dog van. Should be with you in about twenty-five minutes.'

'Received. What's the ETA of the train at Pickering?'

'Well, that's the bad news Mike. It's about twenty minutes.'

This was not good. If things kicked off it'd be me, Fordy and Brenda against the lot of them. Sure, the reports suggested that they were good-humoured, but what was to say there weren't some hardcore saboteur types amongst them? It would not look good on the Pannett CV if the local MP was roughed up, assaulted or goodness knows what on my patch, with me in charge. Christ knows what Birdie would say, and I wouldn't be surprised if I ended up with a direct bollocking from the chief constable herself. It didn't bear thinking about.

When you have a crowd to control, the most basic issue is staffing, and we were nowhere near up to strength. With this job there would also be issues around crowd safety near a railway line. Then if things kicked off, and I decided I needed to make an arrest to control a volatile situation, I'd need enough officers to make the arrests and enough vehicles to accommodate the prisoners. At this stage all we had in prospect was one van – and that would be when Ed eventually arrived. What you want, from the outset, is enough officers to deter any would-be troublemakers – in other words, as we say, a show of strength. At this stage of the proceedings the cards were not stacking up for me. Any trouble, and we were going to find it very hard to cope.

I arrived to find a lot of cars lining the street beside the station, among them a number of four-by-fours. I managed to park up and quickly mounted the steps into the station. There I found quite a crowd, milling around by the booking office and on the platform. The majority of them appeared to be respectable people in country-style clothes: waxed jackets, flat caps, checked shirts and ties. They were chatting amicably amongst themselves, some of them laughing and joking. There was a complete mix of age groups, from the more senior to what appeared to be families with children. Even so, they must have been organised; somebody must have been spreading the word. You don't get three or four dozen people showing up like that by accident – and as I took in the scene I was aware of a steady stream of new arrivals, including one or two gamekeepers I recognised from the moorland estates. So who was in charge?

That was the first question.

I scanned the platform once more, trying to identify an organiser. I saw more familiar faces, one or two farmers I knew from my rounds and people I knew from the Tuesday cattle market, for instance. I was about to collar one of them to find out whether they had a spokesperson when I found myself face to face with a titled lady. I knew Lady C was a keen hunter – indeed, she was the chair of a meet that claims to be one of the oldest in England. She was a woman of some standing in the Malton area, a retired magistrate.

'Good afternoon.' I held out my hand. 'Sergeant Mike Pannett of North Yorkshire police. Can you tell me who's in charge here?'

As I spoke, someone blew a hunting horn. More protesters were coming into the station carrying placards. '59% SAY NO', 'WE WANT QUINN OUT!' I got the impression that people were joining the protest in dribs and drabs, probably arriving by car. But what if a coachload showed up? One or two were on the footbridge already, draping banners from the parapet. 'KEEP HUNTING'. 'FIGHT PREJUDICE. FIGHT THE BAN.' The noise levels were building all the time.

'In charge?' Lady C replied, raising her voice to be heard against the background racket. 'Nobody's in charge. It's all quite spontaneous. This man Quinn has angered a lot of people. I heard he was coming and I thought, let's go and tell him what we think.'

'Look,' I said, 'I don't have a problem with people voicing their opinion. But there are a lot of people here now. The last thing I want is any trouble.'

'Absolutely, officer. But we do want to state our case. I can assure you we will be doing so – politely but firmly.'

You have to be careful how you approach any demonstration or protest. You have to respect people's human rights, but at the same time you have a duty to protect any persons or property that might be at risk. 'OK then,' I said, 'cards on the table. Our aim will be to monitor and maintain order, and allow a peaceful demonstration, but I'm telling you now I will not have any disorderly behaviour. I've heard people in the crowd talking about throwing eggs and flour. That will not be tolerated.'

'Oh.' Lady C looked slightly crestfallen. 'I did actually bring some eggs. Look.' From her pocket she produced an antique silver-coloured egg-box. 'So you're saying that if I throw them at that ghastly man Quinn I'll be arrested?'

'Yes, Lady C, you will. You of all people should know that.'

At that moment Fordy arrived, with Brenda. 'Right Mike, what do you want us to do?'

'Brenda, if you could take a walk along the platform and tell people quite firmly to step away from the track. There's one or two getting a bit too near for my liking. This train will be crawling in, but if someone does go over the edge it can't stop on a sixpence. I want people well back, yes?'

'OK, Mike. Will do.'

'Fordy, just stop here with me a minute, while I think about what we're going to do.'

'1015 to control.'

'Go ahead, Mike.'

'Yeah, we've got fifty to sixty people here now. Still not managed to identify the organisers. It appears they're all here to let Mr Quinn know in no uncertain terms that they don't agree with his views. Quite a rowdy bunch but they're not daft. Passionate yes, stupid no.'

'That's all received, Mike.'

I surveyed the scene once more. Just now it all looked remarkably calm. Were it not for the placards they might have been a group of hikers waiting for the train home. Then Brian came back on.

'Mike, we've had a phone call. There's another group of demonstrators further up the line. On horseback, some of them.'

'On horseback, you say?' I saw Fordy raise his eyebrows. 'Great. Where are they? How far out?'

'*Farwath. It's five miles up the line from you, about two miles south of Levisham. There's a track crossing there and they're right down by the line.*'

'All received. I take it the train's still on time?'

'*Yes, you've got about fifteen minutes till it's due with you.*'

'Right, Fordy. Jump in your car and get yourself over there sharpish. Let me know what the score is.'

'Where exactly is it?'

'It's a little road crossing at Farwath, couple of miles south of Levisham station. I don't like the sound of this. Lady C!' I shouted. 'Where's Lady C?'

She was further down the platform now, waiting for the train. 'Look,' I said when I caught up with her, 'there's another lot turned up at—' But Brian was back on the radio. '*They've got a pack of hounds with them,*' he said.

'Listen, Lady C, this could get serious. There's a load of people, including horsemen, turned up at Farwath. They're down by the track, with hounds. Now, come on, who's organising this thing? 'Cos I need to speak with him – or her.'

'Well,' she said, 'I heard about this by email. Maybe you should get hold of George.'

'George who?' My worry at the moment was that there was no shape to things. If people started acting on impulse, with a train involved, as well as horses and dogs, there could be a very nasty incident. Somebody needed to take charge.

Lady C gave me the guy's name. I recognised it imme-diately. He was a prominent landowner and huntsman, a pretty high-profile figure locally. 'Well, where is he?' I asked.

'I've not seen him yet. He may be up the line somewhere.'

'Has he got a mobile?'

'Yes.'

She read out his number and I dialled it. Nothing. He'd either switched it off or had no signal.

A member of the station staff was standing near me, looking at his watch. 'Have you got any contact with the train?' I asked.

'Not directly, officer. Just via the signalman. It's due in shortly though.'

'*1015 receiving?*' Ed's voice crackled over the radio.

'Go ahead.'

'*Five minutes Mike, with the big van.*'

'Great stuff,' I said. At least we'd have somewhere to put any prisoners should we start making arrests. Moments later the Scarborough dog unit called in to say that he was ten minutes away. With him and Ed, that boosted our manpower by about seventy per cent. Still not ideal, but I was feeling a bit more hopeful.

'*1015, active message.*' Fordy sounded worried.

'Go ahead, Gary.'

'*Right, I've got vision of the track and there are a number of huntsmen and a pack of hounds in the fields next to it. There are also people on foot, and a couple more horsemen right by the side of the track. Red-jacket types. I can also see a member of what looks like the press taking photographs.*'

Before I could answer control were straight in. '*Yeah,*

1015. We've monitored that and I can also confirm we've now had a number of phone calls from people actually on the train stating they have people on horseback galloping alongside.'

Christ, I thought, this is more Hollywood than North Yorkshire. 'Gary, any sign of the train?'

'Yeah, just coming into sight. You're not going to like this, Mike. The train's approaching and I've got what looks like a female now lying across the track. There's no way I can get down to her in time.'

'That's received, keep the commentary going.'

'Yeah, the train's blowing its whistle, but it doesn't look like it's slowing down.'

Why were they trying to stop the train? Were they planning to ambush it? To board it and seek out Mr Quinn? And the woman on the line – she surely wasn't going to stay there, was she? I was just about to redirect Ed and the dog van to Farwath when Fordy was back on the radio.

'Train approaching female. Stand by . . . yeah, she's up on her feet and off the track . . . she's joined by a number of people with placards. Stand by . . . train continuing and passing them now. Should be with you in just a few minutes.'

'That's all received. Good job, Gary. Can you make your way back to the station?'

If they were that organised, and rash enough to try and ambush the train down the line, I had serious concerns now about what might be in store for us at the station. I didn't have much time and I didn't have a lot of options.

There was a wooden stool over by the tea room. I

grabbed it, stood on it, and clapped my hands together. 'Your attention please, ladies and gentlemen. The train will be here shortly. Please do not throw anything. If anybody throws anything they will – I repeat, they will – be arrested. So let's not do anything daft, please.'

My address was met with a few cheers and a ripple of applause. There's a first, I said to myself. Applauded for threatening to arrest people. Bizarre.

We could hear the train now, and then quite suddenly it came into view, round the bend and under the foot-bridge, a string of chocolate-brown Pullman cars pulled by a shiny black steam locomotive, the *Lord of the Isles*. The crowd was suddenly swollen as more protesters came in from outside the station and the tea room emptied, packing the platform. A few trainspotters and railway enthusiasts, who'd been standing at the far end with their cameras and recorders poised, looked on in bemusement as the protesters started up with their slogans. Chants of 'Quinn out! Quinn out! Quinn out!' rose to a crescendo until they were drowned out by the hiss of steam and the squealing of brake-shoes against the huge iron drive-wheels. In among the crowd was a bewildered gaggle of passengers waiting to board the train for the return trip to Whitby.

Suddenly Ed was by my side. 'Thank God you're here,' I said. 'You got the van?'

'Outside, bud.'

I turned to Brenda. 'You two just back me up here, will you? I'm going to protect this man Quinn.' I pulled my woolly hat down. 'If any eggs or flour are thrown I'll make sure they hit me, not him.'

'What carriage is he in?'

'God knows. If I stay towards this end, you walk down the train. Just keep your eyes open.'

'Mike, what does this guy look like?' Ed asked.

'God knows, I've never met him.'

Brenda looked at me questioningly. 'Like an MP,' I said, 'like an MP.'

I was now speaking into my radio mike, keeping control in the picture. 'Train arriving, train arriving right now.'

Instinctively everyone drew back a step or two as the engine cast its shadow over us and steam gushed from the cylinders. Then, much to the surprise of the passengers inside, they surged forward, peering through the murky windows of the carriages. The crowd in front of me was momentarily enveloped by a cloud of steam, so that just their hats and placards were visible. I was drowned out by another round of 'We want Quinn out! We want Quinn out!' One or two of the protesters close by me smelled of alcohol – and I smelled trouble. I needed to find the honourable member before they did.

The train had come to a standstill and the carriage doors were opening. The people trying to get down onto the platform hesitated, clearly shaken by the protesters surging forward and chanting, 'Fight The Ban! Fight The Ban!'

'Brenda!' I shouted, as a group of protesters brushed past me, 'just watch they don't get too close to that edge.' The last thing we needed was someone dropping onto the line.

Fordy was on the radio. '*Mike, for your information, the entire hunt plus hounds are now making their way down the road behind me, at speed, towards the station.*'

'How long's it going to take 'em, d'you reckon?'

'Ten minutes, max.'

'I'll be ready for them. Well, I won't but . . .'

At that moment a smart-looking man in a suit got out of one of the Pullman cars, followed by a man holding a microphone and another with a bulky TV camera on his shoulder. They were a good carriage-length ahead of the main body of protesters. I slipped in behind them, making sure I was between them and the crowd, who'd spotted us and were closing in, shouting 'Boo! Get yourself back to Scarborough, Quinn! You're not welcome here!'

The cameraman was walking backwards, training his lens on the man in the suit. I stayed with our man, determined to protect him. The protesters were now right behind us, still jeering and waving their placards. We'd reached the spot now where the engine was being uncoupled from the carriages. Down on the track a guy with red rubber gloves and a greasy peaked hat was unscrewing the heavy steel coupling. I turned to the man in the suit. 'All right, Mr Quinn?' I asked. He looked at me and gave a puzzled frown. 'I'm not Quinn.' I looked at the gent with the microphone. 'I'm with the BBC *Look North* team,' he explained. 'Norman here, he was fireman on this run – how long ago was it?'

'1965,' said Norman, looking nervously over his shoulder as the protesters cat-called and chanted and jostled and waved their placards. 'It's my retirement journey; that's why they're filming me. What's going on? Why are they all shouting at me?'

I suppressed a grin. 'Right Norman, don't you worry about it, mate. They think you're a local MP.'

'No lad, I'm not into politics. Not me.'

'Good lad,' I said. At that moment another gent in a suit emerged from a carriage doorway and eased his way towards me, through the protesting scrum. He introduced himself as a manager with the North Yorkshire Moors Railway. 'Nothing to worry about,' he said, as quietly as he could. 'Mr Quinn's quite safe.'

'Good. Where is he?'

He shielded his face with a sheaf of papers he was carrying and lowered his voice to a whisper. 'The guard's locked him in the kitchen, down in the restaurant car. Don't worry, nobody'll find him there.'

'Right, how long will it take you to get this train away from here?'

'Normally takes fifteen minutes to turn it round and re-water her. Under the circumstances' – he glanced at his watch – 'I think we can do it in ten.'

'Fantastic, you lads crack on.'

I turned to face the crowd, took a deep breath and cupped my hand to my mouth. 'Now listen,' I shouted at them, putting as much authority into it as I could muster. 'This gentleman is not Mr Quinn. He's a railway man trying to enjoy a retirement trip, so please leave him be. And please, allow these passengers to board the train.'

Immediately people began looking round, confused, disappointed. They thought they'd run their quarry to ground. Now they had to start again. There were shouts of 'Where is he then?' and 'Hiding in the toilet, I bet.' The state of confusion suited me fine. The longer it lasted the better chance we had of a peaceful conclusion. No reason why I shouldn't muddy the waters still further.

'I'm not sure where he is,' I shouted, 'but it could be that he's left the station.'

Someone shouted, 'I bet he's in the car park. Let's try the car park!' Some of them moved off in that direction. Others were looking in through the carriage windows, startling the passengers who'd managed to get on board. If I could keep it like this for a few more minutes then we might just get away with it.

'What's happening, Mike? Where is he?' Ed and Brenda were standing beside me.

It occurred to me that this was really quite amusing. Here we were, the three of us, protecting a man we'd never seen and wouldn't recognise if we did.

'They've put Plan B into operation.' I kept my voice low and they leaned forward, listening intently. 'Apparently the guard's locked him in the kitchen area. We can't go and speak to him or it'll give the game away. If anybody asks you any questions, act confused.' I looked around at the crowd on the platform, leaderless, ebbing and flowing from one point to the next randomly. 'Shouldn't be difficult,' I added. 'This has got me well baffled.'

I'd just finished updating control when the railway manager grabbed me by the arm.

'OK officer, about ready to pull out.'

'Fantastic,' I said. 'Good man. By the way, what was all this about another demo on the line side?'

'Yes, at Farwath, about four miles north of here. There must've been a dozen of them, on horseback, and they had the hounds with them. Close shave. I really thought at one point we were going to hit one of the horses, they were that close. Riding along the line next to the train. Not to mention the woman laid on the track.'

Behind him one or two final carriage doors were being slammed shut, the stationmaster's whistle blew and the *Lord of the Isles* steamed slowly out of the station. As I stood and watched the last carriage glide its way towards the end of the platform, the sound of the engine faded and was replaced by the clattering of hooves in the street outside and a blast on a horn.

'Bloody hell! I forgot the other lot were on their way!' I shoved my way through the disappointed crowd, their placards drooping, their banners being rolled back up. Outside was a small army of huntsmen, many of them sporting the traditional red jackets, their jodhpurs covered in mud and the sweat from their steaming mounts. Around their feet was a full pack of hounds, along with a melee of protesters, onlookers and now a couple of press photographers snapping away.

'Right,' I said, shouting to make myself heard, ' I have no objection to you protesting, but I am telling you that Mr Quinn and the train have left. There is nobody in the station for you to shout at. You've made your point but it's time for you to go home.'

Nobody seemed to be taking a bit of notice. They were too worked up. Around me people were shouting slogans. 'You're not welcome, Quinn! Get him back to bloody Scarborough – we don't want you here!' I suspected they were playing up to the press, and the photographers, of course, were loving every minute of it. I could also tell from their speech that one or two of the huntsmen had been drinking.

Despite what I'd said, people were not dispersing, and the crowd of onlookers were gathered around admiring the horses, the hounds and the general spectacle. Take away the cries of 'Where is he?' and 'Let's run him out of town!' and it might have been a Boxing Day morning in Easingwold. It was part protest, part festivity.

Fordy joined me. 'That was one hell of a sight, Mike, watching this lot come down the road.' He looked around. 'Don't think anybody's been hurt, not as far as I can see.'

'Well, that's a minor miracle,' I said. 'Right, Gary, this lot have blocked the road for long enough. The traffic's backed up both ways. Grab hold of Ed and Brenda and let's try and get them dispersed.'

Out of the corner of my eye I spotted the dog unit parked down the road and the handler standing there. Just the job, I thought. A bit more of a presence. It all helps.

I clapped my hands again. 'Right, can everybody keep calm, please. Who's in charge of the hounds?'

A slightly built man mounted on a bay gelding leaned down and stretched out his hand, introducing himself as the master of a local hunt. I patted his horse and simultaneously shuffled away from another one that was nuzzling my shoulder. 'OK,' I said, 'you've made your protest. That's fine. Now, I can assure you that the man you're after isn't here, and the train has already left. So I think we can wind things up now, can't we, and disperse?'

'Yes, yes, I quite agree. And thank you. I think we've made our point.'

'Aye, and you've got your publicity.' A photographer was squatting down beside me, snapping a shot of the master of hounds. 'How did you lads get wind of this?' I asked.

'We were tipped off,' he said, but before I could ask the question he added, 'Unnamed sources.'

'Yeah, they usually are.'

The guy had taken out his notebook. 'OK if I ask you a few questions?' he said. '*Yorkshire Post*.'

'Maybe when I've got this lot dispersed,' I answered.

At the station entrance a crowd was still milling about, and one or two huntsmen were getting dangerously close. I was determined to stop anyone on horseback entering the station. One man in particular was yelling and carrying on. 'I'm gonna tell that Lawrie Quinn meself,' he shouted. Another was walking his horse, which was lathered in sweat, up and down. 'He's gone,' I said, walking over to the man on horseback. I spelled it out as clearly and deliberately as I could. 'The train has departed.' But he took no notice. He was red in the face and seething with anger. Next thing I knew, he'd dug his heels into the horse's flanks and was making for the entranceway. I ran up the steps, and got there just ahead of him. The horse looked agitated as it loomed over me, snorting and stamping its feet, with the rider shouting, 'Where is the bugger. Eh? 'Cos I'm gonna tell him to his face.' He now had the crowd worried. People were stumbling in their haste as they backed away. A horse will respond to whoever's riding it, pick up their mood – and this guy was full of anger, trying to drive the animal forward, up the flight of steps and onto the platform. In my experience horses don't ordinarily manage steps, never mind station platforms. As the horse tossed his massive head, spattering me with foam, I reached out and grabbed the reins, wrapping them once round my wrist. The beast jerked his head again, violently. I felt a shooting pain in my shoulder, but held on tight.

'C'mon,' I shouted, 'let's have you away from here.'

'He's gone, mate!' someone shouted. 'Quinn's gone.'

At that moment the rider seemed to see sense. He turned his mount, I let go of the reins and he set off down the road towards the town centre. It was then that I realised I'd pulled something in my shoulder. It was hurting like hell.

I approached the master of hounds again and told him, 'You've made your protest, you've got your PR, your photos and videos. It's time to disperse.'

'All right,' he said. 'Will do.' He put his horn to his lips and blew, and the whole lot of them – twenty riders plus all the hounds – set off towards the marketplace. That's great, I thought, just what we need in the town centre on a Saturday afternoon – although I have to say they looked quite a sight. The last thing I heard was one of them laughing as he called out, 'And now for our lap of honour, eh?' The crowd that had been watching, and the demonstrators on foot, all applauded and followed them down the road, some running, some cheering, some snapping away with their cameras.

I sent Fordy and Ed to follow them to make sure everything was OK. I didn't think they were likely to cause any further problems. Most of them were local people. In fact, when Ed came on the radio a few minutes later he reported that the hunt was receiving a round of applause from the shoppers as they paraded through town.

We'd identified only one huntsman as actually step-ping outside the law, and he would be arrested later in the week. Although for a short while there it had looked like a proper demonstration, edgy, with every chance that some spark could set it off, now everything was sweet-ness and light and the whole thing seemed to have turned into a kind of parade.

So, no harm done – other than to Acting Sergeant Pannett's shoulder.

As I left the railway station and headed back towards the car I got on the radio and thanked all of the officers involved. I was just climbing into the car when I was collared by the *Yorkshire Post* reporter. 'Well officer, how did you lot manage to get away with that then?'

I looked him up and down, my shoulder throbbing. He looked about twenty-three. 'Let's say we used diversionary tactics,' I said. 'Anyway, can't talk now. Sorry, I need to get off.'

We'd got away with it. That was my feeling as I drove back to Malton. We'd been told a couple of dozen protesters were at the station. It probably added up to a hundred or more, plus horses, plus hounds, by the time we'd finished. If things had gone wrong – and they could easily have done so if the saboteurs, for example, had got wind of what was happening – we would've been woefully undermanned, and left waiting for backup from across the force. Me, Ed, Fordy and Brenda the PCSO. We'd never have held the line. We would've been well and truly caught with our pants down. Having said that, I'd never known anything quite like it in North Yorkshire. I couldn't help wondering what the photographs would look like when the papers came out. Still, I thought, as I drove into Malton, desperate for a cup of tea and a couple of painkillers, Ann and I had agreed that some frontline experience before my exam would do me good . . .

There were thirty or more of us, filing into the room in silence. PCs from all over North Yorkshire, all in plain clothes. We took our seats, one at each desk, and sat down. From across the room I saw Jayne giving me the thumbs-up as the door was locked behind us. Once we were all settled in our allotted places, the adjudicator started to speak. 'No talking, switch your mobile phones off, nothing on your desk other than two pencils and a sharpener . . .' Well, I thought, we're under starter's orders. I was so nervous I could hardly concentrate on what she was saying. It was like being back at school, only this time much, much more depended on the outcome. The desks, I noticed, were set just the right distance apart, and just at the right angle, to prevent you being able to see the next person's exam papers. 'You have one and a half hours to complete the paper. Please turn over your papers and begin.'

I took a deep breath. Right, Pannett lad. You've read the books and you're battle-hardened. So why's your stomach churning ch?

I turned over the first page. Question one. 'You're out on patrol, at night, and you see a strange illuminated object in the sky. You're sure it's not a plane or a helicopter. What steps would you take to identify it?'

I sighed. Here we go, lad.

Acknowledgements

A special thank you to: Phil Pelham for his dedication to the cause and to everyone at Welcome to Yorkshire for their continued support.

Finally, thanks to the great characters of North Yorkshire, without whom this book could never have been written.

And a little bit extra . . .

Readers from all over the world – and people I meet when I do my talks and other events – often ask me about Yorkshire, so here are some helpful websites:

www.yorkshire.com
www.visityork.org
www.yorkshiretea.co.uk
www.yorkshirerainforestproject.co.uk

And to find out about the train that inspired the cover illustration for this book, have a look at the North Yorkshire Moors Railway at www.nymr.co.uk

Finally, if you want to help a deserving cause – and people who you might need one day – the local Mountain and Cave Rescue teams all do a great job. They're volunteers who go out in all weathers and the service depends on donations, so if you could support them it would be just the job:

Scarborough and Ryedale Mountain Rescue Team:
www.srmt.org.uk
Swaledale Mountain Rescue Team:
www.swaledalemrt.org.uk
Cleveland Search and Rescue Team:
www.csrt.co.uk
Cave Rescue Organisation:
www.cro.org.uk
Upper Wharfedale Fell Rescue Association:
www.uwfra.org.uk

Mike Pannett

Have you read the other tales from the Yorkshire bobby?

MIKE PANNETT

YOU'RE COMING WITH ME, LAD

Policing rural Yorkshire is a far cry from Mike's old job hunting
down drug gangs and knife crime in Central London. Settled back
in his native Yorkshire, however, Mike finds that life as a rural
beat bobby is no picnic.

After a crazed swordsman threatens to take his head off, he finds
himself confronting a knife-wielding couple bent on carving each
other up. When a stag night turns ugly he gets stuck with the
groom, the best man and the bride-to-be all banged up in the cells
– and the wedding just hours away. With record-breaking floods
and politicians to escort, will Mike find time to woo the woman
of his dreams?

Hodder & Stoughton paperback
www.hodder.co.uk

Have you read the other tales from the Yorkshire bobby?

MIKE PANNETT

NOT ON MY PATCH, LAD

Mike Pannett used to work the beat in Central London and when he moved back to Yorkshire he was hoping for a quieter life. But it seems the moors and villages of his native county aren't as sleepy as he once thought . . .

A casual remark about a barn with blacked-out windows leads him to an isolated farmhouse where skunk cannabis is being cultivated on an industrial scale, and at the height of the holiday season a young girl is attacked at a local theme park. As well as handling these serious crimes, Mike is still trying to identify and bring to justice the 'Sunset Gang' who are systematically targeting isolated warehouses and shops on his patch.

On the home front, Ann has moved into Keeper's Cottage and taken a Sergeant's post in York – and people are asking Mike what it's like to be a kept man.

Hodder & Stoughton paperback
www.hodder.co.uk